Business Data Processing and Systems Analysis

Pete Kilgannon FWSOM, MIAM (DIP), MBCS

Senior Lecturer in Computer Studies
South East London College

Edward Arnold

© Pete Kilgannon 1980

First published 1972 as The Student's
Systems Analysis

by Edward Arnold (Publishers) Ltd.
41 Bedford Square, London WC1B 3DQ

This edition published 1980

British Library Cataloguing in Publication Data

Kilgannon, Peter
    Business data processing and systems analysis. —
    2nd ed.
    1. Business—Data processing
    2. System analysis
    I. Title II. Students' systems analysis
    658.4'032   HF5548.2

ISBN 0-7131-2755-4

To Dean and Tracy

Printed in Great Britain by
Thomson Litho Ltd, East Kilbride, Scotland

Preface

Since the orginal version of this book, *The Student's Systems Analysis*, appeared seven years ago, I have been surprised at the many areas of use and many levels at which it has been employed. In addition to the National and Higher National courses for which it was originally aimed, the text has been used in many areas of education from CSE and O Level courses to second year degree work.

Many changes have taken place in the short space of seven years. The world of business education has been overhauled by BEC and BEC/TEC with its integrated, practical, learning objective oriented approach. The computer scene has been revolutionised by the introduction of the microprocessor and the full impact of this on the lives of every individual in the country is only just around the corner. The ability of the computer to revolutionise our lives is now being appreciated by noncomputer people and fears of redundancy, robots and 1984 are being publicly discussed.

Strangely, this emphasis on the machine in the public eye is occurring at a time when the technicalities of the computer are being tamed. No longer is it really necessary to understand in depth how the processor works any more than it is necessary for the user to understand the inside of the telephone. The computer is now assuming its proper place as yet another machine used by man to assist him in his endeavours. Man has always needed to conduct business in some form and always will do. The tools he employs to help him have changed over the centuries and there is no reason to suppose that the computer of today is the ultimate machine.

Apart from the obvious updating of material and the elimination of past errors, I have completely restructured this book, so much so as to warrant the new title. The section on business systems has been enlarged and omissions such as a practical introduction to program writing have been added. I would like to thank all those in Universities, Polytechnics, Colleges and Schools who have contacted me with comment and constructive criticism. I think you will find your suggestions have been incorporated.

Pete Kilgannon 1979

Contents

Module 1
Business systems

Unit 1
The business environment

Learning objective

To be able to identify the component parts of a system and to relate this to the business environment. To be able to identify a business owner's motivation and selected means of need satisfaction and, thus, to justify the primary systems of any business. To be able to identify and justify those parts of the business activity which primarily satisfy the needs of the society in which the business operates.

The business world

This book uses the term business to describe any undertaking that employs resources to satisfy an economic need of society, e.g. product manufacturers, hospitals, banks, newsagents, airlines, supermarkets, local authorities, etc.

Society is the environment of the business world. It can be considered to consist of consumers (customers), producers (suppliers), competitors, legislation, technology, politics, economic factors and social factors.

The economic needs of society are satisfied by:

primary (extracted) goods, e.g. coal, oil, fish, etc.

secondary (manufactured) goods, e.g. cars, shoes, etc.

commercial services, e.g. banking, insurance, transport, etc.

social services, e.g. fire, police, education, etc.

These goods and services are distributed by means of:

direct trading, e.g. wholesale, retail, mail order, etc.

indirect trading, e.g. rates and taxes for police, health, etc.

The resources employed by a business are used in two ways:

prime resources, i.e. resources which are processed to produce the goods and services

producer resources, i.e. those resources which perform the processing.

Society has economic needs. It is made up of individuals and groups with individual and group needs, some economic and some social (*see* Unit 4). Some individuals and groups find that they can satisfy their own needs by satisfying the economic needs of society and so they become business owners. They have an **aim** (their own need satisfaction) and they find a **means** (some business activity) to achieve it. To achieve their aim the activity must be guided. It must be conducted according to a set of rules and so it becomes a **regulated activity**.

The owners need satisfaction is provided by way of **profit**. Profit is the difference between **price** and **cost**. Price is a measurement of the value of goods or services to the consumer depending upon scarcity. It always tends towards a

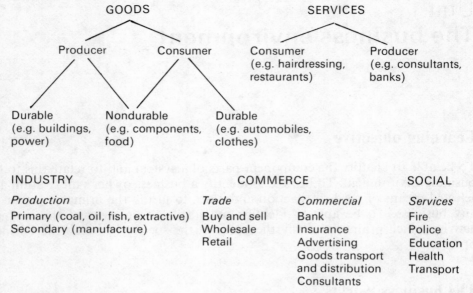

Figure 1   The business world

balance of supply and demand. If supply exceeds demand prices drop and if demand exceeds supply prices rise. A rise in price curtails demand, a fall in price stimulates demand. Price must exceed cost to produce profit, but price is directly related to demand and only indirectly, by method of production and

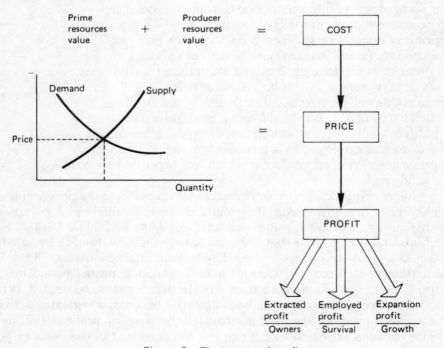

Figure 2   The nature of profit

economy of scale, to cost. Cost is the price of prime resources added to the price of producer resources. Profit satisfies the owner's needs in the following ways:

> extracted profit–goods and services for the owner
> employed profit–to safeguard, maintain and improve the business (continued need satisfaction for owner)
> expansion profit–to enlarge the business (greater need satisfaction)

The business system

A system is defined as 'input subjected to a (regulated) activity to produce (aim-achieving) results'.

Our definition of a business is 'a motivated force (owner) obtaining prime resources (raw materials) and subjecting them to a regulated activity (the business activity) performed by producer resources (premises, staff, machines, etc.) to produce goods or services for consumers (society's need satisfaction) and thus provide profit (the owner's need satisfaction)'.

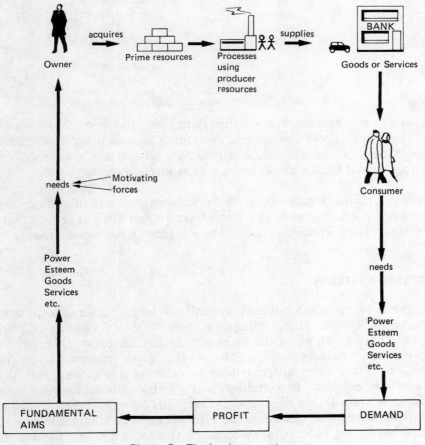

Figure 3   The business system

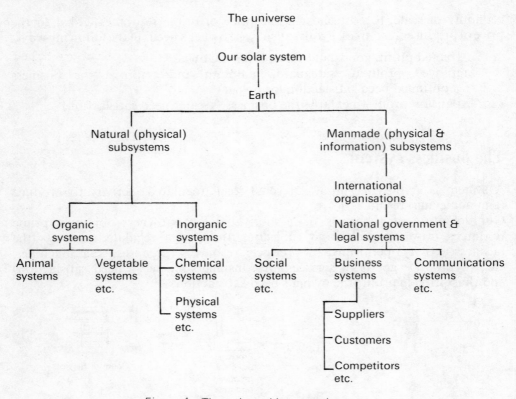

Figure 4   The universal integrated system

A business is a system. Many other things are also systems, although it is argued that there is only one system, everything, and all other systems are subsystems of this. No system exists in isolation, all systems are integrated and, therefore, external factors are as important as internal ones.

One major distinction can be made between natural and man-made systems. It is not known whether natural systems have an aim but it is certain that manmade systems are purposefully devised to produce aim-achieving results.

Integrated systems

It may help to visualise business systems as being rather like a country's transportation system. Just as there are several major systems of transport (road, rail, air) linking all of the main population centres so there are several major business systems linking all of the main processing centres or departments. There are transport links to other countries (sea and air) and there are business links (information and goods) with other businesses and organisations outside the business. In each major city there are individual transport networks (e.g. bus and underground) as in each business department there are individual processing systems. In transport systems the inputs and outputs are people (and goods). These people can get on a train and travel from one city to the next or they can get a bus to take them across the town to their homes where they are 'stored' until they need to travel again. It is important to realise that just as rail, sea, road, or air systems never leave their passengers at a complete dead end, so no business system exists where the resultant output is not used as input to some subsequent systems either inside or outside the business. Just as the aims of the various transport systems may conflict and necessitate some compromise so will the aims of the individual subsystems operating within a business. For example, visitors from another country may wish to visit the capital but the best passenger handling facilities are on the coast or at an airport some distance from the town. They must then make arrangements to travel from the port or airport by some internal transport system. If these passengers wish to travel to some other part of the country they may first have to go to the capital and then travel out again. The aims of the travellers are modified and constrained by environmental factors. The same happens with business systems where the various environmental factors, laws, competitors, politics etc., all affect the ultimate business system.

The points at which one subsystem ends and the integrated subsystem(s) begins are known as system interfaces. The output of each system is the input to one or more subsequent systems, for example train passengers getting on a bus. It is not possible to identify these interfaces, and thus the size of any system, without being purely arbitrary. The division of systems into subsystems

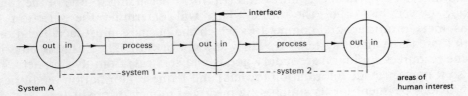

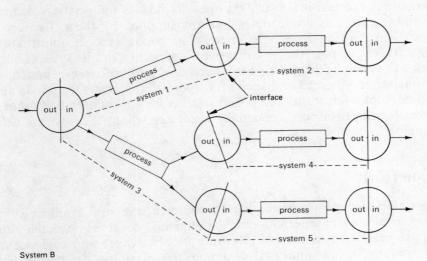

Figure 5   System interfaces

is a subjective process, the limits of a system being set as 'an area of human interest'. The investigator states his own limits or has them set for him. In business this is often determined by the organisational grouping of resources into departments and sections, each with its own targets (aims) to achieve.

Environmental systems (E1, E2, E3)

The business world exists in an environment of many other systems. The two major considerations are of time and space. A business exists at a point in time and continues over a period of time. Any particular moment of the existence of the business is determined by its own history and the historical development and current state of the many influencing factors with which the business must contend. For example, the availability of labour, the prevailing technology, public opinion, etc. will be different in one time period to another. What one could expect in the past, e.g. children at work, monopoly markets etc., may not now be possible. What was once not possible e.g. computer processing, sexual equality etc. may now be taken for granted. It is essential to regard the business environment as dynamic and the process of business must be adaptive in order to survive. This is the basis of management.

The business also exists in space; in a particular location of a particular community in a particular country and continent belonging to one of the three major power blocks of the world. This will determine the selection of consumers, producers and competitors which the business must face. Relations with these three major systems are fairly straightforward. The business buys its prime resources (primary, secondary goods and services) from its suppliers. To do so it must provide information (orders) and request information (enquiries). It provides payment for its supplies by means of money or credit (*see* Unit 3). With respect to its customers the business acts as a supplier and the same interchange takes place—goods, services, information, money. As far as competitors are concerned it is usually a one-way flow of information gleaned by the business about its competitors but not supplied by them. Because a business exists in space and needs to interchange goods, services, information and money there is one universal system common to all systems—the communication system. This can be considered as a producer service system of the environment; commercial and social transportation systems for goods and people and telecommunications and postal systems for information and money. Communication and transport are equally necessary within the business itself (Units 3 and 5).

Legislation (E4)

Laws, rules and regulations pertaining to the structure and conduct of a business are generated at international, national and local levels. Each rule demands interpretation and control to ensure its observance and evidence of this is often required. Sometimes part of the business resources are required in exchange for being allowed to function at certain levels or even at all. All legislation generates work, to be performed by the business either as a separate system or as an additional operation to existing systems in the business.

It is the legal framework which largely determines the fundamental type of business (legal identity) that will be operated.

Sole trader The traditional 'one-man business' consisting of one owner financed by his own or borrowed capital. He is fully liable for all debts, repaying them from his own private assets if necessary.

Partnership Several owners carrying on a business under their own names or a registered business name. The partnership is formed by a verbal or written agreement but the business has no legal identity of its own, each partner being responsible for debts, from their private assets if necessary.

Corporation A company existing as a legal entity in its own right, separate from its owners. It is brought into being by a memorandum of association and has inbuilt rules for its conduct and management. The liability of its owners for debts is limited to the value of the shares they own or the guarantees they have made. Corporations can be private, public or state owned. Variations include producer or consumer cooperatives and publicly owned municipal corporations.

The type of business operated will determine what extra work must be performed to satisfy the environmental needs of legislation. For example, corporations particularly are required to produce information, much of it of an accounting nature, which has little or no value in directly satisfying the owners' needs through profit. This information does, however, provide remote owners (e.g. ratepayers, shareholders etc.) with evidence of the quality of the management they employ and the current value of their investments.

In addition to legislation concerning its legal identity a business is involved with:

Taxation Taxes vary from country to country but among the most usual are sales tax, income tax, health insurance, customs duties, licence fees, pensions, corporation tax, capital gains tax, death duties, stamp duties, local authority rates, etc. Taxation requires additional systems in the business for the purpose of evaluation, collection, calculation and payment.

Employment legislation Laws relating to employment are concerned with health, safety and hygiene, fair wages, training, contracts of employment, termination and redundancy, industrial relations, race, sex and political discrimination, disablement, pensions, trade union activities, security of employment, employee statistics, environmental conditions, etc. Systems are required for the interpretation and observance of these laws.

Trading legislation In addition to the corporation laws mentioned previously, businesses must conform to laws relating to monopolies, trade practices, prices, contracts, patents and trademarks etc.

Criminal legislation All of the normal laws applicable to crime in society apply also in business. In addition, there are laws to cover business crimes such as fraud, industrial espionage, embezzlement etc.

Social legislation Because a business exists in a social framework it must obey such rules that exist to protect society from its activities. Examples are physical and noise pollution, consumer protection, negligence, privacy and other social responsibilities.

Technology (E5)

Technology is concerned with both what the business does and the way that it does it. It is concerned with what is done in so far as the business' goods and services produced will reflect current technological solutions to the problems of society's needs, which change continually. Technology is the practical realisation of ideas, the end product of philosophy as interpreted by science and education. If a business does not need technology it will produce unsaleable, obsolete products. In a changing world, technology requires systems in a business for the purpose of keeping up-to-date with competitors and in step with the world. These systems can take the form of research, training and more enlightened management.

The other aspect of technology is its use in the way prime resources are processed, either by which producer resources are used or by which processing procedures are employed. It is possible to cut steel with a hand saw or a computer-controlled guillotine. Goods can be sold over the counter or by self-service in a supermarket. The first example is the use of a different machine resource, the second the use of a different procedure. New methods and procedures may be forced upon a business as being the only ones available at any point in time or they may be deliberately sought after as a result of economic pressures.

The additional work forced upon a business by the technological environment is largely a question of obtaining information from the relevant sources (learned and scientific societies and professional institutes, equipment manufacturers, trade organisations, etc.) and assimilating this knowledge by education and training.

Politics (E6)

The political environment is a formal expression of the society's aims and ideals. Its effect upon a business is all-embracing. It affects not only how the business is run and who its customers and suppliers will be but even who its owners will be and what their aims can and will be. This in turn determines the structure of the business and the trading environment in which it operates.

Running a cooperative in a capitalist society or a private enterprise in a socialist state can be a pretty lonely affair. Even within a particular power block, political leanings can have a very influential effect. State influence is greater in Europe than in the USA because of socialised medicine, nationalised industries etc. One of the major problems in our society is the conflicting political ideologies of owners and trade unions. The trade union movement includes craft unions (e.g. woodworkers), industrial unions (e.g. mineworkers), general unions (e.g. general and municipal workers) and non-manual unions (e.g. clerical and administrative workers). There are also owner/employer federations or similar groupings formed to protect and represent the interests of this section of society. The major political factor is of course the presiding government and its policies which in theory represent neither of the two preceding factors (employers and employed) but rather represent the will of the majority of the population. It is this element that generates the legislation constraints of the business. The formulation of management policy requires up-to-date and forecast information of the political environment.

Economic factors (E7)

The economic climate determines the level of activity in the business world. In times of depression, business policy will be concerned with reducing costs or even with the survival of the business. When times are good, capital investment and expansion are encouraged. Management needs information about the economy to determine policy with regard to the employment of resources on existing work systems. The state of the economy is indicated by the level of unemployment, the balance of payments i.e. imports and exports, the value of the national currency in relation to others, share prices, national indebtedness, interest rates etc. There are many national and international financial,

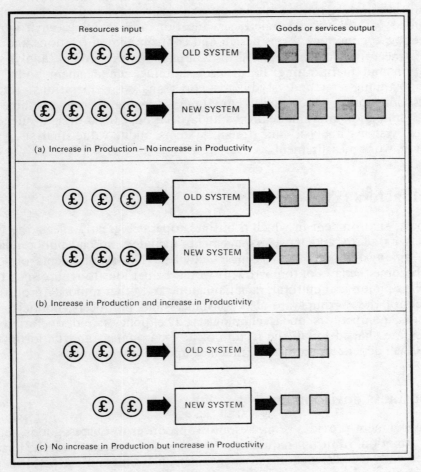

Figure 6   Productivity

commercial and educational bodies and government departments that are concerned with the publication of statistics regarding past and present economic situations and forecast trends. A large part of the management system is concerned with the interpretation and evaluation of this information.

Apart from the general economic conditions prevailing in the society, one major economic factor that concerns the business is its competitiveness. This depends on cost which as we have seen is determined by the price of prime resources added to the price of producer resources. If a way can be found to utilise resources more effectively, costs will be lower and the business will be more competitive. The ratio of input to output, of resources used to goods or services produced is known as **productivity**. An increase in production is not the same as an increase in productivity.

Productivity improvement is something business management has been concerned with since the beginning of business. However, since the Industrial Revolution, the emphasis has been on scientific management with the resulting development of a large variety of formal techniques to replace the intuitive approach. Productivity improvement techniques include automation, brainstorming, business games, cost benefit analysis, cybernetics, decision theory, discounted cash flow, econometrics, education and training, environmental engineering, ergonomics, forms design and control, human relations and social science, incentive schemes, interfirm comparison, investment analysis, job evaluation and merit rating, linear programming, management audit, manpower planning, method study, network analysis, operations research, organisation study, productivity bargaining, queuing theory, resource allocation, simulation and modelling, standardisation, stock design, suggestion schemes, systems analysis and design, systems audit, value analysis, variety reduction, work measurement.

Social factors (E8)

The social environment in which a business operates greatly affects the way it conducts its affairs and most managements include a special public relations system amongst those of its business activities. The requirements of society today become the laws of tomorrow. It would be perilous to ignore such things as public opinion and cultural, racial, religious and other minority groups. The members of these groups are also consumers and producers, politicians and legislators, competitors and technologists. The policies and operation of a business are shaped by all the factors of its environment and its fortune and survival will depend upon these as much as upon its own efforts.

The business environment

The environment provides prime resources, producer resources, goods, services and information. In turn it requires an exchange of resources from the business. To cope with its existence in its environment a business must perform work that is not directly concerned with producing its own output and thus making

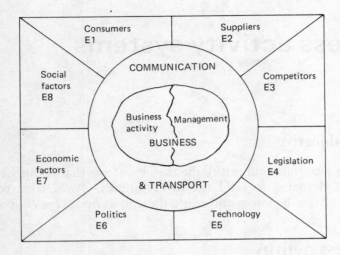

Figure 7   Business and its environment

the profit required to satisfy the owner's needs. Some of this environmental work will be in the form of special systems, e.g. public relations, and some will be in the form of additional operations added to direct business activities, e.g. sales tax added to sales. Much of the environmental work will be in the form of management evaluation of environmental information and policy decision making based on this.

The primary systems of any business thus comprise those activities which satisfy the economic needs of society by producing and selling goods and services, together with those activities which produce outputs required by the environment, and those that process inputs from the environment in order to manage the business.

Assessment tasks

1 Chose three different types of business operating in your locality, identify the owners and discuss and compare their motivation in running them.
2 List the main customers, suppliers and competitors of:
      (a) NASA   (b) Your local brewery   (c) Your local hospital
      (d) The Datsun Automobile Company   (e) Your local bank
3 What changes might occur in the Coca Cola Company if China adopted a westernised form of government?
4 What employment legislation is current and what workload does this entail for a local, medium-sized manufacturing company?
5 List five industries that could not have existed in the year 1937. What factors have influenced their inception and prosperity?
6 Draw a diagram (different to those in the text) to illustrate the influence of the environment on a business.

Unit 2
Business activity systems

Learning objective

To be able to recognise and justify the major systems that comprise the activity of a business designed to fulfil the owners needs. To be able to define the characteristics of each system and relate these to various types of business.

The Business Activity

A business exists in an environment, therefore it must perform certain activities to satisfy the needs of that environment and to ensure its survival and prosperity. However, these activities are not the ones chosen by the owner to bring him the results he needs. He will have seen an economic need in society and have decided to satisfy that need in the form of goods or services. The activities needed to do this are known as the Business Activity. It may be making and selling cars, providing a banking service, running a corner tobacconist's shop or providing local authority services etc. Whatever the means chosen, the work involved will have a common element of providing goods or services to the consumer (marketing) and obtaining goods or services to market (production).

One way of conducting a business is to decide what one is best at producing, provide it and then try to market it. However, if there is little or no demand the business is doomed to failure. A better approach is to find out what goods or services are required by society, choose from these those items that one has expertise in producing and then provide and market them. This approach is marketing oriented.

Marketing systems

Marketing is the primary Business Activity system. It consists of a series of subsystems which exist in any business, from the intuitive work performed by the owner/manager of a one man business to the workload of specialised departments in large corporations.

B1 Market research, analysis and assessment
Market research, analysis and assessment consists of going out to the consumer and asking questions, analysing the data obtained into meaningful groupings of needs by type of consumer and then assessing the relative market size and the ability of the business to satisfy these needs. The data can be gathered by

14

interview, questionnaire, published statistics, sales analysis, competitions etc. The work involves data capture to obtain the data and data processing to total, classify and sequence it etc. The assessment involves comparison with other known data, decision making and policy formulation. This is the work of the management.

B2 Advertising and sales promotion

Advertising and sales promotion is the development of latent markets, the creation of new ones and the exploitation of existing channels. These objectives are achieved by means of communication between the business and the consumer via the media, the press, television, radio, cinema etc., and by personal contact either directly from salesman to customer or indirectly by product to customer. A knowledge of the potential markets is needed together with the ability to motivate the consumer by showing how the product will satisfy his overt or subliminal needs. Advertisements must be devised, tested, placed and assessed. Sales campaigns must be planned and executed. The work involves management, data processing and specialist salemanship skills.

B3 Publicity

Publicity differs from advertising in that it is concerned with communicating information about the nature and availability of the product or service rather than trying to persuade the customer to buy. This information covers such things as price, specification, location, opening times etc, and often it is skilfully intermixed with advertising material. There is a tendency for advertising to be predominant in competitive markets whereas pure publicity is more normal in the social welfare sector.

B4 Customer contact and advice

Customer contact and advice is the interaction between the consumer and the business. Sales can be achieved by retail shopkeeping (counter sales), mail order (postal sales), wholesale credit sales (sales representative or communication based sales), discount stores (cash and carry) and other methods. The salesman can approach the customer, introduce the product and answer questions regarding price, delivery dates, specification, etc., or the customer can approach the salesman. In the latter case some form of customer reception is provided either personally, or by post or telephone. In both cases some form of information storage and retrieval system is provided for the receptionist or salesman. A business may not be providing an 'off the shelf' product or service but instead will produce to order. In this case an additional subsystem of estimation and quotation is involved. Preparing an estimate requires a detailed knowledge of how the product will be produced together with the material, labour and environmental resources that will be used in its production. From this and a knowledge of the cost and resource availability an estimate of the price and delivery date can be made. This is formalised into a quotation which is communicated to the consumer.

B5 Customer order acceptance

At its simplest, customer order acceptance is the shopkeeper taking a verbal order and reaching for the particular item from a shelf. A more complicated example is that of a sales representative noting a customer's requirements in an order book, dictating the day's orders onto tape, mailing the tape to the sales office, its transcription to a number of typed, multi-part order sets and the separation and distribution of the copies of these sets to sales ledger accounts, and production and despatch departments.

B6 Sales inventory and storage

The production of 'off the shelf' goods starts with inventory design which is a management function that determines by policy the range of goods to be stocked and the quantities (stock levels) to be maintained, bearing in mind such factors as size and frequency of demand, shelf life and the cost of unproductive capital. There is always a conflict between the ability to fill customers' orders without delay and the fact that resources tied up in stock usually devalue whereas those invested yield a profit. Sales inventory involves the purchasing or replacement of items consumed from stock and the receiving, checking and storage of the replacements. This system is usually very closely connected with inventory control (Unit 3).

B7 Distribution

Distribution involves inventory selection, packing, addressing, vehicle loading, routing and delivery. In the case of a shop the salesman can just select the item, wrap it and deliver it into the hands of the customer. However, with a service the actual performing of the service normally incorporates the above elements. Addressing, vehicle loading and routing is concerned with goods for customers distant from the business. In its simplest form this can be the mailing of packets via the postal system. More complex processes can involve the managing of the

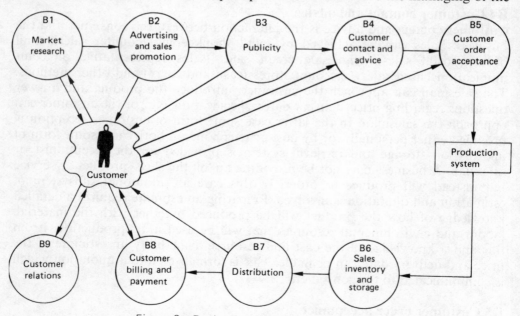

Figure 8   Business activity marketing systems

transport resources of a business, for example by loading vehicles in the reverse sequence to unloading requirements, and the planning of loads and routes so that a vehicle travels at maximum capacity along a route that contains little or no wasted mileage.

B8 Customer billing and payment handling

Payment may be either direct or indirect. A consumer does not receive a direct bill for a social amenity, e.g. parks, roads, etc. This is paid for by rates and taxes and, thus, is costed and payed for indirectly. Cash transactions are usually billed in the form of a sales receipt together with a verbal request for payment. Credit transactions require the checking of customer orders and delivery notes, followed by the production of invoices for distribution to the customer and to sales ledger accounts. This form of trading also requires the production, periodically, of customer statements of account and the chasing of unpaid accounts due. If a business runs a credit account system it will also normally incorporate a credit control subsystem. The receipt of payment is followed by notification to sales ledger, account updating for credit transactions and the banking of all cash, cheque and credit card payments.

B9 Customer relations—queries and complaints

This is an additional system involved in customer contact which is not part of the publicity system concerned with the product but is to do with the goodwill relationship between the customer and the business. It requires access to records detailing all customer contact and transactions and also a knowledge of the potential of the business to remedy any defect. It is an important system as good customer relations will encourage the development of a body of regular customers.

Production systems

Production is the secondary Business Activity system. In essence it is the obtaining of something to sell, as typified by the small shopkeeper. More often the business will make what it sells, either by the production of a service or the manufacturing of goods. As in marketing, a series of subsystems can be identified, applicable to both goods and service production.

B10 Research and development

The progression from an idea to a working model or prototype is the result of research and development. Market research may reveal a consumer need for a product or service that does not yet exist or exists in another form. Alternatively, a potential new market could be revealed by an invention created by the pure research of an advancing scientific and technological environment. The problem is to turn the idea into reality and this is achieved by obtaining resources and working these, often primitively by hand, using craftsmen and scientists. Then the product must be tested and retested, noting performance, finally modified and retested in the field of application. A product is developed when a prototype has passed its exhaustive field tests and has been modified to a state where it is ready for copying and so can be put into production.

B11 Product definition and design

Product definition and design takes the prototype a stage further by taking into account the design aspects not just to make it work but also to enable it to be produced and marketed. The aesthetic and fashionable aspects must be considered to make sure the product looks good to the consumer. The prime resources and producer resources must be defined for production bearing in mind the cost and availability factors. Finally the designer must produce a specification of the product in the form of drawings, charts and resource lists for the complete product and its individual component parts. The specification must include details of all quality and other working constraints.

B12 Methods planning

To prepare the manufacturing resources for the task of providing the product, after it has been designed, requires methods planning. The quantity, quality and availability of the existing resources must be known. Special resources may be required both for the manufacture and testing of the product. Staff may need to be trained and job specifications, procedure manuals and operations lists prepared defining the step by step sequence of work, the physical environment and the equipment and other resources required to produce the component parts and the final product, whether it is goods or service. At this stage a time and cost evaluation can be made as a basis for pricing.

B13 Production planning

The definition, obtaining and preparation of the manufacturing resource requirements is the job of production planning. The volume of production must be obtained from the marketing function, determined by customer order or management policy. The volume will affect the method of production—unit, batch or mass. Productivity improvement techniques need to be applied to devise the most efficient production systems. The working areas must be provided and prepared and the machines and equipment ordered and installed. The necessary staff for supervision and management must be obtained and trained, and the materials provided.

B14 Manufacturing stock inventory

Providing raw materials for the manufacture of the product or service is the function of manufacturing stock inventory. This is a parallel of sales inventory and entails inventory design, replacement purchasing, receiving and storage and is closely associated with manufacturing stock control (Unit 3).

B15 Manufacture or service production

Manufacture or service production is the employment of the productive resources of materials, staff, machines and buildings, in accordance with the production plans and methods to produce the required volume of products to the laid down quality requirements within the specified time limits. Goods may be manufactured, e.g. footballs, computers, canned beans; services produced,

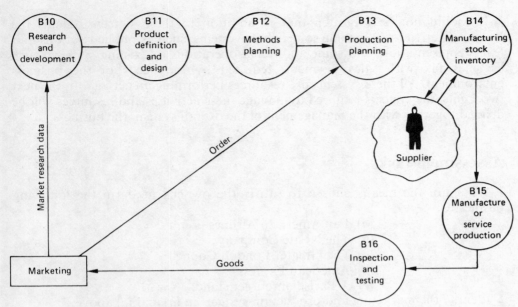

Figure 9   Business activity production systems

e.g. banking, hairdressing, legal advice; or processes operated, e.g. electricity generation, airline operation, tax collection. Many incidental processes are involved such as servicing, which is using less skilled resources to feed the main resource; finishing, which is cleaning up and presentation and packaging, which is putting the product in a container as opposed to packing for delivery.

B16 Inspection and testing

The last stage in production before the product is pronounced saleable is its inspection and testing. This consists of checking the product against the design specification and also giving it a working test, on an individual basis for some products or on a sampling basis for others. Associated with this system, a control system, called quality control, will often be found. This is a way of reducing the need for individual inspection by testing samples and charting results against quality tolerance limits. If errors are revealed which show production is going out of control, investigation of causes can be fed back to production to repair the damage and allow production to flow.

Business Activity systems

The preceding two major systems, containing sixteen subsystems, are common to all types of business under our definition. The provision of a public health amenity or a beauty treatment requires just as much production planning, market research and product design as does the manufacture of a radio set. Not all types and sizes of business have organisational departments for each subsystem and it may be considered a valuable exercise for the student to try to relate the list of subsystems to businesses within their experience.

It should not be forgotten that in addition to these sixteen systems the Business Activity will include some whole systems, such as public relations and legal representation, and some additional operations to existing systems, such as sales tax with sales payment, required by the needs of the business environment. All these systems use resources performing an activity. In the next two Units, the systems required to manage these activities and resources will be defined together with the management of the overall system–the business.

Assessment tasks

1 What are the means chosen to satisfy the owner's needs in the following businesses:

(*a*) Pan American Airlines
(*b*) The Nestlé Company
(*c*) The Greater London Council
(*d*) American Express
(*e*) A Paris hamburger stand.

2 Identify the marketing and production systems in (*a*) and (*e*) above.
3 Produce a chart or diagram to illustrate the relationship between marketing and production systems. Indicate other systems, as yet unidentified, that you think may be found in any business and try to show how they relate to the other systems in your diagram.
4 What, in your opinion, is the value of the analysis of a business into its component subsystems? If systems are concerned with the work required in running a business, what is the relationship between these and the resources employed?
5 What is the connection between the business activity systems and data processing?

Unit 3
Resource management systems

Learning objective

To be able to distinguish between those systems which are required to satisfy the needs of the owners and the society in which the business operates and those systems required to manage the resources employed. To be able to identify the different types of resource and the activities involved in their management. To be able to show how the grouping of resources into organisational areas is related to the work systems performed.

Resources

Resources have a dual nature. There are prime (raw material) resources and producer (performing) resources. The difference lies not in the nature of the resource itself but in the way it is used in the work system, e.g. a lift can 'process' a man or a man can service a lift.

It is useful for the systems analyst to identify resources as follows:

Real resources
> Location: land, premises, floor space etc.
> Materials: animal, vegetable and mineral matter
> Energy: wind, gravity, magnetism, etc.
> Machines, tools and equipment: aids to or substitutes for manpower
> Manpower: human physical ability
> Information: cumulative or stored useful knowledge
> Goods and services: the processed prime resources

Token resources
> Money and credit: representing the value of real resources

Token resources have no value in themselves but are used as a medium of exchange, a measure of value and a store of value.

Management

Work systems employ producer resources to process prime resources to produce the goods or services which meet the aims of the system. They need a motivating and controlling force to make them work and ensure that they hit the target in the same way that a vehicle needs a driver. Management is that force. The job of management is twofold; to manage the resource employed by the enterprise and to manage the work systems involved.

21

Management consists of:

$$\left.\begin{array}{l}\text{planning} \\ \text{effecting} \\ \text{controlling} \\ \text{improving}\end{array}\right\} \begin{array}{c}\text{resources} \\ \text{and} \\ \text{systems}\end{array} \left\}\begin{array}{l}\text{to achieve} \\ \text{the owners' aims}\end{array}\right.$$

Planning implies making provision for the future and the first step is to forecast the situation that will prevail at that time. This forecast will need to take into account all the environmental factors (Unit 1) together with the situation within the business. After the forecast has been made, management will identify requirements and set objectives in terms of system achievement. Then policies will be outlined to be used as continuing decisions in answer to questions relating to the attainment of the set objectives. Policies are positive rulings made known to all to avoid the necessity for on the spot decisions.

The next step is to plan an integrated schedule of work tasks against a time scale indicating sequence and system interfaces. Each activity on the schedule must then be defined in detail in terms of its aims and rules for conducting the activity. This is the work that is delegated by management to the specialist systems designer.

Given all this information, the manager can now plan for the resources required by each system to achieve the required outputs. The plan will consist of specification, quantity, quality and value. Finally, these facts can be assembled into the form of budgets to be used for control purposes.

Effecting is putting the plan into operation and consists mainly of two factors, organising and coordinating. Organising requires the locating and acquisition of the resources and their preparation and grouping for the systems in which they are to be employed, followed by the final placement of these resources ready for use and control. Coordination refers to the utilisation of the resources in the work system and involves the integration, balancing, direction and timing of the system to ensure the right resource is present in the right amount in the right place at the right time. In the same way that a coordinated football team wins the match so a coordinated system achieves its aims.

Organisation is the grouping of resources to facilitate direction and control. This grouping can be considered as a matrix of horizontal and vertical relationships. Horizontal groups usually consist of:

Function organisation: type of work e.g. sales, production
Geographical organisation: location of resources performing systems
Product organisation: resources producing different goods or services
Process organisation: resources operating different processes
Market organisation: specialist groups aimed at different consumers

Usually a mix of several of these types of grouping will be found at different levels in the business. Relationships between groups within any horizontal group type are known as **staff relationships**.

Vertical grouping is concerned with authority and responsibility. Initially the authority over and responsibility for the business lies with the owners. By employing specialist management the owners delegate authority over certain definite groups of work and resources. The responsibility cannot be delegated

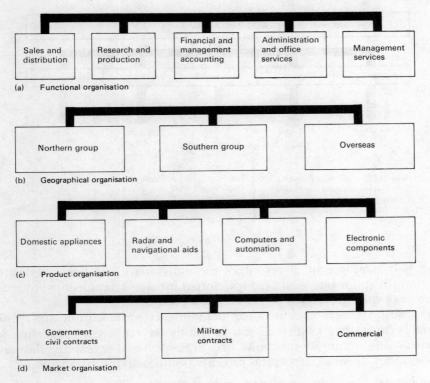

(a)   Functional organisation

(b)   Geographical organisation

(c)   Product organisation

(d)   Market organisation

Figure 10   Horizontal groupings

but multiplies with each delegation of authority. Relationships between vertical groupings are known as **line relationships**. Vertical groups usually consist of:

Group of companies
Individual business
Group or division (by horizontal grouping)
Department
Section
Work station

Each vertical level will require management and the number of staff reporting directly to any manager is known as the **span of control**. This span is based upon the amount of management work required at any level, and varies greatly depending upon the nature of work, quality of staff (and of management) and the degree of responsibility involved.

When authority is delegated, managers must define exactly the area of authority by written and agreed terms of reference; ensure the ability of those delegated to perform the duties involved by training and motivation; be selective in what is delegated and what is retained; set targets of quantity, quality and timing, and effect control to ensure these are achieved; establish good working relationships between all delegated groups.

The matrix of horizontal and vertical grouping is normally represented in the form of an **organisation chart** using boxes to identify the work performed

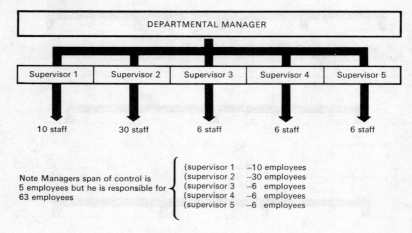

Figure 11   The span of control

by any particular group of resources (or individual) and lines joining these boxes (unbroken for line relationships, dotted for staff relationships) to indicate the formal or informal relations between the groups.

Organisation charts are used for planning, communicating and problem solution because they ensure all job functions have a higher reporting level; they ensure all required functions are present; they reveal overlapping of functions; they illustrate structural incompatibilities and imbalances.

Controlling resources is concerned with security, maintenance and disposal. Security is the protection of a resource from accidental or deliberate loss, damage or misuse. Protection can be preventative or detective and takes the form of physical protection e.g. locks, fire extinguishers; organisation protection e.g. security guards, supervision; systems protection e.g. audit, passwords, inspection.

Maintenance and repair of resources is concerned with the continuing functioning of the protected resources. It can be preventative, i.e. servicing, or operational. The actual form it takes depends, of course, upon the nature of the resource e.g. welfare for manpower, repair for machines, etc. Together with maintenance, alternative provision is made in the form of stand-by facilities and insurance.

The disposal of a resource needs management in the same way as acquisition. Resources are required to be used in a work system and if that work ceases to exist then the resource must be disposed of in some way. If the work continues but the resource is no longer capable of functioning then it must be disposed of and replaced.

Improvement is a continuing task of management and applies both to the work systems being performed and to the resources utilised. Sometimes improvement takes the form of a deliberate attempt at innovation forced upon the business by a changing environment. Often it takes the form of problem identification and solution occurring in the normal day to day operations of the enterprise. Improvement also springs from man's inbuilt need for what he considers progress. Improving entails taking an existing situation, analysing it in terms of

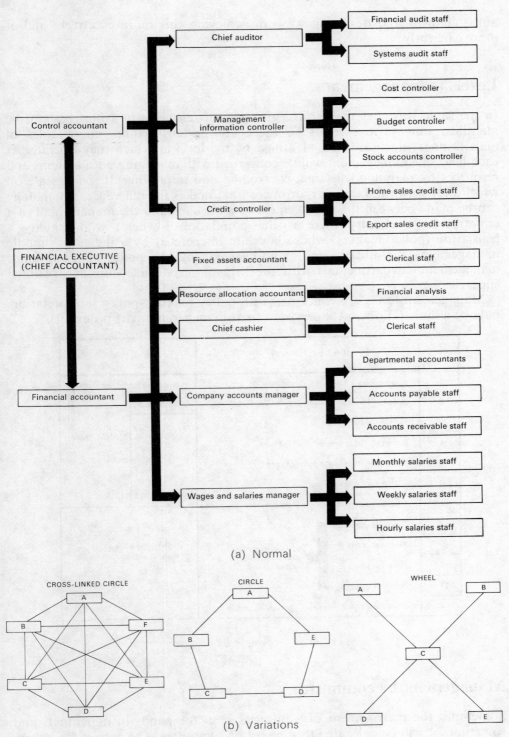

(a) Normal

(b) Variations

Figure 12 Organisation chart

aim fulfilment and designing ways of achieving this more effectively and/or more efficiently.

Levels in management

In the same way that the vertical grouping of resources in a business can be identified into various levels so there are primarily three major roles of management which are best identified by the level at which they operate. At each level, the management will be concerned with managing both systems and resources by planning, effecting, controlling and improving. It is the scale on which they perform, i.e. macro or micro, that makes the difference. An analogy can be made between the management of a business and the management of a country. In a country there is the population (owners) who employ a legislature (policy makers) whose laws are interpreted by a judiciary (middle management—divisional) and administered by a police force (junior management—departmental) with the help of responsible citizens (sectional supervision).

Management levels are concerned with policy making, policy interpretation, policy administration and supervision (part manager and part producer).

LEVEL	JOB DESCRIPTION	JOB TYPE		
1	Shareholders – Council – Committee etc.	owners or elected spokesmen		
2	Board of Directors – Management Committee etc.	Administration		
3	Functional management			
4	Geographical or product management	Executive	MANAGEMENT	
5	Departmental or office management			
6	Supervisory management			
--7--	Section leader – senior clerk grade F leading hand			
8	Producer grade E			
9	Producer grade D	Levels of job skill complexity and responsibility	PRODUCERS, technical, manual and clerical	
10	Producer grade C			
11	Producer grade B			
12	Producer grade A – trainee – junior —unskilled			

Figure 13   Levels in a business

Management by committee

Sometimes the management of a business is in the hands of individuals and sometimes it will be delegated to a board or committee. The reason for having a group of people is to spread the work load and also to allow for subject specialisation. However, the board can only speak with one voice. Group decisions are communicated through one channel of authority.

It is quite possible that each member of the committee will be given a special responsibility or area of investigation upon which to report back at committee meetings. Each member will submit his point of view and then a group decision will be made by discussion and vote. Often the main committee will split into sub-committees or individual members will form sub-committees to examine a particular aspect of the main committee work.

Theoretically all meetings other than seminars and conferences are committees but the term normally applies to a constitutionally set up group conducting meetings on a regularly organised basis. Committees are mainly either policy making or advisory. A policy making committee has built into its terms of reference, the power to act within stated limits on behalf of those appointing it. An advisory committee exists to make recommendations to some higher authority. Sub-committees, therefore, fall into this latter category.

The advantage of the system of group decision is that better informed and well reasoned decisions should be made by employing the energies and opinions of more than one person. However, group decisions often take far longer to reach and put into practice and even if it has the most efficient and well informed members, any group brings with it additional problems of organisation, coordination and communication. The committee system is very good in principle but in practice it is only as good as its terms of reference, its chairman and its membership.

Resource management

A business is worth no more and no less than the value of its resources. The emphasis placed upon finance and accounting in business is due to the fact that money represents the value of real resources and this is one way of managing these resources. There are many other ways of managing resources which are equally important—you do not measure the worth of your mother in terms of money.

Resource management is concerned with the survival of the business, with its day to day efficient running and with its future growth and development. It is concerned with locating and obtaining resources and with their maintenance, security and replacement. Resource management causes much additional work in a business and this work must itself be performed by resources which must be managed. Resource management adds another set of systems to the environmental and business activity systems, all of which need systems management (Unit 4).

R1 Location management systems
Departments such as estates and housing, maintenance, security and cleaning are involved in location management. Some of the work involved will be the concern of top management who must consider the location of markets, communication problems, the availability of staff, etc. Top management policy approval is required when considering the actual location(s) of the business,

the type and size of buildings required, the method of acquisition and so on. Once acquired the buildings must have their floor space allocated and laid out for the type of work that will be performed there. Specialists will become involved to provide floor layouts that satisfy safety, economic, efficiency and aesthetic requirements. Once the premises are occupied they must be kept clean and in good repair; for example, redecoration will be required, light bulbs will need replacing. As the work requirements change so modifications will become necessary. Walls may be knocked down, additions built on and so on. All this work will require a maintenance workforce.

R2 Materials management systems

The manufacturing stock inventory (B14) and the finished goods sales inventory (B6), and also all other materials that are used by the business e.g. stationery, building materials, canteen foodstocks, are the concern of materials management systems. As with manufacturing materials, these must be planned for, acquired, organised, made secure and maintained and, finally, disposed of. Most materials management systems are built around a paperwork model of the actual stock situation. This shows the amount of stock of each item and as the goods flow in and out of the stores the model is updated. The model will contain details of minimum and maximum stock levels, re-order quantities, source of supply etc. and will automatically produce requisitions when stocks reach re-order level. Such systems are generally called stock or inventory control systems. In addition, large firms usually have some form of internal materials handling systems to move materials and finished goods from store to production line etc.

R3 Energy management systems

The provision and maintenance of such services as electricity, gas, compressed air, etc. must be organised. The smaller business will obtain its supply from the various utilities boards but larger firms sometimes provide their own supplies or at least have stand-by provision in case of utility failure. Energy, like any other resource, must be planned for, acquired and organised. Often, the responsibility for this and the maintenance of supply is grouped organisationally with the location management systems.

R4 Machines management systems

Machines management systems also cover tools and equipment. They are either based in the department that uses the machines, e.g. screwdrivers, pens, typewriter ribbons, or involve the services of a specialised department, e.g. transport maintenance, typewriter repair. For specialised or large machines the services of an outside agency might be called in, e.g. computer maintenance. Planning for the machines and equipment is normally done in the department in which they will be used but the purchasing, placement and record-keeping will generally fall to some centralised buying department.

R5 Manpower management systems

The most important resource in business is staff, who are not only the source of motive power but also the generators of knowledge. Furthermore, staff are not like inanimate premises, materials or machines but have feelings which can affect their performance in both a disruptive way (strikes etc.) and a positive way (enthusiasm). In systems terms, staff can be considered to be probabalistic systems (Unit 4).

One of the main considerations when dealing with the manpower resource is the trade union movement. In addition, some trades are covered by wage councils which fix wages and conditions of work. Employment legislation covers a vast area to provide minimum terms of employment but many firms go much further than this, realising that it is in their own interests to have a healthy, happy workforce. Extras such as sports and social clubs, goods discounting and non-contributory pension funds are provided and sometimes worker participation in management and profit sharing schemes are also found.

Manpower management begins with the forecasting and identifying of manpower requirements in terms of quantity, quality, type and value. Such techniques as work measurement, job evaluation and job specification are often employed at this stage. The next step is recruitment which involves advertising, appraisal, interview and selection. Education and training follow, then placement and induction. Security of the manpower resource is effected by employment legislation, insurance, accident prevention, the discouragement of staff poachers and the prevention of bad working habits. The resource is maintained by the keeping of personnel records for promotion evaluation and welfare, and providing health and first-aid facilities, canteen, cleaning and remuneration systems together with the provision of stand-by services in the form of overtime and temporary staff. Within the province of the manpower management system are the problems of redundancy, retraining and dismissal.

R6 Information management systems

Like the other resource management systems, information management systems are concerned with the planning for, acquisition, organising, maintaining and disposal of the resource which in this cases is information. Until recently this work was achieved on a local basis, department by department. However, with the concept of business database becoming more popular, the trend is towards centralised databanks and specialised information retrieval systems. Information is required to manage the business overall and all its resources and subsystems. The planning for the required information must therefore be performed by management although usually with the specialised assistance of organisation and methods (O & M) and systems designers. Data acquisition is normally called data capture and is followed by encoding and validation. The data is then transmitted for storage in the database which is organised by record, file and database structure design.

Security is achieved by physical, organisational and 'software' methods and maintenance involves the modification of the data by file management and update procedures. Some data is required to be stored for a certain period of time as historical records, and database management systems will contain details of storage life and provision for disposal as required. The distinction between data and information is simply that of usefulness. Data is just facts

		MATERIALS	MANPOWER	MACHINES	ENERGY	LOCATION	MONEY	INFORMATION
SPECIFY	**PLAN**	Forecast specify	Identify requirements	Identify requirements	Evaluate requirements	Space planning	Budget	File design
SCHEDULE		Ordering	Job planning	Job planning	Job planning	Job planning	Management accounting	System design
PURCHASE	**EFFECT**	Receive Inspect	Advertise Interview Select	Purchase Lease Rent	Negotiation with utilities	Purchase Lease Rent	Loans Shares	Data capture
PREPARE		Pre-production	Training Induction	Set up	Install services	Decoration	Cash Credit facilities	Data preparation
INSTALL		Storage	Placement	Install	Connect	Installation	Allocation	File conversion and update
PROTECT	**CONTROL**	Materials control	Welfare	Security	Security	Security	Bank Audit	Data controls
MAINTAIN		Cleaning Storage	Payroll	Machine maintenance	Utility maintenance	Building maintenance	Investment	File maintenance
DISPOSE		Scrap Reject	Retirement	Depreciate	Disconnect	Sale	Dividends	Distribution
IMPROVE	**IMPROVE**	Quality control	Training	Modify	Boost	Modify	Productivity	Systems analysis

Figure 14   Resource management systems

about a situation or environment and if these facts are readily useful then they are called information. If not, they can be regarded as raw material from which information is produced by data processing (Unit 5).

R7 Money management systems

Money management systems should not be confused with work systems which process monetary data for purposes of control by management. Money management systems are concerned with managing money as a token business resource. Planning for money is achieved by budgeting and cash flow analysis. Acquisition is effected by the issue of shares, obtaining loans, investing excess profits etc. The acquistion and disposal of money is also covered by the various cash handling systems involved in the receipt of customer payments and the payment of business debts. Other cash handling systems are petty cash, expenses and banking.

One of the major jobs in business is the accounting system, a large proportion of which is devoted to the security of the money resource in the day to day operations of the firm. Bookkeeping, with all the ledgers, journals, double-entry etc. that are entailed in the preparation of final financial accounts, is all for the purpose of money security representing real resource security. There are also physical systems involved including such things as safes, security guards, the issue of cash and so on. Specific security procedures include audit and credit control routines. The disposal of money involves either the issue of cash, cheque payments and the depreciation and write off of book assets.

Summary

Resource management systems are less easy to define than the business activity systems as only in certain cases, e.g. personnel records, inventory control are they found to exist as a completely separate system in their own right with their own organisational department devoted to their operation. More often, the work of resource management is found to be delegated to the management and staff of a department whose prime function is operating one of the business activity systems. This facilitates organisational structure as the grouping incorporates responsibility for the resources used by the business activity system in question but it should be realised that this is not the only approach to resource management, particularly with the advent of global information processing systems.

Assessment tasks

1 List all the separate resource management systems you can think of under the resource headings.
2 You are asked to form a business for the manufacture and sale of model aircraft kits. You must define your objectives:
Marketing objectives:
What kind of model—wood, plastic, metal etc.?

What range of products—how many lines?
Expected sales area?
Expected sales volume for each line?
Percentage profit required from each kit?
Work involved
Sales method—mail order, retail shop, wholesale distribution, etc.?
Production work involved?
Resource requirements?
What work other than sales and production is required?
What price will be charged for each kit?
3 Produce an organisation chart for any business known to you. For each box on the chart, list the work systems performed.
4 How can the management task of improving (p. 24) be effected on each of the resources (real and token) found in business?

Unit 4
Systems management

Learning objective

To be able to identify and justify the work systems in a business which are required to manage all work systems, notably the business activity systems of marketing and production and the resource management systems. To be able to define the different types of system found in a business and the varying levels of system and their components. To be able to apply this knowledge and relate it to the function of systems management. To be able to justify how a knowledge of the similarities and differences in the human resource can be useful in systems management. To be able to specify the different types of standards used for systems control.

System levels

A system is defined as '**prime resources** subjected to a **regulated activity** to produce **aim-achieving results**'.

This definition can be applied to almost any man-made activity whether large and complex or small and simple. The business as a whole can be regarded as a system. The sub-activities within the business are also systems, subsystems of the whole. We use different names for systems at different levels in the business organisational structure.

A **system** is an activity which exists as a continuous entity in more than one organisational department. It is comprised of two or more procedures.

A **procedure** is an activity which is a continuous entity existing in one organisational department. It is comprised of one or more operations.

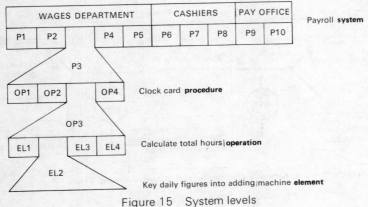

Figure 15   System levels

33

An **operation** is an activity which is a continuous entity performed at one organisational work station. It is comprised of one or more work elements.

An **element** is the smallest system which can usefully be identified in a business.

System types

The output from a system is in the form of aim-achieving results. The degree of aim-achievement unfortunately varies from something less than 100% to near failure. Systems can be identified according to their aim-achievement properties.

Determined systems always act the same way and will always produce the same results from a given input. These systems are also referred to as 'mechanistic' systems and all machines can be regarded as determined systems. Where the

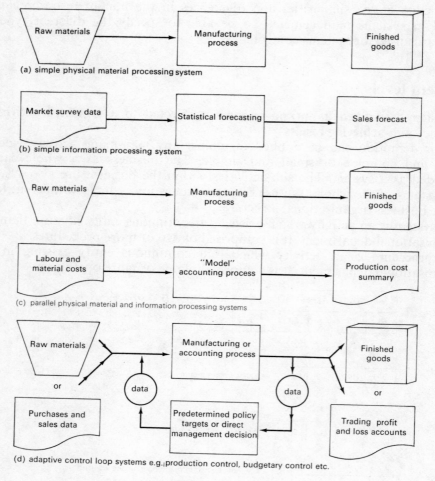

Figure 16   System types

rules are fixed, and the environment, resources and activity do not vary, the output results are determined.

Probabilistic systems cannot have their output determined. It may be possible to make a statistically based forecast of the probable outcome with some degree of accuracy but each individual result is unpredictable. Probabilistic systems are also called uncontrolled systems.

Homeostatic systems are adaptive and self-controlled. They are designed as such to combat entropy which is the tendency towards random, unregulated activity found in man-made systems. This is achieved by the addition of a second, control feedback system to the main system. These systems have inbuilt management and are automatic systems.

Competitive systems are the most common type of business system as they are environment controlled adaptive systems. It is the presence of management that makes them adaptive to environmental changes. To produce the results required by changes in the environment management can change the aims, the rules, the activity or the resources of the system. If the management make the correct decisions and changes the system will adapt to the environment and prosper; if not it will fail.

Systems can also be identified according to their function.

Prime systems exist in their own right and can be either physical material processing or data processing.

Model systems are models of prime systems usually in the form of data processing systems used in the management of prime systems.

Feedback systems are systems which convert outputs from prime or model systems into controlled inputs which are fed back into the system to control its performance.

System components

To manage the work systems it is necessary to understand not only the various levels and types of system but also the breakdown of the component parts of a system.

Prime resources are the items that are processed. They can be physical matter (coal, steel, plastic, etc.), machines (in a repair system), raw data (e.g. expenditure on expenses for financial accounts), money (a cheque received in payment, etc.) or any of the resources listed in Unit 3.

System rules are the rules covering the activities in the system defining what processes and decisions must occur, the sequence in which these are performed, the direct limits and constraints (quantity, quality, time, etc.) within which they must be achieved, and the integrated systems environment in which they exist.

Systems activity is the employment of organisationally grouped **producer resources** in a **physical environment** working according to a particular **method**. There is a distinction between system rules and method. The rules determine the ideal system whereas the method is the chosen (or compromise) way of realising this ideal.

Results from a system will be in the form of changed prime resources. These may be added to, subtracted from, grouped and merged or dismembered in some way.

System aims are the most important component, whatever the type of system, whatever the level. If a system has no aim then it has no validity and should be scrapped. If the aim is unknown or imperfectly stated, how can the results be achieved? Each system aim must be contributory to the aims of the higher level system of which it is a subsystem. The ultimate business aim is the need satisfaction of the owners. All subsystem aims should lead to this.

Systems management

Resource management is concerned with obtaining, maintaining and disposing resources used in business systems. Systems management is concerned with formulating the aims, devising the systems, operating and controlling them. Systems management must ensure that all systems necessary to the achievement of the business aim are present and that they are effective, achieve their aims, and operate at the highest level of productivity possible i.e. they are efficient.

Planning work systems is a prerequisite of planning resources (Unit 3). They are planned, within a framework of objectives, policies and work schedules, by the management in conjunction with a specialist systems analyst/designer. Effecting systems consists of putting the producer resources to work according to the system rules. If the system were a purely mechanistic one comprised of inert producer resources, like buildings and machines, the problem of effecting the system would be simply the matter of pressing a button. The most common producer resource, however, is man and a far more understanding approach is needed when attempting to utilise this resource in a work system. It is not enough to give an order and expect it to be obeyed. Men need to be motivated to give of their best and to do this, management need an understanding of human relations.

Human relations

The work of a manager utilising the human resource consists of selecting the staff suited to the job specification; training the staff for job skills and promotion; appraising the employee's efforts; rewarding the employee's contribution; providing opportunities for participation; providing channels of communication and direction; counselling employees on problems, welfare and grievances.

To understand why these activities are necessary, it is important to have an idea of how people behave and why.

Differences in individuals are both physical and personality based. People have different work experience, mental abilities and aptitudes, interests and temperaments.

Work experience can be ascertained from a person's past history and can range from skills experience, e.g. typing, selling, to actual systems experience e.g. invoicing, auditing.

Mental abilities and aptitudes are usually revealed by various carefully designed tests. Among the more common classifications are:

Mechanical comprehension—perception of mechanical relationships

Intelligence–the ability to learn by experience

Literacy–fluency with words and vocabulary

Numeracy–the ability to reason in numeric terms

Spatial perception–reasoning in abstract terms

Clerical ability–speed and accuracy of perception.

Interests are usually determined by interview and questionnaire and can be artistic, musical, computational, social, outdoor, scientific, persuasive, mechanical, clerical, literary, etc.

Temperament is a measure of an individual's adaptation to his physical and social environment. There are several classification systems, all defining how an individual reacts towards his environment. One example uses components of temperament, the weighted mix of which comprises a person's character.

Normal–integrated, self controlled behaviour

Hysteroid–self interested behaviour

Manic–active and sociable behaviour

Depressive–pessimistic and retarded behaviour

Autistic–shy, sensitive and introspective behaviour

Paranoid–aggressive, argumentative and stubborn behaviour

Epileptoid–plodding, matter of fact, single-minded behaviour.

The use of the knowledge of differences in people allows the manager to select and place staff in the most suitable jobs and to provide corrective training where necessary. It also helps in the building of organisational group structures to provide harmonious working relationships.

Similarities in individuals are based upon human needs. All normal human behaviour is goal directed (motivated) towards the aim of need satisfaction. These needs are universal although the degree of personal priority will vary according to the degree of individual satisfaction and the individual's past experiences and his adaptation to these. Needs can be classified as biological or social. The latter group subdivides into ego needs and dependency needs.

Biological needs are the needs for survival and take priority over social needs. They include food, sleep, warmth, health, sex, shelter and dreams. It is difficult to say when a biological need is satisfied and further satisfaction is social not biological, e.g. water or champagne, cottage or palace?

Ego needs are developed if a person's experience teaches him that other people in society frustrate his need satisfaction. If this is the case, he will adapt by developing behaviour that will derive satisfaction outside of or in spite of society. Ego needs are

physical independence–financial and job security

mental independence–individuality and self expression

mental security–freedom from criticism

self determination–opportunity to follow one's own aptitudes and succeed

self protection–against not being wanted and failure

personal reward–for one's own individual abilities and efforts

stimulation–new experience to combat monotony and boredom.

Dependency needs develop if a person's experience leads him to obtain his need satisfaction from within society. They include

social acceptance–inclusion in group activities
social approval–to be liked/loved by others
companionship–comfort and agreement from others
group inclusion–to have a say in group aims and policies
social reward–for group abilities and efforts
social status–recognition of value to the group.

All individuals have all the above needs but with various priorities according to the person's past experience and circumstances. Knowledge of these needs and the ability to recognise them in his staff will enable a manager to motivate his human resources towards the mutual satisfaction of the needs of his staff and the needs of the working systems in which they are employed. To effect his systems, the manager must show his staff how, by performing the work activity in the systems they will, at the same time, satisfy their own needs. This is the equivalent of pressing the button in a mechanistic system and will cause the resources to work of their own volition.

Frustration is the opposite to motivation. If an individual perceives that something obstructs his need satisfaction, he will react with a behaviour pattern that is definitely non-productive. The reaction will depend on the temperament of the individual concerned and could be

direct agression–open hostility and anger at the frustrator
transferred aggression–towards the nearest available object or person
introverted aggression–self blame and punishment
direct compensation fixation–illogical return to original position
indirect compensation fixation–selection of an irrelevant substitute goal
rationalisation–distorting the motives of the frustrator
flight–physical refusal to face up to the situation
day dreaming–as a substitute for action
repression–substandard behaviour justified by faults in others
regression–childish behaviour referring all decisions to others.

The manager must learn to recognise these symptoms of need satisfaction frustration in order to be able to remedy the situation and thus put his systems into effect.

Group behaviour must be managed and understood in much the same way as the behaviour of invidivuals. Each individual belongs to three groups.

The primary group–the home and family
The secondary group–friends, workmates, superiors and subordinates
The mass–people dealt with but unknown (e.g. in shops and offices).

Each group builds up its own collective aims, needs and behaviour patterns. Each individual in the group tends to adopt the generally accepted attitudes of the group and behaves and reacts accordingly, sometimes even against his own personality. The needs of the individual both affect and are affected by the needs of the groups to which he belongs.

Group roles have been analysed as being

problem solving–adaptable
creative–unregulated

productive–output orientated
procedural–by the book
compromise–unstable
dependent–indecisive
aggressive–unadaptable
flight–abdication of responsibility.

The group role affects the behaviour of the individual in the group by forcing a level of conformity. This is achieved by a process of first persuasion (logical and emotional), then force and ultimately, if conformity is not obtained, exclusion.

Systems management consists of planning and designing the work systems and then motivating the human producer resource to employ the other producer resources in the regulated activity of the system.

Systems control

Once working, the systems must be maintained and controlled so that they function both effectively and efficiently. Systems control consists of setting targets; communicating targets; capture and measurement of results; comparison of results with targets; revision of targets.

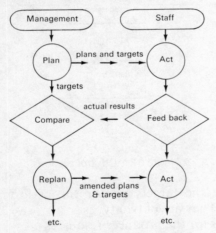

Figure 17   Systems control

Management systems control can be effected in two ways.

Direct control–where the comparison and revision of targets are carried out by direct management intervention.

Automatic control–where overall targets are set for a period of time and the comparison and revision are computed automatically by the system.

Whichever form of control is adopted, it is achieved by the addition of a feedback system to the controlled prime system. In direct control the prime system is controlled by a management information system interfaced with a management system. In the case of automatic control, the control system is a pure data processing system.

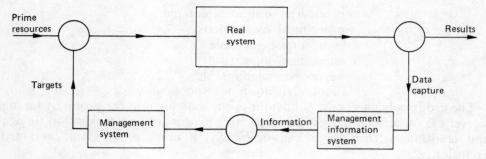

(a)   Direct control system

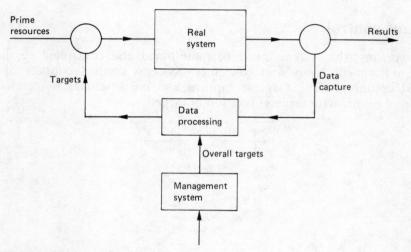

(b)   Automatic control system

Figure 18   Control systems

Systems standards are the targets set for the performance of the regulated activity in the system. They are of two types.

Methods standards for the producer resources

Performance standards (quantity, quality, time, etc.)

For each system and subsystem in the business activity and resource management areas, there will be a performance target which will be monitored by a direct or automatic management control system. Some of these control systems will be large enough to occupy a complete organisational department and are identifiable in their own right. Examples of these might be production control, budgetary control, quality control and cost control. In these systems a large model system is constructed to cover the areas of the prime system controlled and results and changes in the prime systems are used to update the model and deficiencies against target are noted. Corrective action can then be taken.

Where a control system is localised or is not large enough in itself to exist as an organisational grouping, it will consist of departmental management control operating within the framework of a management information control system. The management information control system of a business is a network feedback system operating through all organisational departments which enables departmental, divisional and overall business control to be coordinated by the various levels of management. This is primarily a data processing system and will be covered in Unit 5.

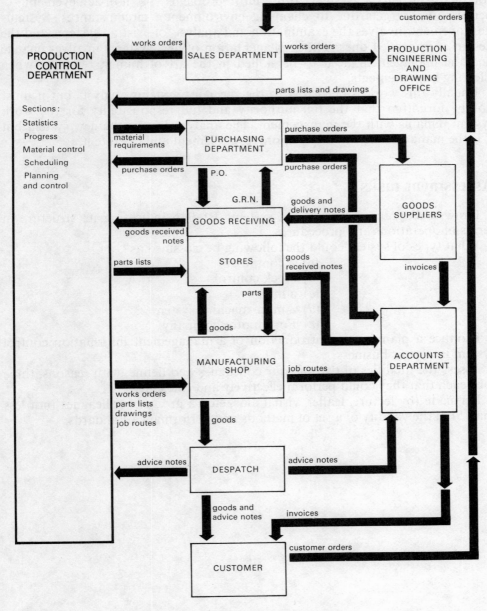

Figure 19   Production control system

Systems improvement

Management have a duty to improve existing systems in the business and to make them more efficient and effective. One method employed is systems audit which is a positive approach to evaluate the effectiveness of an existing system by the measurement of its achievement against its aims. More often, however, systems improvement comes about as the result of a trouble-shooting exercise conducted when a system runs into problems of non-achievement of performance targets due to changing environmental circumstances. Systems improvement involves the examination and analysis of existing systems and the design of improved ones. The implementation of new systems involves change and the management need to be skilled in the art of human relations when effecting improvements.

Usually this work is delegated to the specialist systems analysts but it must not be forgotten that the full authority and full responsibility for the work system remains with the management. The analyst designs the new system but it is the management who must approve, implement and operate it.

Assessment tasks

1 Draw a diagram of one of the systems B1-B16 indicating its structure in terms of operations and procedures.
2 What types of system could the following be classified as?

                (*a*) a computer
                (*b*) stock control
                (*c*) a man
                (*d*) a man–machine system
                (*e*) Ford motor company.

3 Produce a plan for the introduction of a management information control system into your business.
4 Assess the qualities of two of your colleagues and define, with reasons, three jobs each that they could perform effectively and efficiently.
5 Persuade (by lecture, leaflet, visual aids, etc.) a group of colleagues (not less than 5) of the validity of a set of methods and performance standards.

Unit 5
Data processing systems

Learning objective

To be able to identify and justify the major data processing systems in a business. To be able to distinguish these as being prime systems, subsystems of prime systems, model systems or feedback control systems. To be able to identify the components and mechanisms of data processing systems and to distinguish between the operations and procedure types involved and the methods employed to effect them. To be able to explain the significance of data processing in a business and its relation to the business activity and its management.

Types of data processing system

Some systems process physical prime resources such as wood, steel, chemicals, etc. to produce output goods or services. Data processing systems process the prime resource, data, to produce output information. In the same way that unprocessed steel and plastic differ from a refrigerator, so data is different from information. To the housewife, a refrigerator is useful. To the businessman, information is useful. Data processing systems are the same as any other man-made system, producing aim-achieving results by processing prime resources.

Some prime systems are data processing systems. For example, system B1, market research; system B13, production planning. Some prime systems are made up of some physical resource processing and some data processing subsystems. For example, system B8, customer billing (data processing) and payment handling (physical resource processing).

Some data processing systems are model systems running in parallel to the prime system they model. Stock inventory (part of system R2, materials management) and personnel records (part of system R5, manpower management) are examples of this.

Some data processing systems are feedback control systems taking their input as data concerning the prime system output and providing information to be used to update the prime system targets. All the systems introduced in Unit 4, in particular the management information system, belong to this category.

Extent of data processing systems

A system is an area of human interest. Any attempt to define the systems in a business is purely arbitrary, based on the method of categorisation. We have examined one such method which has listed the business systems as the marketing system (subsystems B1–B9); the production system (subsystems B10–B16); the resource management system (subsystems R1–R7).

Each of the marketing, production and resource management subsystems, B1–B16 and R1–R7, need themselves to be managed, and so we can add a further 23 systems management subsystems, S1–S23, to the above, in which the work of those subsystems is planned, effected, controlled and improved.

Finally, the business as a whole requires managing with the aid of the management information system (M1).

In total, this method of analysis identifies 47 major subsystems of a business, under 5 categories. If we attempt to specify which of these systems are physical resource processing and which are data processing, we must, bearing in mind that many systems are composed of a mix of both types of subsystems, invent a method of classification. A deliberately imprecise classification method would give us:

Mainly physical resource processing
B6, sales inventory
B7, distribution
B10, research and development
B14, manufacturing stock inventory
B15, manufacturing or service production (in some cases)
B16, inspection and testing

About equal physical resource and data processing
B2, advertising and sales promotion
B3, publicity
B8, customer billing and payment handling
B11, product definition and design
R1, location management
R2, materials management
R3, energy management
R4, machines management
R5, manpower management

Mainly data processing
B1, market research
B4, customer contact and advice
B5, customer order acceptance
B9, customer relations
B12, methods planning
B13, production planning
B15, manufacture or service production (in some cases)
R6, information management
R7, money management
S1–S23, systems management
M1, Business management—management information system

Under these headings, we have 6 physical resource processing systems, 9 partly physical resource, partly data processing systems, and 33 data processing systems.

This classification method may distort, in that it does not compare size of

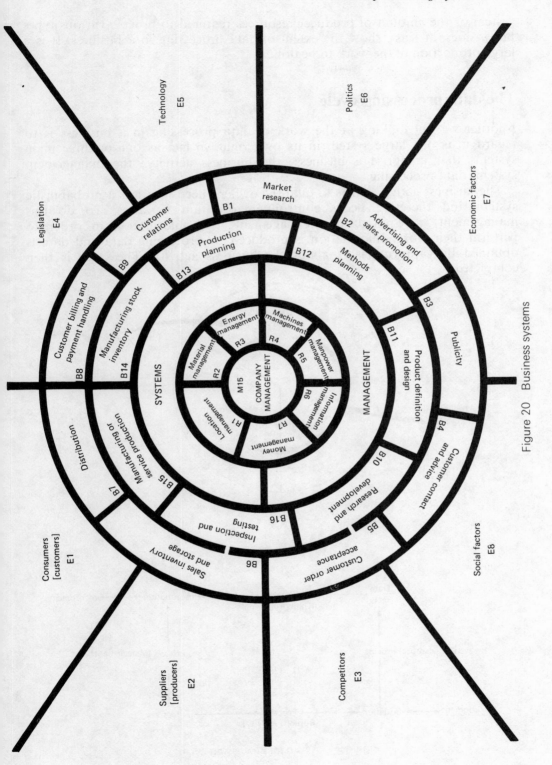

Figure 20   Business systems

system or the amount of producer resources required to process various types but it does, at least, show the extent of data processing in a business. It is a large proportion of the work to be done.

The data processing cycle

Another way of looking at the work of data processing in a business is to regard it as one large system in its own right, in fact as one of three main systems that comprise a business: the business activity; the management system; data processing.

The business activity exists to fulfil the owner's needs but it is a probabilistic system and therefore needs controlling to attain its aims. To do this management is required, but management need information in order to perform their work. Information is produced by processing data and data is obtained by capturing facts about the business activity. The cycle is then completed.

(a)

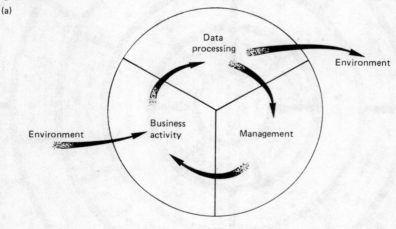

(b)

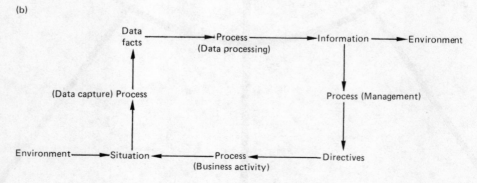

Figure 21   The data processing cycle

When using Figure 21 it should be remembered that sometimes the business activity itself can be data rather than physical resource processing (e.g. banking, insurance). There can, therefore, be two kinds of data processing: business activity (prime) data processing and management data processing. It is the latter, consisting of model systems, feedback systems and communication systems which is identified as data processing in the diagram. This is the resource management system R6, information management, identified in Unit 3, with interfaces both within the business and to the external environment. Data is acquired, prepared, processed, stored, safeguarded, maintained and disposed of just like any other resource, providing a source of current and historical information for use by management at all levels in their work of making comparisons and decisions before issuing directives, policies and targets.

Analysis of business in this way can help to clarify the purpose of each activity but it should be realised that most businesses are still organisation oriented and resource and systems management are carried out at a procedure (subsystem) level by departmental management without much regard for the integration aspects. Another factor inhibiting the systems approach is the traditional accounting method which tells how much a particular type of purchase (e.g. light and heat) has cost but not what any system has cost in production of its aim-oriented results.

Management information

There are as many management information systems as there are businesses as each one depends on the structure, size and organisational resources of the particular business concerned. There are, however, many common factors and it is possible to identify the main items of information required by any business management. We can consider the type of information, the information time coverage and the information activity coverage.

Management could not operate if it were faced with mountains of facts about every single activity carried out in the business. The first requirement is for consolidated facts—totals, summaries, etc. Often, these totals are provided on a sectional, departmental and divisional basis although, as mentioned above, there can be great advantages in providing totals by system rather than organisational grouping. Even with consolidated totals, management work would be unnecessarily retarded if it were required to give attention to aspects of the business that were proceeding satisfactorily and for this reason a policy of management by exception is normally adopted. This means that for day to day operational management, totals that deviate from the standard (above or below) are given priority so that immediate corrective action can be taken. These standards, usually performance but occasionally methods standards, are either the system aims targets or organisational group targets.

In addition to the provision of individual exception reporting totals, which are totals compared to standard, management often wish to make other comparisons and it is common for information to be provided in the form of ratios, which are the comparison of one item relative to another, or in the form of an analysis, which is the provision of a set of related totals broken down by classification headings. The above information is numeric and quantitative. Often management require descriptive, qualitative and other non-numeric information presented in the form of a report which can be detailed or an outline.

Information requirements

Management need to plan for the future and control the present. To plan for the future requires a knowledge of future conditions and performance under such conditions and this can only be predicted, i.e. guessed at, estimated or statistically forecast, based on past and current performance and trends. The particular system being managed will determine the frequency of information reporting. Some systems, not usually found in business, require second by second reporting. These are usually fully automatic control systems such as are found in weapon or spacecraft guidance and are known as real real-time systems. Some systems require minute by minute reporting, e.g. airline or hotel reservation systems, and are known as **real-time systems**. Most business systems require reporting on a less frequent basis, i.e. day by day, week by week, or month by month, and are known as **batch systems** as the data is allowed to accumulate into a batch before it is processed and the information reported. Usually the higher the management level, the longer is the reporting period. Departmental management may want to know the day by day situation whereas the top business management may only require monthly reporting with annual review. Typical reports will include current totals (for the time period used); cumulative totals for the year to date; moving annual totals; previous time period totals and totals for this time last year.

The above also applies to ratios and any other report form.

The actual information areas covered by a management information system will include:

Environment

Customers–analysis of potential market by quantity, type identity, location and relative prospects

Suppliers–analysis of potential suppliers by quantity, type identity, location and relative advantages

Competitors–analysis of potential competitors by quantity, type identity, location and relative strengths

General–intelligence report on opportunities and risks produced by legislation, technology, politics and social and economic factors.

Business

Resources–an analysis by identity in terms of quantity and value of inputs, outputs, current balances and utilisation against standard, for each of the real resources of location, materials, energy, machines and manpower

Money–a complete set of accounts covering trading and profit and loss accounts and balance sheet for the period (usually a month) expressed in terms of standard, actual and variance

Product–details of inputs, outputs and balances in terms of quantity and value for actuals, standards and variances, for each of the major systems of production and sales

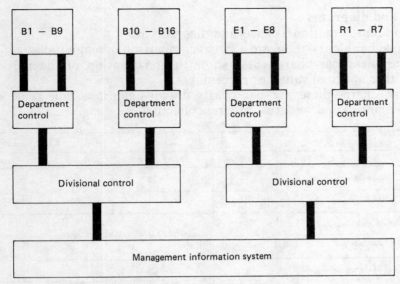

Figure 22   Systems control coverage

Information–intelligence report on the various business potentials in terms of technology, skills, etc. Also details of current problems and bottlenecks.

Presentation of information

Information is normally presented in the form of tabulations, charts and diagrams, graphs and written reports.

Tables
The type of table adopted will depend upon the information to be presented and the purpose for which it will be used.

Informative classifying tables–these present material in the best sequence (usually chronological) for easy reference. Not used for analysis or comparisons

Reference tables–these contain summarised information as a source for information retrieval, not analysis

Interpretive tables–relevant or significant aspects such as ratios, averages, percentages are presented for classification, analysis and comparison

Frequency distribution tables–these are a tabulation of the number of items in a distribution (dependent variable) of different sizes or attributes (independent variable)

Time series tables–these are values tabulated over a time scale with the value as the dependent variable.

Simple tables present the quantities of one dependent variable against a set of independent variable classifications, e.g. the number of families living in varying size houses.

Complex tables display measurements of several dependent variables against a common set of independent variables and are often divided into groups to provide relationship comparisons.

Charts and diagrams

The main representational charts and diagrams are

Simple bar charts–these are a visual comparison of magnitudes

Component bar charts–these show the relationship of the parts to the whole either in actual values or percentages

Gantt charts–these are bar charts drawn against a time scale used to indicate planned and/or actual progress of activities

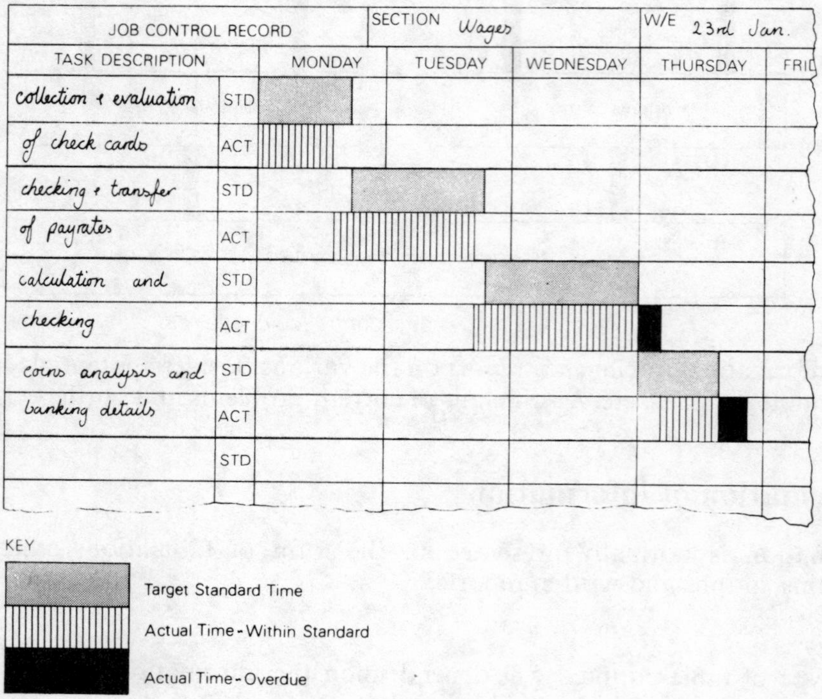

JOB CONTROL RECORD		SECTION *Wages*			W/E *23rd Jan.*	
TASK DESCRIPTION		MONDAY	TUESDAY	WEDNESDAY	THURSDAY	FRID
collection + evaluation	STD					
of check cards	ACT					
checking + transfer	STD					
of payrates	ACT					
calculation and	STD					
checking	ACT					
coins analysis and	STD					
banking details	ACT					
	STD					

KEY

Target Standard Time

Actual Time - Within Standard

Actual Time - Overdue

Figure 23   A Gantt chart

Pie charts–these are component charts showing relationships

Pictograms–these are pictorial bar charts using outline shapes, e.g. men, forms, machines, products

Statistical maps–these are actual maps with shaded areas or other markings

Histograms–these are vertical bar charts illustrating frequency distributions.

Graphs

The main forms of graph are

Historigrams–these are graphs of a time series, e.g. the cartoonist's typical sales figures representation

Normal graphs–these are graphs depicting the relationship of any two variables

Z charts–these are current, cumulative and moving annual totals against a time scale

Band curves–these are moving component bar charts on a time scale

Ratio scale graphs–these are semilog graphs illustrating relative not absolute change

Break even charts–these are charts of costs against volume where the point of intersection of cost and sales price indicate the break even volume above which profits are made.

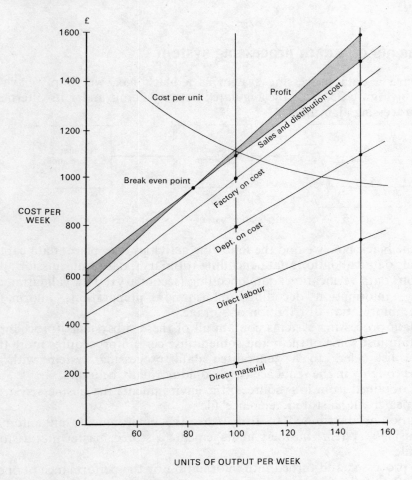

Figure 24   A break-even chart

Written reports

Written reports should have a clear purpose and a known distribution. The frequency of reporting and period covered should be relevant to the purpose. The content should be brief, simple, clear, visual and positive covering only known, accurate facts. The presentation should include

Cover–details of date rendered, period covered, units of quantity used, source and circulation, glossary and explanation.

Title–exactly describing content
Index–content headings and pages
Summary–necessary if the content is complex and voluminous
Introduction–defining subject(s) and scope of report
Body–stating problems, working methods and conclusions or solutions
Conclusion–emphatic restatement of conclusions reached and actions requested with time limits etc.
Appendices–tables, diagrams, etc. that are too large or complex for the report body.

Components of a data processing system

If we regard a data processing system as a **black box**, we simply have the situation in Figure 25, with the regulated activity going under its alternative name of **processing algorithm**.

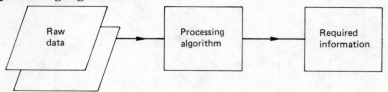

Figure 25   A data processing system—black box representation

Inside the black box, we find the following activities take place: data capture or retrieval; data validation; data encoding (primary); data transmission; data preparation; data verification; data encoding (secondary); data validation and processing; information decoding; information preparation; information validation; information distribution or storage.

Some data processing systems contain all of these subsystems (procedures), some contain just some of them and some utilise certain procedures more than once. The list refers to a generalised data processing system with the procedures roughly in the sequence they would normally be found.

Data is obtained from four sources: the environment; the business systems; a stored 'master' file; a stored 'reference' file.

Information is distributed to five areas: the environment; an automatic control business system; business management; a stored master file; a stored reference file.

Data is processed and turned into information by the performance of one or more of the following activities: communicating; comparing–checking; writing; comparing–classification; sorting; copying; calculating; filing and retrieval.

Summary

A business is an activity (system) that is made up of physical resource processing subsystems and data processing subsystems. These two types of

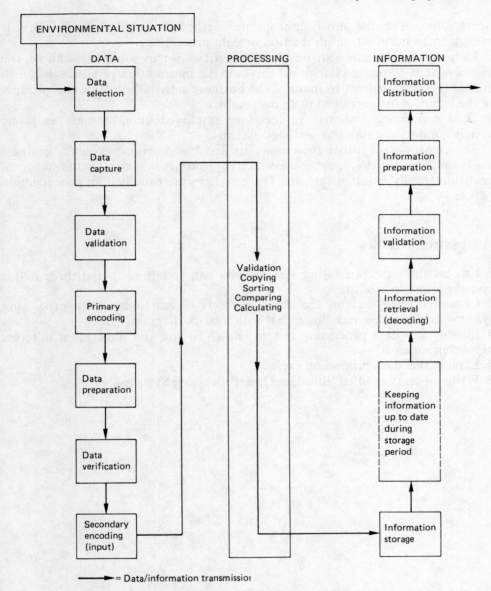

Figure 26   A data processing system—general procedures

subsystem are found in the three major activities of the business—the business activity, management and management information production (usually just called data processing or the office).

Management is concerned with resource management (planning for, effecting, controlling and improving resources) and systems management (devising, operating, controlling and improving systems). To manage effectively and efficiently requires accurate and timely information of the right quality in the correct quantities. This is achieved by capturing facts about a situation or environment (data) and processing these by an assortment of up to eight operations using the most appropriate methods (*see* Module 2). This is management information production or data processing.

Data processing can also be found as part of, or in some cases all of, the business activity prime systems. In this case the information produced is not to enable the management to manage the business activity but is an end product of the business (or part of it) in its own right.

Data processing systems are therefore employed in a business as prime systems, model systems and feedback systems.

The environment (other than suppliers and customers) in which a business exists adds work to the business activity prime systems in the form of environmentally required systems. These systems are usually data processing in nature.

Assessment tasks

1 List all the data processing systems you can recognise in the three major systems found in a business.

2 Choose one of each of the three methods of employing data processing systems in a business and illustrate it with a block diagram.

3 Identify any data processing system known to you and illustrate it in terms of its components.

4 Explain the 'data processing cycle'.

5 Write an essay entitled 'Business Data Processing Systems'.

Module 2
Business data processing

Unit 6
Data and information

Learning objective

To be able to identify the prime resources processed by data processing systems and to differentiate between the various forms these take. To be able to explain the different types of data and information structures and the reasons for these. To be able to analyse data and information into its content, its medium and its encoding.

Data representation

Data is simply unprocessed facts about a situation or an environment and therefore not directly useful for a given system purpose. For example, there may be six lights in a room, the moon may be out, it may be cold in the room, the person sitting there may be sleepy. These are all facts, just a small selection of the limitless number of facts that go to make up a situation in an environment. By listing the few above, we have made a selection. We have also encoded them into the form of alphabetic characters of a certain kind and then further encoded them into words in the English language. The selecting and encoding of facts is called data capture. There is a third aspect of data capture and that is concerned with the medium that is used to carry the encoded representation of the facts. The medium used for this book is printer's ink on paper. The book contains ideas which are encoded into characters (alphabetic, numeric and special, e.g. +, %, ?) and diagrams and retained for display on the ink and paper media.

The ideas in this book are also facts about situations. We tend to use the word facts as meaning truths but this is not necessarily so. Things—situations and physical environments—exist, just that. As soon as you introduce an observer you also introduce a bias or predudice in the form of the observer's perception. Two observers can survey the same situation and perceive different things because the sensory data that is being received is modified both by the quality of the observer's sense organs and by how his brain interprets what is received. Machine observers are no better. For example a photographic lightmeter will give one reading for white light strength but a false reading for light of one colour only, and no reading at all for temperature or boredom. It is limited to doing the one thing it is designed to do and by the quality of the mechanisms it is provided with to do it. Ideas, therefore, are perceived or projected facts, which may or may not conform to reality. Strangely, this possibility of error does not matter too much providing the information we derive from our perceived facts enables us to act usefully. The idea of a flat earth was wrong but it did not matter until man needed to travel the globe. Newton's physics are fine unless you wish to split the atom or travel to the stars. Then you need the perceived ideas of Einstein.

To summarise, data processing systems use data as a raw material which is first captured by

selection—which facts are needed for a certain system purpose
perception—observation and interpretation by human or machine senses and
    mechanisms
encoding—how the facts are represented in the mechanism
recording—onto a physical medium.

Information is usually required by humans, possibly after machine storage, and is, therefore, required in human intelligible code. In our environment this means in a human language, number system, standard symbols or pictures. These are built from a few standard codes of alphabetic characters, numeric characters and special characters.

A B C D E F	0 5	£ ! " ; : '
G H I J K L	1 6	+ − * / = %
M N O P Q R	2 7	. , ? & @ $
S T U V W X	3 8	( ) # [ ] ↑
Y Z	4 9	← > < ƀ(space)
Alphabetic (26)	Numeric (10)	Special (28)

Figure 27   A standard 64 character code

Data structures

Whilst information is normally required by humans, data can be captured and processed by man or machine. Information used by machines is called control signals. There is a wide range of primary codes used to represent the facts. In the same way that human alphabetic characters are further coded or organised into language structures e.g. English, French, so data is organised into a heirarchical structure to facilitate communication and processing.

The lowest level of code used to represent data is the binary digit or bit. In our alphabetic system we have 26 variations of code, A–Z. In the decimal number system we use, there are 10 variations , 0–9. In the binary system there are just 2 variations, 0 and 1. This makes it ideal for use in mechanical or electronic systems as it is easy to represent the two codes, e.g. a lever up or down, a switch on or off, the presence or absence of electrical current, etc.

Being a simple code, binary is also limited in what it can represent unless its characters are grouped together into a higher level code, each grouping representing a different idea. This is like human alphabetic characters being grouped into words, words into sentences, sentences into paragraphs, paragraphs into chapters, chapters into a story. The hierarchical system of data structures is shown in Figure 28.

Note that a **digit** is the name given to the occurrence of a character. In the number 27437 there are four characters but five digits. In the word 'shoes' there are four characters but five digits.

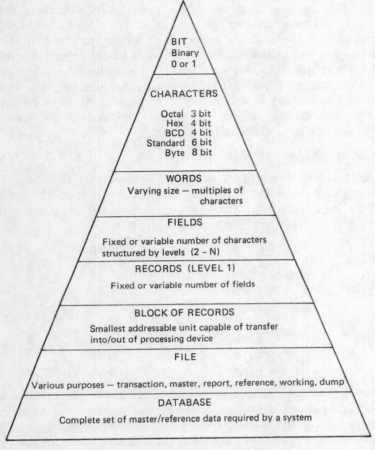

Figure 28   Data structures

Number systems

The number system we are all familiar with is called the decimal number system. A typical number in this system might be 10.75 and we all know this means ten and three quarters. But why does it mean that? What does ten and three quarters mean? We are so used to numbers that we rarely stop to think about them. We use them and that is that.

Numbers are just the symbols we use to express ideas about the quantity of things. Ten and three quarters has no meaning unless we are talking about ten and three quarters of something. But why does the set of characters 10.75 mean ten and three quarters? It obviously has to do with the particular characters chosen; it is not the same as 24.63, and even if we use the same characters, 10.75 is not the same as 57.01. The difference lies in the sequence of the characters but not just the sequence. 10.75 is not the same as 1.075. Numbers in our numbering system indicate their value by the choice of characters from ten symbols 0–9, and the sequence of the characters in relation to the point.

There are two digits to the left of the point (called the **radix point**) in the number 10.75, and two digits to the right of it. The digits to the left are called the integral part of the number and express whole numbers or integers. The digits to the right are called the fractional part because they express fractions or parts of whole numbers. We can count the positions both left and right of the radix point calling them first left, second left, third left, first right, second right, etc. This is clumsy and a more convenient method is to express each position by powers of R, where R = radix. The first position to the left is always indicated by R^0 and so we have a system

$$R^{+n} \ldots R^{+3} R^{+2} R^{+1} R^0 \text{ radix point } R^{-1} R^{-2} R^{-3} \ldots R^{-n}$$

The small number above the R is called the exponent. It indicates the value of the position and shows the number of times R is multiplied by itself and then multiplied by (or divided into if the exponent is negative) unity, which is the value of the first position to the left of the radix point, R^0.

$$R^{-n} = 1 \div R \times R \times R \times \ldots \text{etc. (n times)}$$
$$R^{-3} = 1 \div R \times R \times R$$
$$R^{-2} = 1 \div R \times R$$
$$R^{-1} = 1 \div R$$
$$R^0 \ = 1$$
$$R^{+1} = 1 \times R$$
$$R^{+2} = 1 \times R \times R$$
$$R^{+3} = 1 \times R \times R \times R$$
$$R^{+n} = 1 \times R \times R \times R \times \ldots \text{etc. (n times)}$$

This gives us the general rule for all numbering systems. All we need to do for any particular number system is to substitute the actual radix for R. The radix (or base) of any numbering system determines two things: the number of symbols (character set) in the system and the multiple value for each successive position from the point.

Thus in our decimal system number the radix is 10. The ten symbols are 0 1 2 3 4 5 6 7 8 9 and the value of 10.75 is determined as follows:

position	number		general rule	decimal		value
R^{+1}	1	=	$(1 \times R)$	$(1 \times 10) \times 1$	=	10
R^0	0	=	(1)	$(1) \quad \times 0$	=	0
	.	radix point				
R^{-1}	7	=	$(1 \div R)$	$(1 \div 10) \times 7$	=	$\frac{7}{10}$
R^{-2}	5	=	$(1 \div R \times R)$	$(1 \div 100) \times 5$	=	$\frac{5}{100}$
	total	=		$10 + 0 + \frac{7}{10} + \frac{5}{100}$	=	10.75

The example number is given in what is called **fixed point representation**. In this format numbers follow the rule

sign (+ or −)   integral part   radix point   fractional part

If the number is positive, it is normal to omit the sign. If there is no fractional part, it is normal to omit the radix point. The more positions added to the left of the radix point the bigger the number. The more positions added to the right of the point the more precise the number. Any number given can only be presumed to be accurate to the number of positions in the fractional part. Some numbers can never be given in fixed point form with complete precision. The value of pi, for example, is often given as 3.14 or as 3.142. To seven places (fractional part positions) it is 3.1428571. We would continue to one thousand places and still not define it with one hundred precent accuracy. In cases like this, it is often better to use the alternative representation 22/7 (**fractional representation**) which does not imply any precision at all.

A third format for expressing numbers is called **floating point representation**. Numbers can be expressed in the following way

> sign   a fixed point number   a radix   an exponent

An example might be $(+)0.273_{10}{}^5$ which means in fixed point representation (where R = 10):

$$0.273 \times 10^5 = 0.273 \times (1 \times R \times R \times R \times R \times R) = 0.273 \times 100000$$
$$= 27300$$

Binary, octal and hex

A number system may have any radix. The one we use most frequently has no special significance, but was adopted simply because man originally used his fingers for counting. Some civilizations adopted a radix of 60 or even 360 (based on rough calculations of the movements of the earth and sun in a year) or of 20 (based on finger and toe counting). The most useful number systems at present in use for machine data processing are binary (radix 2), octal (radix 8) and hexadecimal (radix 16). These follow the general rules stated above and we therefore have the following positional values:

number systems	*etc.*	R^4	R^3	R^2	R^1	R^0	R^{-1}	R^{-2}	R^{-3}	*etc.*
binary	etc.	2^4	2^3	2^2	2^1	2^0	2^{-1}	2^{-2}	2^{-3}	etc.
decimal	etc.	16	8	4	2	1	$\frac{1}{2}$	$\frac{1}{4}$	$\frac{1}{8}$	etc.
octal	etc.	8^4	8^3	8^2	8^1	8^0	8^{-1}	8^{-2}	8^{-3}	etc.
decimal	etc.	4096	512	64	8	1	$\frac{1}{8}$	$\frac{1}{64}$	$\frac{1}{512}$	etc.
hex	etc.	16^4	16^3	16^2	16^1	16^0	16^{-1}	16^{-2}	16^{-3}	etc.
decimal	etc.	65536	4096	256	16	1	$\frac{1}{16}$	$\frac{1}{256}$	$\frac{1}{4096}$	etc.

To indicate the quantity in any position we have the following characters:

binary	0 1
octal	0 1 2 3 4 5 6 7
hex	0 1 2 3 4 5 6 7 8 9 A B C D E F

Typical numbers in these numbering systems might be:

binary	1001	110.101	101010.1
octal	257	165.13	54.6
hex	990	4AB.9C	E 28.0A

Numbers not possible (illegal characters) might be:

binary   1002.304   octal   594.380   hex   91K.2G1

To distinguish numbers in different systems which could be otherwise confused (e.g. 257 decimal   257 octal), the radix can be given after the number thus:

decimal $257_{(10)}$ octal $257_{(8)}$

The general rule for converting any other number system to decimal is

$$N_{(10)} = N_{(R)} = \text{etc.} \ldots (D \times R^2) + (D \times R^1) + (D \times R^0) + (D \times R^{-1}) + \text{etc.}$$

where N is the number, R is the radix and D is a digit in any position.

Some examples of conversion to the decimal system are:

binary $1001.01_{(2)}$

$$= (1 \times 2^3) + (0 \times 2^2) + (0 \times 2^1) + (1 \times 2^0) + (0 \times 2^{-1}) + (1 \times 2^{-2})$$
$$= (1 \times 8) + (0 \times 4) + (0 \times 2) + (1 \times 1) + (0 \times \tfrac{1}{2}) + (1 \times \tfrac{1}{4})$$
$$= 8 + 1 + \tfrac{1}{4}$$
$$= 9\tfrac{1}{4} \text{ or } 9.25_{(10)}$$

octal $52.4_{(8)}$

$$= (5 \times 8^1) + (2 \times 8^0) + (4 \times 8^{-1})$$
$$= (5 \times 8) + (2 \times 1) + (4 \times \tfrac{1}{8})$$
$$= 40 + 2 + \tfrac{4}{8}$$
$$= 42\tfrac{1}{2} \text{ or } 42.5_{(10)}$$

hex $A9.C_{(16)}$

$$= (A \times 16^1) + (9 \times 16^0) + (C \times 16^{-1})$$
$$= (10 \times 16) + (9 \times 1) + (12 \times \tfrac{1}{16})$$
$$= 160 + 9 + \tfrac{12}{16}$$
$$= 169\tfrac{3}{4} \text{ or } 169.75_{(10)}$$

Number systems conversion

To convert from a decimal system number to any other system, two processes must be followed.

(1) Integral part: successively divide the integral part by the new radix, the successive remainders becoming the integral part of the new number in reverse sequence.

(2) Fractional part: successively multiply the complete fractional part by the new radix, the successive carrys becoming the fractional part of the new number in the sequence derived until the required precision is reached.

Some examples of conversion from the decimal system are:

To octal

$$874.39_{(10)} = 874 \div 8 = 109 \text{ remainder } 2$$
$$109 \div 8 = 13 \text{ remainder } 5$$
$$13 \div 8 = 1 \text{ remainder } 5$$
$$1 \div 8 = 0 \text{ remainder } 1$$

$$874_{(10)} = 1552_{(8)}$$

$$.39 \times 8 \ = 3.12$$
$$.12 \times 8 \ = 0.96$$
$$.96 \times 8 \ = 7.68$$
$$.68 \times 8 \ = 5.44 \text{ etc.}$$

$$.39_{(10)} = .3075 \ldots \text{etc.}_{(8)}$$

$$874.39_{(10)} = 1552.3075 \ldots \text{etc.}_{(8)}$$

To hex

$$874.39_{(10)} = 874 \div 16 = 54 \text{ remainder } 10 = A$$
$$54 \div 16 = \ 3 \text{ remainder} \quad 6$$
$$3 \div 16 = \ 0 \text{ remainder} \quad 3$$

$$874_{(10)} = 36A_{(16)}$$

$$.39 \times 16 = 6.24$$
$$.24 \times 16 = 3.84$$
$$.84 \times 16 = 13.44 = D.44$$
$$.44 \times 16 = 7.04 \text{ etc.}$$

$$.39_{(10)} = .63D7 \ldots \text{etc.}_{(16)}$$

$$874.39_{(10)} = 36A.63D7 \ldots \text{etc.}_{(16)}$$

To convert a binary number to an octal number (or the reverse) can be a very simple matter if you can remember the binary equivalents for the eight octal characters.

$$7_{(8)} = 111_{(2)} \quad 6_{(8)} = 110_{(2)} \quad 5_{(8)} = 101_{(2)} \quad 4_{(8)} = 100_{(2)}$$
$$3_{(8)} = 011_{(2)} \quad 2_{(8)} = 010_{(2)} \quad 1_{(8)} = 001_{(2)} \quad 0_{(8)} = 000_{(2)}$$

For example,
$$1042_{(8)} = 1_{(8)} \qquad\qquad = 001_{(2)}$$
$$0_{(8)} \qquad = \qquad 000_{(2)}$$
$$4_{(8)} \qquad = \qquad\qquad 100_{(2)}$$
$$2_{(8)} = \qquad\qquad\qquad 010_{(2)}$$
$$= 001 \quad 000 \quad 100 \quad 010$$

and
$$1000100010_{(2)} = \qquad\qquad\qquad\qquad\qquad 010_{(2)}$$
$$100_{(2)}$$
$$000_{(2)}$$
$$001_{(2)}$$
$$= 1 \qquad 0 \qquad 4 \qquad 2 \ _{(8)}$$

A similar procedure can be adopted for converting binary to hex and the reverse except that the binary number is broken into sets of four digits starting from the radix point instead of three as in octal. For example,

$$A979_{(16)} = 1010 : 1001 : 0111 : 1001$$
$$= 1010100101111001_{(2)}$$

One special form of coding used, based on the preference for binary by machine processing, is binary coded decimal (BCD). In this system, a decimal number is converted into sets of four binary digits (four being the minimum digits required to represent the highest decimal character 9). This system eliminates the need to be able to convert large numbers to pure binary and can be operated by anyone who knows the binary for the ten character decimal set 0–9. For example,

$$76326_{(10)} = \quad 7 \quad\quad 6 \quad\quad 3 \quad\quad 2 \quad\quad 6$$
$$= 0111 \quad 0110 \quad 0011 \quad 0010 \quad 0110_{(BCD)}$$

Primary coding systems

In capturing data, we encode it into symbols; numeric, alphabetic and special. If we are going to machine process it, we may further code it into one of the binary based number systems above. These elemental codes are very much determined by the capturing and processing devices (human or machine) that are employed.

Data is also coded for system purposes, as opposed to device purposes. This is most often done to compact as many facts as possible into one small data item, to use this item both as a carrier of facts and as an identity and further to use this identity as a basis for a logical storage and retrieval system.

The most common types of code include

simple sequence code—a straightforward numerical sequence, practical for a limited number of items only, e.g. 1 = boy, 2 = girl, 3 = single man, 4 = etc.

block sequence code—sequenced blocks of numbers allocated to groups of like things, economic in its use of digits but not easy to remember, e.g. 1–10 stereo records, 1 = male vocal, 2 = female vocal, etc., 11–20 mono records, 11 = male vocal, 12 = female vocal, etc.

group block codes—blocks allocated to like things based on leftmost digit and structured within this into sub-blocks, one for each digit, e.g. 1000 = vehicles, 1100 = commercial transport, 1200 = passenger transport, 1210 = buses, 1220 = cars, 1221 = sports cars, 1222 = etc.

faceted codes—arranged so that particular digits indicate further facts about the item. e.g. 1000 = vehicles, 1100 = 100 bhp vehicles, 1050 = 50 bhp vehicles etc., 1000 = new vehicles, 1010 = new Fords, 1020 = new Fiats, 1030 = new etc., 2000 = second-hand vehicles 2010 = second-hand Fords, 2020 = etc.

universal decimal—originally devised as Dewey decimal system for subject index classification, e.g. 100 = the arts, 110 = theory of art, 120 = fine arts, 121 = art history, 121.1 = ancient art, 121.11 = ancient European art, 121.12 = etc.

alphabetic sequence—possibly mnemonic, if used to the full (26 alpha, 10 numeric) gives wider range, e.g. m = male, f = female, 1 = London, etc; or a = 1st item, b = 2nd item, c = 3rd item, etc.

mixed codes—codes can be devised using any mixture of the above but it should be remembered that coding costs money in terms of encoding, validating, decoding and directory maintenance and the system chosen should be simple, unambiguous and flexible.

Characters, bytes and words

Facts about things are captured by selection and encoding on to a medium. This initial encoding may be in the form of numeric, alphabetic or special symbols belonging to a conventional human communication system (e.g. the English language, the decimal number system) or in the form of one of the special primary coding systems above. This captured data may then be stored or processed by machine (or it may have been initially captured by machine) in which case a further encoding stage takes place, transforming the facts into a series of groups of binary digits conforming to the rules of one of the numbering systems mentioned or into groups of binary digits arranged in a

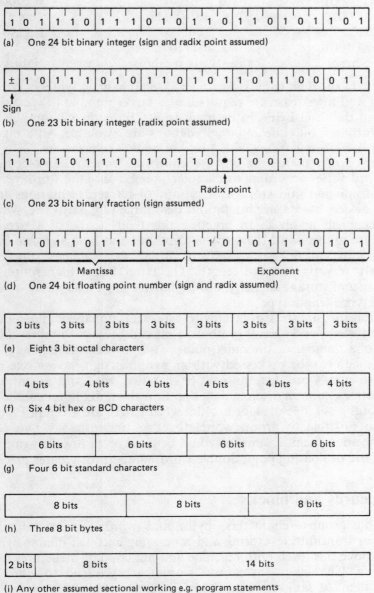

(a) One 24 bit binary integer (sign and radix point assumed)

(b) One 23 bit binary integer (radix point assumed)

(c) One 23 bit binary fraction (sign assumed)

(d) One 24 bit floating point number (sign and radix assumed)

(e) Eight 3 bit octal characters

(f) Six 4 bit hex or BCD characters

(g) Four 6 bit standard characters

(h) Three 8 bit bytes

(i) Any other assumed sectional working e.g. program statements

Figure 29 Various uses of a 24 bit word length

code for representing non-numeric or mixed numeric and non-numeric symbols.

These blocks of binary digits are called **characters**, bytes or words according to their size, for example the 3 bit octal character, 4 bit hex character and 4 bit BCD character, which have already been discussed. There is also the standard 6 bit representation:

0 = 000000	A = 010001	% = 011101
1 = 000001	B = 010010	+ = 010000
2 = 000010	C = 010011	etc.
etc.	etc.	(see Figure 27)
9 = 001001	Z = 111001	
ten symbols	twenty-six symbols	twenty-eight symbols

Normally, in the 6 bit code, only upper case alphabetic symbols are coded. If both upper and lower case are required, or a larger number of special symbols needed, then the 8 bit **byte** can be used. In a 6 bit code, 64 combinations are possible, with an 8 bit code 256 combinations are available. An 8 bit byte is a convenient size when working with 4 bit hex or BCD characters.

Bit groups larger than eight bits are known as **words**. The exact number of bits to a word varies according to manufacturer because the word, which is the unit of transmission and storage of groups of bit representations inside the processing device, has its size limitations determined by hardware, which is the actual mechanism involved. In practice, this tends to be of a size that will accommodate multiples of the various character and byte sizes we have seen, e.g. multiples of 3, 4, 6, 8 such as 12, 16, 24, 32, 48. Machines can be of fixed word length or variable word length. The latter has a higher utilisation of transmission and storage capacity, but in practice most machines nowadays are of the fixed word length type.

In addition to using bits in groups to represent alphabetic, numeric (in any numbering system) and special symbols, a bit can be used to represent the sign (+ or −) of a number or the radix point of a number. Alternatively, numbers of the same sign can be processed with an assumed sign, saving one bit of the word length and word lengths can be handled with the assumption that different sections contain discrete data and thus the radix point can be omitted. Examples of the possible uses for a 24 bit word length are given in Figure 29.

It is also possible to group words together and use, say two words, to represent one data item. Examples would be fixed point double word numbers for greater size or floating point double word numbers for greater precision.

Fields, records and blocks

Bits and bit groups (characters, bytes and words) are the fundamental structures for transmitting, storing and processing encoded human symbols by machine. Above this level, both machine and human data structures follow the same pattern. Characters (bytes and words) are grouped together to form meaningful items of data known as **fields**. For example in the following data

John Smith, Number 6958, born 3.7.1966, Wages department

there are four fields (name, works number, date of birth, department) each made up of a selection of characters. Fields are often grouped together in levels. In the above example, the name field can be thought of as made up of two lower level fields, first name field and surname field. The lowest level field is the smallest meaningful group of characters which is qualitative or descriptive of some real phenomenon.

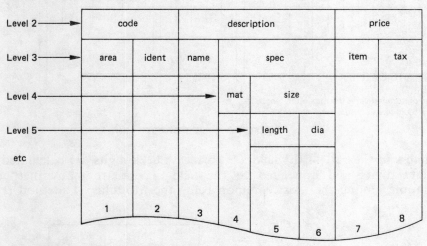

8 Fields — five at level 3, one at level 4, two at level 5

Note. The whole 8 field group forms a **record** (which is level 1).

Figure 30   Data fields and levels

A group of field levels comprise level 1, a **record**. A record is therefore a set of data about an identifiable thing or occurrence. When data is captured a record(ing) is made about the facts of the situation. Records may be captured for processing once only (transaction records), for storage and continual processing (master records) or for storage and reference (reference records).

The fields within a record not only belong to a certain level but also will be of a certain length (either fixed or variable) containing either numeric, non-numeric or mixed characters. This information can be specified by **pictures** which use symbols to depict character type and field size either by repeating the symbol or placing the quantity in brackets after it.

The normal symbols are

A (non-numeric characters)
9 (numeric characters)
X (mixed numeric and non-numeric)
V (decimal point)
B (space).

Whilst a character is a representation to denote or distinguish data, a digit is the name given to an occurrence of a character. Therefore field 5 in Figure 31 has 5 digits but only 4 characters.

Sometimes digits are used not for data but in order to check that the

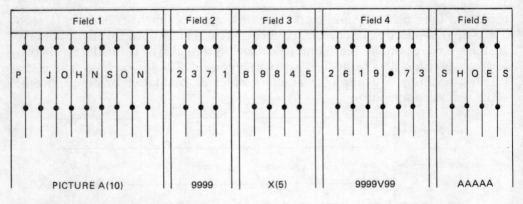

Note. The picture indicates the maximum length
      of a fixed length field

Figure 31   Field pictures

characters in the rest of the field are correct. **Check digits** are calculated from the data digits and appended to the field. There are many methods of calculation, among the most common being the Modulus 11 method (Figure 32).

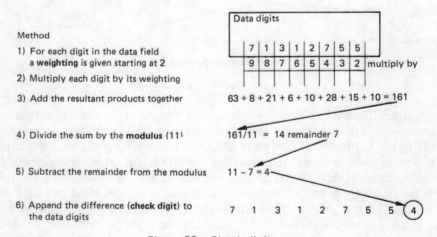

Figure 32   Check digits

When specifying the content of a field, it is often useful to indicate the minimum and maximum values in addition to giving the picture. This, like the check digit, enables checks to be made on the validity of the data digits.

Pay number	Name	Payrate	Tax code	Insurance
Picture X(5)	Picture A(20)	Picture 999 Maximum value 105 Minimum value 35	Picture 9(4) Maximum value 3071 Minimum value —	Picture 9V99
A1073	Jenkins B	64	1043	1·05

Figure 33   Minimum and maximum value validity data

A record is a group of fields all relating to one logical subject. For purposes of identification and retrieval, one of the fields is designated as the **key field**. The field designated as the key may vary within the same record for different processing applications. Records can be of fixed or variable length depending on whether each record in a group of records has the same number of fields or not.

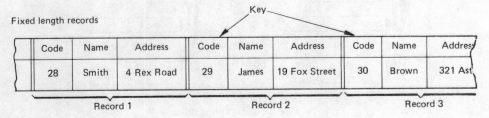

Figure 34   Fixed and variable length records with keys

If records are of variable length, they usually contain either a record length field or an end of record marker field (Figure 35).

Record length field

Record length	Item	Order 1	Record length	Item	Order 1	Order 2	Order 3	Record length	Item
2	123	74298	4	124	11126	77211	77324	2	125

End of record marker

Item	Order 1	Order 2	End of record marker	Item	Order 1	Order 2	Order 3	End of record marker	It
123	74298	44162	99	124	11126	77211	77324	99	12

Figure 35   Record length indicators

For data processing purposes, records are organised into **blocks**. A block is the smallest addressable unit of data which can be transferred into or out of the processing device at one time (rather like a folder containing records in a manual filing system which is transferred into or out of a filing cabinet).

Blocks (or files) may contain a fixed or variable number of records. As records can be of fixed or variable length, blocks can therefore be classified as being one of four possible types: (a) fixed number/fixed length records; (b)

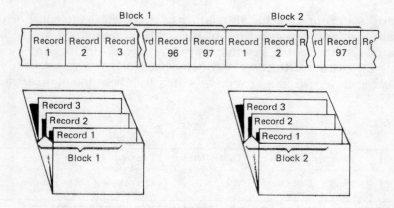

Figure 36   Record blocks

fixed number/variable length records; (c) variable number/fixed length records; (d) variable number/variable length records.

When records/blocks are grouped into files, they can be considered from two viewpoints: (a) the physical grouping and (b) the logical grouping. Physically, records placed one after another contiguously are grouped serially. However, the logical grouping may be

(1) Full sequential (serial sequential)
(2) Part sequential (partitioned or indexed sequential)
(3) Nonsequential (random).

Sequential files are arranged in a certain sequence according to a key field.

Fixed fixed

	Block 1				Block 2				Block 3				Block 4	
1	2	3	4	1	2	3	4	1	2	3	4	1	2	3

Fixed variable

Block 1   Block 2   Block 3

| 1 | 2 | 3 | 4 | 1 | 2 | 3 | 4 | 1 | 2 | 3 | 4 | 1 |

Variable fixed

Block 1   Block 2   Block 3   Block 4

| 1 | 2 | 1 | 2 | 3 | 4 | 5 | 1 | 2 | 3 | 4 | 5 | 6 | 7 | 1 | 2 | 3 |

Variable variable

Block 1   Block 2   Block 3   Block 4

| 1 | 2 | 1 | 2 | 3 | 4 | 1 | 2 | 3 | 1 | 2 | 3 | 4 | 5 | 1 |

Figure 37   Fixed and variable block size

Serial sequential organisation of records in file

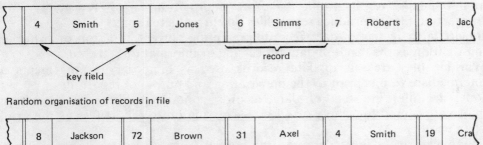

Random organisation of records in file

Figure 38   Serial sequential and random file organisation

Partitioned organisation involves grouping records sequentially within several **members**, each member having a unique identity name or number. The file must also contain an index of the member identity cross-referred to its physical location start address.

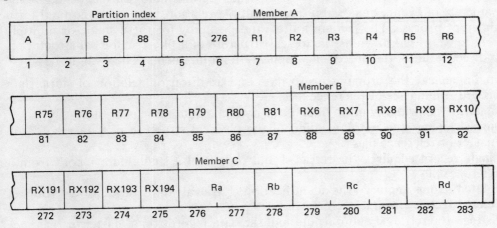

Figure 39   Partitioned file organisation

Record structures: files

The record is the main data item. It can be considered singly or in groups. When a group of records (physically organised into blocks) are put together for processing according to some application system purpose, this grouping is known as a **file**. There are several types of data file, identified according to the role they play in the processing sequence.

Transaction files are sets of data records containing source data used in the maintenance or update of master files or as the raw data to be processed in the production of report files.

Master files are sets of data records containing static (e.g. name and address) and dynamic (e.g. current balance) information, used repeatedly with transaction files to produce report files on current situations.

Report files are sets of data records presenting current situation or historical information as the result of data processing or information retrieval.

Working files are sets of data records used as temporary arrangements or intermediate results prior to the preparation and output of report files.

Reference files are sets of data records containing historical or current information used for whole or selective copying on to report files as the result of an enquiry.

Dump files are sets of data records copied from any of the above files to provide duplicate copies for security purposes.

A data record contains facts about things or situations (entities) in the real world and certain characteristics (attributes) of these entities. When a set of records are put together for some processing system purpose, these records will have certain common aspects (relationships). It may be that the only relationship is that they are all required by the same processing system or it may be that the entities or attributes belong to the same set of something.

There may be a direct relationship such as chronological sequence of the same set of events or possibly even multiple relationships, each required for a different process. The recognition of, and grouping for these single or multiple relationships is known as the logical structure of a file. The logical structure is a direct result of the processing application requirements. These might be

maintenance – the bringing up to date and addition or deletion of static data records on master or reference files

update – the bringing up to date of the dynamic data on master files

housekeeping – the reorganisation of the physical structure of data records on master or reference files

single record enquiry – the retrieval and output of a single data record from a reference file

related group enquiry – the identification, retrieval and output of a group of related records from a reference file

listing – the retrieval and output of all the data records on a master or reference file

calculation report – the matching of data records on transaction and master files, calculation based on data from both and the output of the results on a report file

validation and edit – detection and correction of data records on any file type.

In each of the above applications, the requirements of access to a record or group of records in the file, together with the available physical devices for storage, will determine how the logical (relationship) structure of the file is implemented.

Logical structures

The logical structure of any file can be considered as

simple sequential – entity relationship (alphabetic or numeric) or attribute relationship (size, quantity, etc.) sequence by record key field

multiple sequential – as simple sequential but with multiple keys for varying system applications

nonsequential (random) – no relationship of records other than membership of same file set.

Sequential records may be required individually or in sequenced sets. Nonsequential records are normally only accessed individually unless these form an intermediate working file which is accessed serial sequentially.

The physical implementation of logical file structures is concerned with the record key or keys; the physical location address; the means of locating that address; provision for data overflow of storage location.

There are several methods for locating records by key on a physical file: straightforward searching of the file in a serial (contiguous store location) sequence; using an index to locate an address and then proceeding directly; locating index pointers or tags in the preceding record; generating the address by calculation. The method adopted is influenced by the system requirements and the available storage devices which determine whether the data records are stored in serial sequence, part serial sequence or in nonserial sequence.

The structure of a file changes either as more records are added, as the size of variable length records grows or as the calculation of a storage location address, based on the record key, outgrows the available storage area. In all of these cases, **overflow** can occur producing further needs for storing and locating the overflow data.

Physical implementation

The main methods of physically implementing logical structures are

Serial sequential storage – locate by serial search or calculate address from key and then locate direct

Skip sequential storage – calculate start address from key and then locate from start by serial search

Partitioned storage – records are grouped sequentially within several members. The file contains an index of member identity and start location address. Locate by serial search index – direct to member start or serial search member

Indexed sequential storage – records are stored in serial sequential manner within sets (tracks on disc). These sets are themselves filed in groups (cylinders on disc), the total groups comprising the file. Records are located by first serial searching a coarse (cylinder) index for the start address of the highest key in that group containing the record. The start address contains a fine index of the highest key and start address of each set. Final location is achieved by direct access of that start address and then serial search of the set (track)

Chained (threaded) list storage – chaining is achieved by locating the address of the next in sequence record in the preceding record. Location is direct to that address

Multilist (multiple threaded) storage – as for chaining but with multiple pointers to the next sequential record for varying applications

Inverted list storage – records containing the same key data are stored at

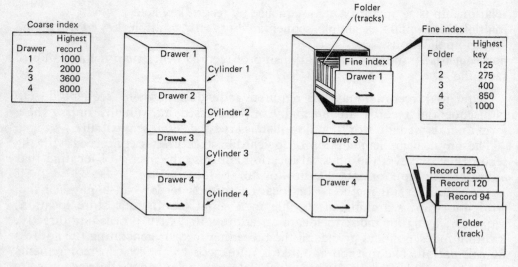

Figure 40   Indexed sequential file organisation—a manual filing analogy

random or according to other keys throughout the file. Location of all the records with the same key is achieved by first referencing the key to an index which cross refers to an inverted list file. The referenced inverted list location contains pointers to the addresses of all the records with that key which can then be located by direct access

Key/location address random storage – the record is stored and located by generating its location address by an arithmetic formula or address generation algorithm (e.g. division of the key by a prime number, squaring the key)

Full index random storage – records are stored at random and located by serial search (binary split, etc.) of key index

Full random storage – intermediate working files only

Progressive overflow storage – the data overflow is stored in the next available empty location and is found by serial search

Chained overflow storage – the overflow is stored either in the next available space or in a special overflow area. Its address is stored in the main part of the record as a pointer

Tagged overflow storage – the whole of the overflowing record is relocated and the address tag of the new address stored in the previous (too small) location.

When overflow occurs, there is a need for periodic housekeeping, that is rewriting of the complete file to reallocate overflows and rewrite the index.

Record structures: database

Manual and serial database

A **database** is the complete set of master and reference file records required by a system. It is stored in a **databank**. Up to the 1950s, the database of clerical systems was stored in filing cabinets, desk drawers, bound and loose leaf ledgers, notebooks, etc. Business was organised functionally (sales, accounts, production, etc.) and each function had its own data processing centre (office). Each office selected those facts it required to set up its own individual model of reality and because these functions were not isolated but integrated, e.g. production made things that were sold at a price that had to be accounted for, the models, of necessity, contained many duplications of each other. The office database tended to be grouped into files made from one entity and its related attributes. Relationships between one file and another were ignored, being catered for by duplication. These files were organised serial sequentially. As data processing was carried out manually, at human speeds, the updating of these files was carried out at human convenience. Maintenance and updating data was captured either as it occurred or historically and was then piled up into batches until there was enough work for a human to turn into a worthwhile job. The more frequently these files were referred to, the more need there was to keep them up to date by more frequent processing but rarely did this mean more than once daily batch processing.

During the 1950s and early 1960s, office work began to be computerised. At first the machines were limited by available hardware facilities, then, as these improved, the limitations were imposed by inexperience and man's traditional methods of working. The initial attempts at electronic data processing were restricted to the pure mechanisation of the old manual methods which brought both advantages and disadvantages. The computer at that time, being largely an electronic calculator, speeded up the actual updating and processing of the facts stored, but there was then the problem of data preparation and integrity vetting, and also the organisational disadvantages of centralisation. Although, under the manual system, the processing had been slow, information retrieval, based on files readily to hand in books, binders and desk drawers, was achieved at manual speed real-time, i.e. at the moment of the enquiry event in the real world. Computerisation brought fast computer batch processing but slow batch information retrieval from magnetically stored (and therefore accessed only by computer run) files at a place physically remote from the origin of the enquiry.

Direct access database

Towards the mid-1960s, new hardware developments together with the appropriate software (magnetic discs, multiprogramming, operating systems) brought about an interest in the relationships between the various functional processing systems and their related master data files. Attempts were made to design integrated systems or, at least, to computerise functional systems progressively according to an integration plan. The first attempts were based on serial access magnetic tape files, where, it was hoped, by careful preplanning one would be able to use, or modify for use, heirarchically organised master files as the database for more than one functional system. New ways of using the computer were also being pioneered. Direct access disc led to multiprogramming and thus to timesharing, which led to the development of remote, communications based, access to the computer, its processing facilities and its physical databank. It now appeared feasible to combine the two ideas to provide a large, integrated file which could be available to many users simultaneously via a real-time communication system. This would solve many of the disadvantages of the batch processing computer systems, such as elimination of duplication, real-time access and decentralised flexibility, whilst providing all the speed advantages of an automatic system. By the end of the 1960s, the database task group CODASYL had been set up to investigate and report on the implications of this new mode of computer application.

The initial hopes were for an ideal system where all the data requirements of a whole business could be made available to all users, in one giant database. However, the complexities of related record storage and retrieval, together with the enormous investment in hardware, software and development required has meant that the database systems implemented up till now, whilst forming large parts of an organisation's information requirements, fall short of being a total business system. This may not in itself be a bad thing, for, with the very rapid development of microprocessors, the time might not be far off when we reach full cycle and most business processing returns to a local, decentralised functional base, but this time with the speed of real-time automation and duplication no longer being a problem, at least in terms of chip based storage space.

Database implementation is discussed in Unit 14.

Assessment tasks

1 Take any real, completed business document (e.g. invoice, payslip) and analyse this in terms of its fields, levels, pictures, and characters. How might this be represented in the form of binary digits?

2 Write a report giving your recommendations for the optimum word length for a computer which will specialise in banking applications. Give your reasons.

3 Discover and present in graphical or tabular form the details of the database of your firm or college.

4 Prepare a tape-recorded radio lecture on the topic of data structures for information retrieval.

5 Construct a small physical model to illustrate the concept of capturing facts from the environment and encoding them on to a suitable medium for processing by any method.

Unit 7
Processing theory and methods

Learning objective

To be able to identify some of the common processing requirements used to turn data into information. To understand that these requirements can be achieved by a variety of methods, each with its own advantages and suitability for a given system situation. To be able to recognise suitable applications for non-computer processing and to further recognise that computerised systems contain very large areas of manual processing.

The basic elements

In Unit 5, we identified eight basic elements of data processing. Those that do not change the form of the data being processed are communicating; comparing and checking; writing; filing and retrieval. Those that change the arrangement of the data by resequencing or selection but do not add to or change the data itself are classification; sorting; copying. However, the last basic element, calculating actually transforms the data into a new form. It is, therefore, worth knowing about some of the basic forms of calculating.

Arithmetic operations
A few reminders on terminology may be of use at this stage.
(i) **Operands** are subjected to an **operation** to produce a **result**
(ii) Addition: **augend + addend = sum**
 (if the sum is to appear in location of one operand it always replaces the augend)
(iii) Subtraction: **minuend − subtrahend = difference**
(iv) Multiplication: $\underbrace{\textbf{multiplicand} \times \textbf{multiplier}}_{\textbf{factors}} = \textbf{product}$

 (repeated addition of multiplicand)
(v) Division:

$$\frac{\textbf{dividend}}{\textbf{divisor}} = \textbf{quotient} \text{ (possibly with } \textbf{remainder}\text{)}$$

(vi) Exponentiation: the **exponent** (to the power of) is the number of times the operand must be multiplied by itself to give the result.
 When working in number systems other than decimal these same arithmetic operations can be performed. As computers work primarily in binary we need only consider the following three concepts.

(1) Binary addition rules:

$$0+0 = 0 \text{ carry } 0$$
$$0+1 = 1 \text{ carry } 0$$
$$1+0 = 1 \text{ carry } 0$$
$$1+1 = 0 \text{ carry } 1$$

(2) Binary subtraction: this is achieved by **complement addition**. In decimal notation this is done as follows.

normal subtraction	true (10s) complement addition
794	794
–	+
256	744 (complement of 256)
= 538	1538
	= 538 (ignore carry)

The complement of 256 was found by subtracting 256 from a power of 10 higher than the number (i.e. $1000 - 265 = 744$).

In binary the 1s complement can be formed by simply reversing all the bits involved. To change this to the true (2s) complement we only have to add 1. The following example shows binary subtraction performed by complement addition.

binary complement addition:

minuend	(794)	1100011010
subtrahend	(256)	0100000000
1s complement of subtrahend		1011111111
add 1		+ 1
= 2s complement of subtrahend		1100000000
add minuend		+ 1100011010
= ignore carry (538)		(1)1000011010

(3) Binary multiplication and division: multiplication can be achieved by multiple addition (also exponentiation) and division by multiple subtraction (complement addition).

Logical operations

The exact definition of a logical operation is an operation where the operands and result have only one digit. In practice a logical operation in computer terms usually means a Boolean operation (see Unit 8, p. 105). For now it is enough to say that as far as information processing is concerned, logical operations may be thought of as conditional operations, that is operations which are performed as a result of a certain condition being fulfilled.

Examples of conditional operators are:

> greater than
< less than
= equal to
≠ not equal to
⩾ greater than or equal to
⩽ less than or equal to

By this means checking may be achieved by the comparison of two answers; sorting may be done by comparing keys; etc.

Processing data

Numeric processing
Certain numeric formulae look frightening due to the unfamiliar symbols used. Here are a few of them:

$$x = \text{individual items}$$
$$\bar{x} = \text{(bar x) arithmetic mean}$$
$$\Sigma = \text{(large sigma) the sum of}$$
$$n \text{ or } N = \text{total frequencies } (\Sigma f)$$
$$f = \text{frequency}$$
$$x^1 = \text{assumed mean}$$
$$d^1 = \text{deviations from assumed mean}$$
$$i = \text{class interval}$$
$$\sigma = \text{(small sigma) standard deviation (SD)}$$
$$w = \text{weight}$$

The next few examples should explain the use of these symbols.

Averages
An average is just a figure that is taken to be representative of a group of figures. This is why there is more than one type of average as the most common one (the mean) is not always representative. There are four types of average: arithmetic mean; geometric mean; median and mode.

(1) Arithmetic mean
This can be calculated from a **simple series**

$$£20 + £16 + £12 = £48 \div 3 \text{ items} = £16 \text{ (mean)}$$

or from a **frequency distribution** (weighted mean)

$$£20 \times 100 \text{ items} + £16 \times 200 \text{ items} + £12 \times 50 \text{ items} \div 350 \text{ items}$$
$$= £16.57 \text{ (mean)}$$

or from a **grouped frequency distribution**

1	*2*	*3*	
Group	*Mid-point*	*Frequency*	*2 × 3*
21–25	23	6	138
26–30	28	17	476
31–35	33	22	726
		45	1340

$1340 \div 45 = 29.8$ (mean)

or alternative method (**deviations from assumed mean**)

Mid-point of groups taken as assumed mean (i.e. from above $35 + 21 \div 2 = 28$)

1 Group	2 Mid-point	3 Frequency	4 Deviations	3 × 4
21–25	23	6	−1	−6
26–30	28	17	0	0
31–35	33	22	+1	+22
		45		16

Note. Deviations from assumed mean are in class interval units (5)

$16 \div 45 = 0.36$

0.36×5 (class interval) $= 1.8$ (average deviation)

$1.8 + 28$ (assumed mean) $= 29.8$ (true mean)

(2) Geometric mean

This is calculated as Nth root of product of N values

$$5, 3, 7 = \sqrt[3]{5 \times 3 \times 7} = \sqrt[3]{105} = 4.72$$

However, as obtaining Nth roots can be difficult an alternative method is to use logarithms:

(a) obtain log of each value

(b) add the value logs

(c) divide sum by number of items

(d) obtain antilog of result.

(3) Median

The median is the central value when items are arranged in sequence of magnitude. For example:

(i) Simple series 2, 3, 4, 5, 6, 7, 8, 9, 10

Formula: Position of median $=$ (number of items $+ 1) \div 2$

9 (number of items) $+ 1 = 10 \div 2 = 5$ (position of median)

5th item is median $= 6$

(ii) Grouped frequency distribution

Group	Frequency	Cumulative total
21–25	6	6
26–30	17	23
31–35	22	45

Formula:

(a) position of median $=$ cumulative total $\div 2$

(b) position in median group $=$ overall position $-$ cumulative total of preceding groups

(c) median $=$ first item in median group $+ ((\text{position} \div \text{frequency}) \times \text{class interval})$

(a) $45 \div 2 = 22.5$ (overall position)

(b) $22.5 - 6 = 16.5$ (position in median group)

(c) $26 + ((16.5 \div 17) \times 5) = 30.85$ (median)

(4) **Mode**

When the mean is not representative, due to extreme values, and the median is unrepresentative, due to uneven distribution, the mode which indicates the majority of cases is used. For example:

(i) Simple frequency series

Class	1	2	3	4	5	6	7	8	9
Frequency	4	9	15	24	38	26	18	13	7

Highest frequency = 38
Mode = 5

(ii) Grouped frequency distribution

Group	Frequency
21–25	6
26–30	22
31–35	17

L = lower limit of modal group
i = class interval
fa = frequency following modal group
fb = frequency preceding modal group

Formula: $\text{Mode} = L + \left\{ \left(\dfrac{fa}{fa + fb} \right) \times i \right\}$

$$= 26 + \left\{ \left(\frac{17}{17 + 6} \right) \times 5 \right\}$$

$$= 29.7 \text{ (mode)}$$

Measures of variation

When data is obtained over a large population no one figure (average) can be fully representative of the distribution of items. It is often desirable to supplement this with some further information to indicate how typical the average is. For this we use measures of **dispersion** and **skewness**.

Measures of dispersion
These are designed to indicate the deviation of each item in the distribution from the chosen measure of central tendency (average). The most commonly used are: range; quartile deviation and standard deviation.

(1) **Range**

The range is simply the difference between the maximum and minimum values in the distribution. It is simple to derive and understand. However, one extreme value renders it useless and, where classifications are open-ended, arbitrary decisions must be made which make this unreliable as an indication of distribution.

(2) Quartile deviation

Quartiles are quarter points in the distribution being found simply by the formula:

Lower quartile $(Q^1) = N \div 4$
Upper quartile $(Q^3) = 3N \div 4$

Quartile deviation is equally easy to calculate

$$QD = (Q^3 - Q^1) \div 2$$

The resultant quartile deviation is a figure only meaningful in comparison with other known quartile deviations. The smaller the figure the less the dispersion of the middle half of the items about the median average.

The advantage of using quartile deviation is its simplicity of calculation and the fact that measuring only the middle half of the items eliminates the risk of extreme items distorting. Its disadvantage is that it is only representative of half of the items and not the whole distribution.

(3) Standard deviation

This is a development of an earlier method, the mean deviation, which was not suitable due to problems with the arithmetic signs of the deviations.

Its advantage is that it includes every value and is the result of a correct mathematical process on the values so that further processing may be performed on it without error.

(i) Simple series

The standard deviation is found by:

(a) Calculate arithmetic mean
(b) Calculate the sum of the square of each individual difference between each value in the series and the mean
(c) Divide this sum by the number of items in the series

This produces a figure known as the **variance** (used later)

(d) The standard deviation (σ) is the square root of the variance.

(ii) Grouped frequency distribution (assumed mean method)

Example: Assumed mean $= 38$

(a) Given groups and frequencies select assumed mean (largest frequency) and calculate mid-points and deviations in class interval units
(b) Calculate frequency $\times$ deviations (fd^1)
(c) Calculate $fd^1 \times d^1 = fd^{1^2}$
(d) Total frequency, fd^1, and fd^{1^2} columns
(e) If desired, true mean can be calculated:

$$\text{assumed mean} + \left(\frac{\text{sum } fd^1}{\text{sum } f} \times \text{class interval} \right)$$

$$38 + \left(\frac{-134}{392} \times 5 \right) = 36.3 \text{ (true mean)}$$

(f) Calculate standard deviation

$$\text{Standard deviation} = \frac{\text{Square}}{\text{Root}} \left\{ \left(\frac{\text{sum } fd^{1^2}}{\text{sum } f} \right) - \left(\frac{\text{sum } fd^1}{\text{sum } f} \right)^2 \right\} \times \frac{\text{class}}{\text{interval}}$$

1 Group	*2* Mid-point	*3* Frequency	*4* Deviations	fd^1 3×4	fd^{1^2} $fd^1 \times 4$
11–15	13	6	−5	−30	150
16–20	18	12	−4	−48	192
21–25	23	30	−3	−90	270
26–30	28	53	−2	−106	212
31–35	33	77	−1	−77	77
36–40	38	96	0	0	0
41–45	43	54	1	54	54
46–50	48	37	2	74	148
51–55	53	19	3	57	171
56–60	58	8	4	32	128
		392		−134	1402

Calculation:

$$= \sqrt{\left(\frac{1402}{392}\right) - \left(\frac{-134}{392}\right)^2} \times 5$$

$$= \sqrt{3.46} \times 5$$

$$= 1.86 \times 5 = 9.3 \text{ (standard deviation)}$$

As with the quartile deviation the SD is a figure only meaningful in its own context. It is used to supplement the arithmetic mean, the larger the standard deviation the more variable the distribution.

As it is the best measure of dispersion the standard deviation is very important in the statistical theory behind sampling techniques. In the section on activity sampling (p. 255) the formula given is for 95% confidence limits. This in fact means that the data lies within a range of 1.96 standard deviations. For the more accurate 99% confidence limits the range is 2.58 standard deviations. Students should note this figure is not the SD figure but a multiple of it.

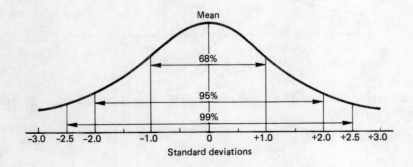

Figure 41   Normal curve

If all of the items in a set of data are plotted in a diagrammatic form and the result is a completely symmetrical curve around the mean then this is known as a **normal curve** and the characteristics would be as shown in Figure 41.

The lines indicate that at one SD either side of the mean 68% of the area and therefore 68% of the values are contained. The figures for ± 2 and ± 2.5 SDs are 95% and 99% respectively.

Skewness

Skewness is a measure of the degree of asymmetry in a distribution and apart from its use in sampling is of lesser importance in statistics than dispersion.

A distribution can be symmetrical as in the normal curve and it can also be skewed or asymmetrical as illustrated in Figure 42.

One measure of skewness is the extent that the three averages differ from one another. In a normal curve of course the three averages coincide.

There are several mathematical methods for determining measures of skewness based on the mean, median, mode, quartiles and standard deviation but the analyst need not concern himself with them unless specialising in statistics.

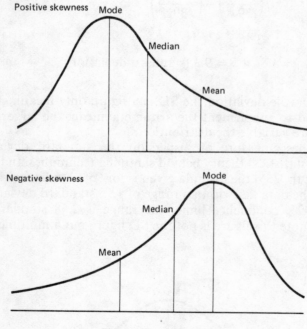

Figure 42   Skewness

Formulae

As a quick reference for the analyst the following formulae for computing averages are provided.

Arithmetic mean

(a) Simple series $\bar{x} = \dfrac{\Sigma x}{N}$

(b) Frequency distribution $\bar{x} = \dfrac{\Sigma fx}{\Sigma f}$

(c) Grouped frequency distribution $\bar{x} = \dfrac{\Sigma fx}{\Sigma f}$ (x = mid-point)

(d) Assumed mean-method $\bar{x} = x^1 + \left(\dfrac{\Sigma fd^1}{\Sigma f}\right) \times i$

Geometric mean

(a) Simple series $\text{antilog}\left(\dfrac{\Sigma \log x}{\Sigma x}\right)$

(b) Frequency distribution $\text{antilog}\left(\dfrac{\Sigma w \log x}{\Sigma w}\right)$

Standard deviation

(a) Simple formula $\sigma = \sqrt{\dfrac{\Sigma fd^2}{\Sigma f}}$

(b) Assumed mean method $\sigma = \sqrt{\left(\dfrac{\Sigma fd^{1^2}}{\Sigma f}\right) - \left(\dfrac{\Sigma fd^1}{\Sigma f}\right)^2} \times i$

Probability

Once the analyst has obtained a set of data he may not only wish to know how representative it is but he may also want to use this data to calculate something in the future. The use of past results to predict future results depends on knowing the basic laws of probability.

The probability or expectancy of an event occurring is measured against a scale which ranges from zero for absolute impossibility to one for absolute certainty. Nothing can have a probability greater than one.

There are certain events for which we can predict by instinct the expectation of occurrence; for example, that a spun coin will land heads for 50% of the time and land tails the other 50%. The probability is then:

heads p = 0.5; tails p = 0.5; heads or tails p = 1.0

This reveals the first law of probability, *the addition law*: The chances that **either one or other event will occur** in a set of possible events is determined by adding the individual probabilities of each event in the set.

How do we decide the individual probabilities in cases other than those known by instinct? It is done by relating to past results. For example if one keeps a record of the mail deliveries over the past year one may discover that they fall into the following categories:

No mail	60	deliveries
Personal letters	50	deliveries

Bills	120	deliveries
Circulars	240	deliveries
Professional journals	130	deliveries
Total	600	deliveries

The probability is calculated:

p = individual number of occurrences ÷ total number of events

No mail	60 ÷ 600	p = 0.10
Letters	50 ÷ 600	p = 0.08
Bills	120 ÷ 600	p = 0.20
Circulars	240 ÷ 600	p = 0.40
Journals	130 ÷ 600	p = 0.22
Total	600 ÷ 600	p = 1.00

so the probability of getting either a bill or a circular in my next postal delivery is $0.20 + 0.40 = p = 0.60$.

The probability of getting no letters is $0.10 + 0.20 + 0.40 + 0.22 = p = 0.92$ and so on.

The second basic law is the *multiplication law* (both–and). The chances that **any set of events will occur together** is determined by the multiplication of the individual probabilities for each event.

Therefore the probability of getting

Both a letter and a bill = 0.08×0.20 p = 0.016

Both a circular and a bill = 0.40×0.20 p = 0.08

Both a journal and a bill and a letter = $0.22 \times 0.20 \times 0.08$ p = 0.00352

This law applies not only to simultaneous events but to events in sequence. The probability of getting a bill two consecutive days would be $0.20 \times 0.20 = p = 0.04$.

Combinations are sets of possibilities. For example Y,D,A is a combination of three alphabetic characters out of the possible 26. These three characters can occur in any sequence in a combination. However when we are concerned with a particular sequence this is known as a **permutation**. Therefore D,A,Y, is a permutation of the combination quoted.

To determine the total number of permutations of any given combination the following formula is used:

Where N = number of permutations
       n = number of items in the combination
      N = factorial n (n!)

e.g.   If n = 3 N = n! N = $3 \times 2 \times 1 = 6$
      If n = 6 N = n! N = $6 \times 5 \times 4 \times 3 \times 2 \times 1 = 720$

Binomial distribution

If the analyst knows from past data the number of times an event occurred and the number of times it did not occur he can use the binomial distribution to predict the likelihood of its occurrence in any sample taken. If for example he knows from previous records that 10% of invoices issued have discount, the other 90% have not, the chance of finding a discount invoice at random is 1/10 (0.1).

By the multiplication law the probability (p) of finding two discount invoices in a row is

$$p = \frac{1}{10} \times \frac{1}{10} = \frac{1}{100} \, (0.01)$$

Therefore, it can be deduced that the chance of finding n discount invoices is

$$p = \left(\frac{1}{10}\right)^n$$

and the chance of finding n normal invoices is

$$q = \left(\frac{9}{10}\right)^n$$

In other words the total chance of finding
One random selection
One discount (p = 0.1) *or* one normal (q = 0.9), p + q = 1.00
Two random selections
Two discount (p = 0.01) *or* two normal (q = 0.81), $p^2 + q^2 = 0.82$ etc.

We can deduce from this that, as the total probability must equal 1, that from a sample of two random selections the chances of finding one discount and one normal is:

$$1 - (p^2 + q^2) = 0.18 \ (2 \text{ chances } p \times q \text{ and } q \times p = 2pq)$$

This is illustrated in Figure 43.

2 selections		
both discount p^2	discount + normal 2pq	both discount q^2
3 selections		
3 discount p^3	2 discount + 1 normal $3p^2q$	1 discount + 2 normal $3pq^2$	3 normal q^3

Figure 43   Probability table

From algebra we know that $p^2 + 2pq + q^2$ is the expansion of $(p+q)^2$ and that $p^3 + 3p^2q + 3pq^2 + q^3$ is the expansion of $(p+q)^3$, therefore we can deduce the general rule for binomial distribution:

The probability for any combination of events occurring in a random sample of n items from a population containing p occurrences and q non-occurrences can be found by evaluating the expansion of $(p+q)^n$.

The expansion to any level can be obtained by the use of Pascal's triangle (Figure 44).

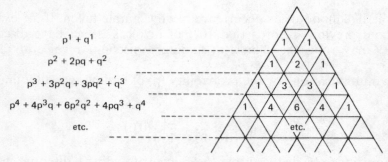

$p^1 + q^1$

$p^2 + 2pq + q^2$

$p^3 + 3p^2q + 3pq^2 + q^3$

$p^4 + 4p^3q + 6p^2q^2 + 4pq^3 + q^4$

etc.

Figure 44   Pascal's triangle

You will see that this triangle itself can be deduced as the lower number is obtained by the addition of the two numbers above it.

Poisson distribution

In certain cases the analyst may be faced with a problem slightly different to the above where he knows the number of times an event occurs but not the total possible number of occurrences and therefore the number of non-occurrences (n and q in the binomial distribution).

An example of this might be the number of computer breakdowns in a week which can be counted; but how many non-breakdowns were there?

Poisson distribution uses the mathematical conception of the exponential law which has at its base the constant e where

$$e = \frac{1}{0!} + \frac{1}{1!} + \frac{1}{2!} + \frac{1}{3!} + \ldots \text{etc.}$$

Evaluated and taken to four decimal places this gives

$$e = 1 + 1 + 0.5 + 0.16667 + \ldots \text{etc} = 2.7183$$

which is the basis of Napierian logarithms.

Developed from this we are given two formulae to use for Poisson distribution.

Formula 1 (where the expected average number of occurrences (z) is known)

$$\text{Total probability (1)} = e^{-z}\left(1 + z + \frac{z^2}{2!} + \frac{z^3}{3!} + \frac{z^4}{4!} + \frac{z^5}{5!} + \ldots \text{etc.}\right)$$

Each item within the brackers multiplied by e^{-z} gives the individual probability of successive increments of numbers of times event will occur.

e.g. $1 \times e^{-z} = 0$ occurrences

$z \times e^{-z} = 1$ occurrence

$\frac{z^2}{z!} \times e^{-z} = 2$ occurrences

$$\frac{z^3}{z!} \times e^{-z} = 3 \text{ occurrences}$$

Formula 2 (where the average expected number of occurrences has a high variability rate for any individual occasion)

$$\text{Total probability } (1) = \left(\frac{c}{c+1}\right)^p \left(1 + \frac{p}{c+1} + \frac{p(p+1)}{2!(c+1)^2} + \frac{p(p+1)(p+2)}{3!(c+1)^3} + \dots \text{etc.}\right)$$

c is calculated	$c = z \div (v - z)$
v is the variance	(square of standard deviation)
p is calculated	$p = z \times c$

As previously each item in the brackets represents the successive probabilities.

Summary
This has been a very brief introduction to some of the basic ideas used in statistical processing. Few commercial analysts will need to use anything more complex in their routine work unless they become involved in operational research problems.

Vectors, matrices and scalars

One final mathematical concept with which the analyst should be conversant is that of vectors and matrices as this also is basic to any progression to more advanced mathematical systems work.

When dealing with situations that involve data concerned with more than one aspect of the problem (e.g. forces which have both direction and value) it is convenient to be able to work on these in the abstract using an algebraic technique called vector analysis.

A **vector** is a line with **direction** and **length**. It can occur on any plane in space and is represented by its coordinates on a graphical representation.

Figure 45 illustrates some two-dimensional vectors, and the numeric coordinate representation of these. Notice that the x axis coordinate is given above the y axis one. Vectors can be multidimensional. A three-dimensional vector might be numerically represented

$$\begin{pmatrix} 4 \\ -5 \\ 6 \end{pmatrix}; \text{ four dimensional } \begin{pmatrix} 2 \\ 3 \\ -7 \\ 2 \end{pmatrix} \text{ and so on.}$$

Vector Arithmetic
Vectors with the same dimensions may be

$$\text{added e.g. } \begin{pmatrix} 2 \\ 3 \end{pmatrix} + \begin{pmatrix} 7 \\ -1 \end{pmatrix} = \begin{pmatrix} 9 \\ 2 \end{pmatrix}$$

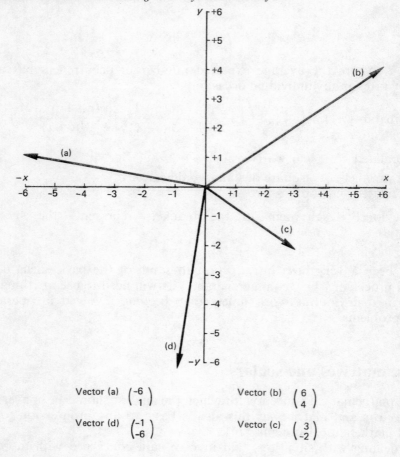

Vector (a) $\begin{pmatrix} -6 \\ 1 \end{pmatrix}$ Vector (b) $\begin{pmatrix} 6 \\ 4 \end{pmatrix}$

Vector (d) $\begin{pmatrix} -1 \\ -6 \end{pmatrix}$ Vector (c) $\begin{pmatrix} 3 \\ -2 \end{pmatrix}$

Figure 45   Vectors

and subtracted e.g. $\begin{pmatrix} 4 \\ 9 \end{pmatrix} - \begin{pmatrix} 5 \\ -1 \end{pmatrix} = \begin{pmatrix} -1 \\ 10 \end{pmatrix}$

If you plot the two original vectors on a grid as in Figure 45, you can see the result of the arithmetic by comparing it with a plot of the result vector.

Multiplication

Vectors may be multiplied by a **scalar** which is in effect (on graphical representation) a factor which lengthens or shortens the vector line. All vectors are in fact scalar multiples of other vectors along the same path in space.

Multiplication is achieved by multiplying all of the vector coordinates by the scalar, e.g.

$$\begin{pmatrix} 2 \\ 3 \end{pmatrix} \times 5 = \begin{pmatrix} 10 \\ 15 \end{pmatrix}$$

$$\begin{pmatrix} 4 \\ -6 \\ 2 \end{pmatrix} \times \tfrac{1}{2} = \begin{pmatrix} 2 \\ -3 \\ 1 \end{pmatrix}$$

$$\begin{pmatrix} 2 \\ 3 \\ -4 \\ 1 \end{pmatrix} \times -4 = \begin{pmatrix} -8 \\ -12 \\ 16 \\ -4 \end{pmatrix}$$

Figure 46 introduces the concept of basis vectors from which (by multiplication by scalars) other vectors can be produced.

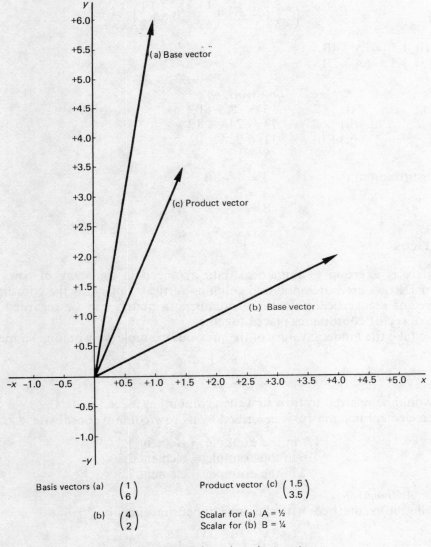

Basis vectors (a)	$\begin{pmatrix} 1 \\ 6 \end{pmatrix}$	Product vector (c)	$\begin{pmatrix} 1.5 \\ 3.5 \end{pmatrix}$
(b)	$\begin{pmatrix} 4 \\ 2 \end{pmatrix}$	Scalar for (a) A = ½
		Scalar for (b) B = ¼

Figure 46   Basis and product vectors

Given   base vector a $= \begin{pmatrix} 1 \\ 6 \end{pmatrix}$

base vector b $= \begin{pmatrix} 4 \\ 2 \end{pmatrix}$

and product vector c $= \begin{pmatrix} 1.5 \\ 3.5 \end{pmatrix}$

we can deduce the scalar for vector a (A) and for vector b (B) by reducing the problem to simultaneous equations

$$\begin{pmatrix} 1.5 \\ 3.5 \end{pmatrix} = A \times \begin{pmatrix} 1 \\ 6 \end{pmatrix} + B \times \begin{pmatrix} 4 \\ 2 \end{pmatrix}$$

(i) $1.5 = 1A + 4B$
(ii) $3.5 = 6A + 2B$

	Steps	Working
Solving	(i) $\times 2$	$3 = 2A + 8B$
	(ii) $\times 4$	$14 = 24A + 8B$
	(ii) $-$ (i)	$11 = 22A$
		$A = \frac{1}{2}$
by substitution in (i)		$3 = 1 + 8B$
		$8B = 2$
		$B = \frac{1}{4}$

Matrices

A matrix is a group of numerical data arranged in an array of rows and columns. Rows are horizontal and columns vertical. In fact, as the coordinates of a vector are vertical columns of numbers, a matrix can be regarded as a group of vector coordinates placed together.

If we take the numeric values of the previous example we would get a matrix

$$\begin{pmatrix} 1.5 & 1 & 4 \\ 3.5 & 6 & 2 \end{pmatrix}$$

This would be referred to (row first then column) as a 2×3 matrix.

Each element in a matrix is described by its row/column coordinate, e.g.

1.5 in the example = element 1,1
6 in the example = element 2,2
2 in the example = element 2,3

Matrix Arithmetic
As with vectors, matrices with the same dimensions may be

added $\begin{pmatrix} 2 & 3 \\ 1 & 4 \end{pmatrix} + \begin{pmatrix} 6 & 3 \\ 5 & 9 \end{pmatrix} = \begin{pmatrix} 8 & 6 \\ 6 & 13 \end{pmatrix}$

and subtracted
$$\begin{pmatrix} 7 & -9 \\ 4 & 8 \end{pmatrix} - \begin{pmatrix} 2 & 1 \\ 4 & -1 \end{pmatrix} = \begin{pmatrix} 5 & -10 \\ 0 & 9 \end{pmatrix}$$

Multiplication

Matrices may only be multiplied together if the number of columns in the first matrix equals the number of rows in the second matrix. This means that it is sometimes necessary to rearrange the relative positions of the matrices or to transpose (change the rows to columns) the elements in a matrix before multiplication can take place.

A simple trick helps us to determine both the possibility of multiplication and the size of the resultant answer.

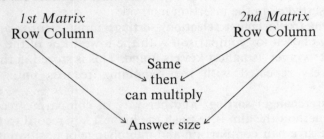

Multiplication is achieved by putting, in the relevant element position in the answer matrix, the sum product of multiplying those rows and columns of the original matrices respectively whose position is indicated by the answer element coordinates, as shown in Figure 47.

```
         Column 1  Column 2     Column 1  Column 2     Column 1  Column 2   Answer
Row 1   /A        B\          /E        F\          /1,1      1,2\          matrix
Row 2   \C        D/    x     \G        H/    =     \2,1      2,2/          elements

Element 1,1  =  A x E + B x G
        1,2  =  A x F + B x H
        2,1  =  C x E + D x G
        2,2  =  C x F + D x H


Example:   /2    3\    x    /6    3\   =   /27    33\
           \1    4/         \5    9/       \26    39/


Element   1,1  =  2 x 6 + 3 x 5  =  27
          1,2  =  2 x 3 + 3 x 9  =  33
          2,1  =  1 x 6 + 4 x 5  =  26
          2,2  =  1 x 3 + 4 x 9  =  39
```
Figure 47   Matrix multiplication

Sorting techniques

(1) **Distribution sorting:** the block of records input are put into ten groups according to the last digit of their key field. These groups are then resorted by the penultimate digit of each key and so on until each character of the key has been processed. The block will then be in sequence and it is output to backing store and a new block read in.

(2) **Insertion sorting**: each record of the input block is examined in turn and compared with each of the already sequenced records in an output area of store. When a record in the sequenced area is reached that is greater than the key in question this and all subsequent records are moved up one place and the new record inserted. Again this process is repeated until all input records are sequenced when the whole string is output to backing store and a new block read in.

(3) **Binary split sorting**: records are taken in turn from the input block and compared with the highest record of the lower half of the already sequenced records to ascertain which half it should be put into. This process is repeated with the subsequent 'correct' halves until the exact location is reached and the new record inserted as in the insertion method.

(4) **Tournament (replacement selection) sorting**: input records are paired and the lowest key chosen for comparison with the lowest key of the next pair and so on until the 'winner' (smallest key) is found. This is stored in the output area and the process repeated with the remaining records until the block is exhausted.

(5) **Bubble (interchange) sorting**: another way of comparing records in pairs but with this method the aim is to push the highest key record to the end of the block by successive pair comparison and interchange of position if a higher key record precedes a lower one. This process must be repeated $n-1$ times until the block is in sequence when it is then output and a new random block read in.

(6) **Scan sorting**: a simple scan of the input block for the lowest key record which is, when found, deleted from the input block and placed in position in an output area. This is repeated to exhaust the block.

(7) **Basic merge**: This consists of taking several strings and comparing the initial records of each, the lowest key becoming the first record of a new larger string. The record chosen is deleted and the next record of that string takes its place. The process continues until the group of strings is exhausted, and then the next set of strings is input and so on until the new record of larger strings is complete.

This new record is subjected to the same process repeatedly until finally a complete sequenced file is obtained.

(8) **Classical sort merge**:

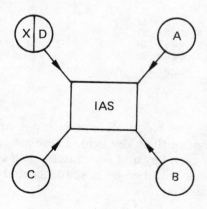

Where X is the original file of sequenced strings the process continues as follows:

1st pass two strings from X merged on to A
two strings from X merged on to B
repeat until X exhausted

2nd pass two strings from A merged on to D
two strings from B merged on to C
repeat etc.

This process is repeated until two of the files have one string each. These two strings are then merged to one sequenced file.

(9) **Other techniques**: there are several other sort–merge techniques getting progressively more sophisticated. They are (i) cascade sorting; (ii) polyphase sorting; and (iii) oscillating sorts.

Batch and real-time processing

There is a fundamental difference in the processing of data determined by the time scale in which it is done. This difference is highlighted in the section on database in Unit 6. There are two kinds of data processing jobs—those that can wait and those that cannot. If you are gathering data about the amount of work an employee has performed so that you can pay his bonus, not only can the processing of this wait but it has to until you have the complete set at the end of the week. However, if a customer phones up to ask for his order or details of his account, it is no good waiting until you have enough enquiries before looking at the file, you must answer him at once. The first situation, and any similar to it, is known as batch processing, as it is a method by which one processes a batch of items and not just a single item, which of necessity means that the answers will refer to a situation some time in the past. The second situation is called real-time processing, as the processing is performed as the event happens and, therefore, in real time and not the past of the happening.

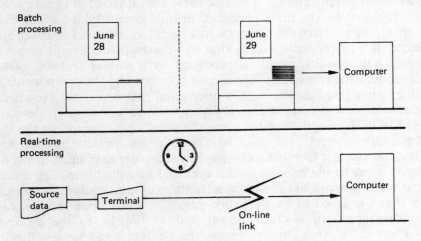

Figure 48   Batch and real-time processing

Real-time processing is generally more expensive than batch as the processing device (man or machine) must await an enquiry, whereas batch processing can be carried out at a moment convenient to the processor. One way to reduce this cost commitment is to give the processor other work to do while it or he is waiting. This requires the ability to handle several jobs at once and of making priority decisions. Humans can generally achieve this. In machines this ability must be built-in and is known as multiprogramming. If the processing device (man or machine) has the ability to be used by more than one user at the same time then this is called time sharing, the time of the processor being shared by its users. This can be done, not only face to face (in human terms) but also over the telephone. In this case we have a remote access application. If there are two processors answering questions between them, the situation is known as multiprocessing.

All these terms are interrelated in some way, but all have a precise meaning of their own and should not be used loosely or regarded as being interchangeable. You should be able to define and use properly the terms: batch processing; real-time processing; multiprogramming; time sharing; remote access processing; multiprocessing.

Processing methods

The whole field of data processing equipment is changing very rapidly at the present time due mainly to the impetus of the electronic component industry. Only a few years ago accountants were using small mechanical rotary calculators, which were replaced by initially expensive electronic pocket calculators. These became relatively inexpensive and widely used but, if you want to pay a little more, you can buy a wrist-watch calculator or a pocket programmable calculator.

In a similar way, only ten years ago, computer terminals, developments from the telex type teleprinters, were a novelty. Today it is possible to obtain a pocket-size computer terminal. The electronic circuit panel of twenty years ago was first replaced by the mass produced printed circuit board which required to be filled with electronic components such as resistors, capacitors and transistors. It was then discovered that the functions of several components, and then whole circuits, could be produced by a similar technology to that used to produce the transistors. The circuit now became the component. As the technology progressed, it was rapidly discovered that it was not even necessary to join several circuit components together to form a functional device, these too could be mass produced in the form of a small chip component the size of a cigarette filter. Strangely, the main advantage of these micro devices is not so much the size since, if they are to be used by man, the keys must fit his fingers, the display must be big enough for his eyes and he will still require a man size desk and chair to work at. The main advantage of miniaturisation comes from the fact that the speed of an electronic device depends upon the resistance of the electronic path to electric current and, obviously, to the distance the current must travel. In a smaller device, the electricity has far less distance to cover and thus the device is faster. In this way, small, inexpensive devices although simple can, in some ways, equal the power of much more costly, large sophisticated machines.

Machines, of any kind, are built to extend man's capabilities, either physical, as in the case of cars, lifts, etc., or mental, as in the case of calculators, computers and so on. However, there are many fields in which man has much greater ability than any machine he has yet invented. I would rather read a human poem than a computer one and much rather kiss a girl than a robot. The same applies to data processing. There are some applications best suited to machine processing and others best suited to human processing. It is useful to identify four main methods of processing data, i.e. of carrying out the eight basic elements identified earlier.

Manual processing—a human with just simple equipment, e.g. pen and paper, rule, etc.

Office machine processing—a human controlling a machine which is designed to perform one or two of the basic elements.

Unit record processing—a human controlling a more sophisticated configuration of machines which perform most or all of the basic elements.

Computer processing—a configuration of machines that can perform all of the basic elements automatically, that is under the control of another machine obeying predetermined sets of instructions.

These are very broad categories and may well change over the next few years. It is very likely that methods (2) and (3) will diminish and finally disappear before the end of the century.

Advantages of mechanisation
  quicker results
  more accurate results
  more legible results
  clerical staff saving
  staff space saving
  more detailed analysis
  new, complex processing techniques possible
      (e.g. critical path analysis, simulation, etc.)
  increased workload capacity
  less 'peaking' problems
  increased standardisation of methods
  compatability with other mechanised installations

Disadvantages of mechanisation
  capital cost depreciation
  maintenance costs
  work development costs
  training and installation costs
  decreased flexibility
  depersonalised service
  coding illegibility
  security and stand-by costs
  under-utilisation
  specialist staff problems

Figure 49   Advantages and disadvantages of mechanisation

Manual methods

We will start by examining those methods available for performing the basic elements of data processing which do not involve the use of machines in the normal sense of the word. These methods do, however, use equipment or materials in most cases.

(1) **Communication** On a purely manual basis we can communicate information by direct speech or by the passing of written messages by hand. We can also make use of notice boards or any other visual display equipment, and in certain circumstances, e.g. racetrack meetings, stock exchange floor, manual signalling can be employed.

(2) **Writing (and imprinting)** Obviously the most used manual method is to handwrite information on paper. This can be a memo or letter or it can be the filling-in of a preprinted business form. In fact this method is used with the most sophisticated computers for capturing data for optical mark document readers. Punched cards may also be marked by hand for punching by mark sense readers. Another way of writing information is by means of rubber or stencil stamping devices. Where the same data must be frequently repeated this is a very cheap and effective method.

(3) **Copying and reproducing** Copies may be made manually by straightforward copying from an original document to a blank sheet. More normal, however, is the use of interleaved carbon paper, carbon backed originals, or chemically treated papers to produce multicopies at the time of origination. Special pieces of equipment known as forms registers, and posting boards are available to hold copies in registration and produce duplicates or file information in one operation.

(4) **Filing and retrieval** There are in fact few machines (until we reach computers) available for filing and retrieval. There is, however, a great variety of equipment, mainly for housing paperwork (Figure 50).

Manual punched (or needle sort) cards, are more of a system for selection and retrieval, although there is also special equipment for housing these cards.

(5) **Checking and classification** These two items are classed together not because they have the same purpose but because the processing involved is basically the same. Checking involves either the repetition of a process and the comparison of results or the comparison of a set of data with a reference. Classification is also performed by the comparison of the data to be classified with a reference either mentally or visually (at the manual level). There is not much in the way of manual equipment available for this process. Overlay checking templates can be used and various measuring devices such as balance scales, measurement rules, etc. can possibly come into this category although these are primarily data capture or detection devices which are normally associated with writing and imprinting. Reference tables and index labelling devices are also associated with classification.

(6) **Sorting** As with filing, until we get to a rather sophisticated level, sorting is primarily a manual plus equipment process. Sorting is usually associated with document handling on this level. The normal manual process is to sort documents on a desk but simple equipment such as pigeon-holes or flap sorters

Document filing	Book binders (ring or post)
	Box files
	Drawer cabinets
	—folders
	—suspended folders
	Lateral filing units
	Fire resistant cabinets
	Safes
Card filing	Plain boxes (blind filing)
	Rotary boxes
	Card wheels
	Visible edge card trays (Kardex)
	Vertical ledger card visible records
Plan filing	Drawer filing
	Vertical plan files
	Lateral plan files
Strip index	Book binders
	Trays
	Rotary trays
Wall charts	Plan boards—visible, magnetic
	Peg boards
	Manual entry
Manual punched cards	Edge punched
	Body punched

Figure 50 Filing equipment

make this a more manageable task. Other things can be sorted such as coins, but this is not information processing as such.

The only real sorting device on a manual level has already been mentioned in connection with filing–that is manual punched card systems. With these various random items can be selected and therefore sorted although in fact one of the advantages of these cards is that they are a random access device and therefore there is no need to sort them or store them in sequence.

(7) **Calculating** The simplest form of manual calculation is mental arithmetic. When this gets above our powers we can make use of ready reckoners, tables and simple office aids. A further step is to use one of the versions of slide rule available. Apart from these (if we discount the use of the abacus as far as the Western world is concerned) all other calculating is done using machines.

The field of office data processing machines

As you will have seen, in some areas the normal office work routine is still very much on a manual basis. In others, such as writing or calculating, it is hard to imagine an office that would operate with the methods described so far. The following is a list of some of the machines to be found in data processing.

Communication
1.0 Centralised dicatating system
1.1 Closed circuit and transmitted television
1.2 Data transmission, telex and teleprint equipment
1.3 Facsimile transmission equipment
1.4 Internal, public and radio telephones and amplifiers
1.5 Office intercom, paging and public address systems
1.6 Signalling equipment
1.7 Teaching machines, slide and cine projection equipment
1.8 Trolleys and transport equipment
1.9 Tube and belt document conveyers
Writing and imprinting
2.0 Addressing machines
2.1 Automatic paper and magnetic tape typewriters, flexowriters
2.2 Cheque writing and signing machines
2.3 Embossing and perforating machines
2.4 Numbering and encoding machines
2.5 Office printing–stencil and rubber stamping devices
2.6 Office typewriters–manual and electric
2.7 Portable typewriters
2.8 Postal and slogan franking machines
2.9 Stenographic and special purpose typing machines
Copying and reproducing
3.0 Hand registers, carbon copying devices, posting boards
3.1 Spirit duplicating – office and systems machines (line selectors)
3.2 Dictating machines – disk, belt, tape, wire, sheet and roll
3.3 Microfilming equipment – roll, aperture, and microfiche, etc.
3.4 Photocopying – silver salt, gelatin, diazo, heat and electrostatic
3.5 Offset lithographic equipment
3.6 Stencil duplicating and reproducing machines
3.7 Still and cine filming equipment
3.8 Telephone answering recorders
3.9 Videotape and special purpose recording equipment
Filing and retrieving
4.0 Book, box and loose leaf filing systems
4.1 Card files – blind, visible, wheel and mechanised devices
4.2 Cupboards, desks, laminators and shredders
4.3 Drawer cabinets – folder and suspension units
4.4 Lateral filing equipment
4.5 Plan boards, peg boards and wall charts
4.6 Rotary filing units
4.7 Safes, shelving and storage boxes
4.8 Strip indexes and plan files
4.9 Visible record ledger card files
Sorting and paper handling
5.0 Binding, stapling and tying machines
5.1 Coin and note sorters and change-giving machines
5.2 Desk-top sort files

5.3 Document collators
5.4 Edge and body manual punched card equipment
5.5 Folding machines
5.6 Inserting and sealing machines
5.7 Joggers and stacking equipment
5.8 Letter openers and guillotines
5.9 Pigeon holes and racking

Calculating

6.0 Slide rules, ready reckoners and simple office aids
6.1 Simple key depression, dial reading adding machines
6.2 Manual and electric key depression adding and listing machines
6.3 Calculating machines – nonprint, simple or full keyboard, lever set, manual and electric key drive
6.4 Printing calculators, simple keyboard, electric key drive
6.5 Electronic dial calculators – simple key board, pocket calculators
6.6 Full numeric keyboard, accounting and book-keeping machines
6.7 Accounting machines with numeric and alphabetic keyboard
6.8 Large electronic accounting machines or configurations
6.9 Invoicing machines and electronic desk computers

Checking and classifying

7.0 Automatic numbering and encoding machines
7.1 Cash registers
7.2 Coin and note counting machines
7.3 Indexing and labelling devices
7.4 Overlay checking templates
7.5 Size measuring devices
7.6 Tally equipment and counting devices
7.7 Telephone-call timers
7.8 Time recording devices
7.9 Weighing scales

Unit record processing

Strictly speaking, the items 6.6–6.9 on the list of office data processing machines come under the heading of unit record equipment. These are so called because they are designed to process records which, due to the nature of the carrying medium used, are dealt with as discrete individual units and not as a set of records on a page or a group of records on, say, a magnetic tape.

There are three main groups of unit record equipment: traditional accounting machines; punched card processing equipment; and visible record computers (VRCs). Both the first two types are now virtually obsolete having been replaced, by the last type, VRCs, if it is essential to retain a visible (printed) record of the historical transactions, and by the microbased desk computer (see Unit 8) if it is not. Punched card equipment retained a foothold in the field of data preparation for the first 20 years of commercial computing but now this also has been replaced by other more direct or faster and more flexible methods.

Accounting machines

At one time all accounting was actually done in ledgers, that is large books with a page for each account, customer, supplier, etc. In some small businesses this is still so, but for larger businesses individual books are soon filled. This led to the introduction of loose-leaf records where each page (kept in book form in lockable binders) could be inserted or extracted as required. The work could then be split up between various clerks and thus finished sooner, and full records could be replaced with fresh sheets.

It was soon realised that these loose pages could be inserted into a printing calculator and thus gain further speed advantages as well as increased accuracy and legibility. Machines were developed by various manufacturers, some starting from typewriters that were adapted to calculate and others from calculators that were modified with alphabetic printing mechanisms. A third source of machine which could classify information was derived from cash register mechanisms.

The simplest form of unit record machine is the **book-keeping machine**. It has a moving carriage to accommodate the ledger card (page), limited printing facilities that can identify items and print simple codes and dates and a feature for accepting opening balances and accumulating closing balances. Book-keeping machines can have manually operated carriages, carriages that alternate between only two posting positions (shuttle), or automatic tab stop carriages.

More complex machines of the same principle are called **accounting machines**. These have additional registers capable of accumulating many balances, more sophisticated printing mechanisms ranging up to full alphabetic and numeric keyboards and program mechanisms which allow a choice of several types of work to be preset by a button which activates a program control bar or panel set up by the manufacturer at the rear of the machine. All accounting machines are capable of addition and subtraction and some have all four arithmetic operations available. This extends the type of work capacity to include invoices, payroll, etc. The most sophisticated of these machines can have many registers allowing analysis of up to several hundred separate totals.

Visible record computers

With the increase in knowledge of electronics in all spheres, the first all-electronic calculating machines were brought out. These became very popular as they are quiet, simple to operate and fast. It then became possible to add small electronic registers, electronic program boxes and automatic input units. This led to the development of electronic accounting machines either for the purpose of ledger accounting or for calculating work such as billing. These machines were made available to accept batched input data by means of punched card, punched paper tape or edge punched cards as well as the normal keyboard method. The register/storage area was enlarged and sometimes a moving print head substituted for the moving carriage.

With all the extra equipment it was found that this was best presented built in to a desk-type working station.

One further step has been taken to increase the potential of these visible record machines. In order to speed up processing we have seen that automatic input was added. There remained the problem of picking up opening balances, which if done by keyboard operation could be a comparatively slow process. Taking an idea from the big computers, a magnetic medium was used to record and store this information at each processing run so that it could be automatically picked up at the next run. This was achieved by placing a stripe of magnetic material on the reverse of the ledger card (Figure 51).

The main feature of these machines is at the same time their major limitation. Their popularity lies in the fact that they still provide a visible record of transactions (unlike a completely magnetic tape system). However, this means that they are limited to the speed of the printing device used and the speed at which the cards can be loaded. The result of this is that they tend to be special purpose machines employed full time on one job such as stock control, payroll, ledger work, etc. This also applies to the other machine type derived from automatic typewriters and not using ledger cards. These will normally be found used solely for invoicing, internal accounting or similar applications. One potential benefit from these machines is that they are able to produce by-product paper tape or punched cards which can then be input into the main computer system.

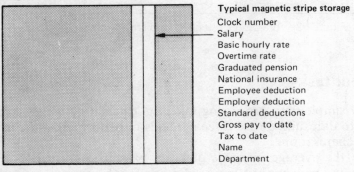

Typical magnetic stripe storage
Clock number
Salary
Basic hourly rate
Overtime rate
Graduated pension
National insurance
Employee deduction
Employer deduction
Standard deductions
Gross pay to date
Tax to date
Name
Department

Magnetic ledger stripes

Magnetic ink ledger stripes store data in magnetic pulse form. Upon insertion data is read from magnetic stripes into the main memory. After operator indexes the variable data, the machine using information from the magnetic stripes, automatically computes, accumulates, and prints output in any desired format. Upon ejection of ledger, machine automatically stores the updated information on magnetic stripes.

Figure 51   Magnetic ledger card

Punched card processing

If you are a newcomer to computing you may not have realised that punched cards and computers are completely independent of each other. It is perfectly possible to have a computer installation that has nothing to do with punched cards. In the same way punched card processing is a method of data processing that was established well before computers were invented.

We have seen that machines are available to perform the individual elements of data processing, and also machines that combine several of these elements. In punched card processing we had a group of machines, some independent, others linked together, which taken as a whole could perform all of the elements of information processing.

The machines involved were: card punch; card verifier; interpreter; sorter; collator; tabulator; reproducing punch; calculator; and mixed element machines.

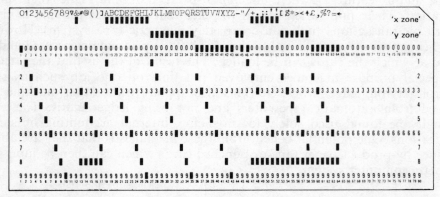

Figure 52 Interpreted punched card showing character coding

Assessment tasks

1 Take any simple data processing task, e.g. calculating wages, keeping stock records up to date, and devise three methods of performing these using various levels of mechanisation.

2 Calculate the average intervals of buses passing a given point. Justify the method you use as being the most valid one for the purpose and give a visual presentation of your findings.

3 Give a tape recorded talk on the usefulness of standard deviation. Explain how this can be of use in data processing work and give examples.

4 Use probability theory to forecast some volume/frequency statistics about the number of items of data occurring in a given set of records.

5 Choose some real problem that can be solved by the use of matrices. Prove you are correct by doing it.

6 Put the ages of all your work colleagues or fellow students on individual cards, put them into a hat and use one of the described sorting methods to put them in ascending sequence.

7 Describe two data processing applications suited to batch and real-time processing. Justify your answers.

Unit 8
Automatic processing methods–hardware

Learning objective

To be able to appreciate the similarities between the main processing methods—manual, man/machine and automatic in terms of hardware and software. To be able to define the differences between analog and digital devices. To be able to explain, in broad terms, the internal workings of a digital processor and to recognise the essential 'configuration of parts' aspect of digital computers. To know the current range of peripheral and ancillary devices used in digital computer configurations and understand their specifications to the extent of being able to define an efficient and effective hardware solution to given applications problems.

Hardware systems

In Unit 1, a system was defined as input subjected to a regulated activity to produce aim-achieving results. A motor car can be regarded as a system in that it receives input in the form of petrol, oil, water as well as other input in the form of pressure on its pedals and steering wheel and contact with road surfaces. As a result of these inputs, something happens in the car (regulated activity) which achieves the aim of getting you from one place to another. What actually happens inside the car may be known to you or it may not. You can just regard the inner workings of the system as a black box. Knowing that inside the black box is a regulated activity will help you a little but you may not know (or care) what the activity is or what the rules are that govern it. Providing your aim is achieved then that is good enough.

In data processing, the regulated activity can be carried out by any of the three methods: manual; man/machine; or automatic machine (machine/machine).

All methods contain two aspects, the work effector mechanism (activity) and its control mechanism (regulated). However, the control mechanism cannot actuate the effector without a set of rules to follow so, to understand how the black box works, we must consider three things: the processing device; the control device; the application (job) rules.

In a manual system, the processing device is the human body together with that part of the brain that performs calculations, logic, etc. The control mechanism is that part of the human brain that makes our limbs and muscles respond to our wishes. Both of these aspects are physical, i.e. the hardware of the system. The rules of how to do the job (known as an **algorithm**) are not part of our body although they may be stored in that part of our brain known

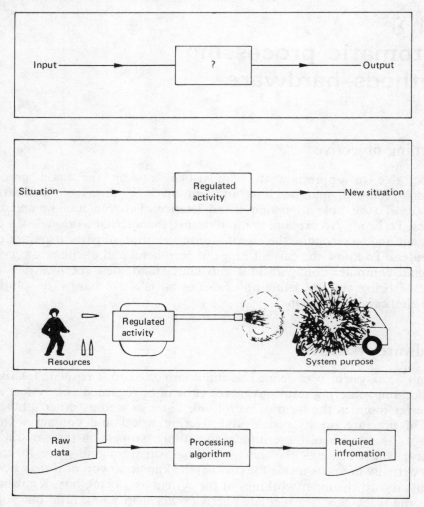

Figure 53   Systems

as memory. These rules are an aspect of the system separate from the hardware. They are known as software.

The most common form of system found in business, and in all areas of human activity, is the man/machine system, e.g. a man driving a car, a person using a telephone, a typist using a typewriter. In this system, it is the machine that is the processing device and the human body that is the control mechanism.

The system illustrated is actually three systems: the overall processing system (man-machine); the machine processing system; the human control system. In each of these systems can be found five stages: the input receptor stage; the input decoder stage; the processing stage; the output coding stage; the output effector stage.

One further factor must be considered. The systems operate in an environment and the control/processor interaction is dependent upon the

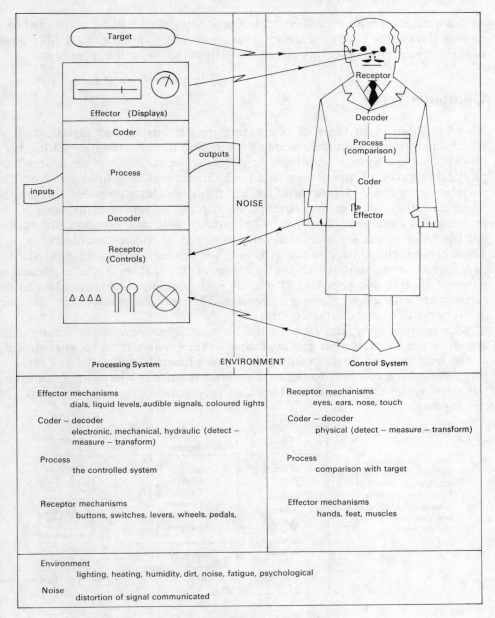

Figure 54   A man/machine system

communication of information from one system to the other. If there is interference (noise) in the environment, there will be distortion or loss of signal in the communication causing a loss of complete control. For example, if the lighting were poor the dials could be misread.

An automatic system is a system with inbuilt control mechanisms. In fact, the human body is just that, as it contains a brain with capacity for both processing and control. In data processing terms, an automatic system usually means a machine with inbuilt control, a processing device being controlled by a control device, the hardware working automatically following the requirements of the software rules. It is this automatic system that we call a computer.

Computer types

There are two main types of computing device, **analog** and **digital**, each of which operate on different principles. An analog device works by setting up a model of the problem to be solved, representing the variables of the problem by physical aspects of the device itself which are made proportional to the variables concerned. In terms of an electronic analog computer this means using variations in electrical voltage or current to represent aspects of the problem. By manipulating these using various electronic components, results are obtained which are measured and displayed by meters, oscilloscopes, etc. These can be related back to the aspects of the problem being investigated.

A digital device requires all the variables of the problem to be expressed in terms of discrete numbers (digits). These are then manipulated according to the rules of arithmetic and number systems and the results expressed in numeric, or numerically coded character, terms.

Both types of computer play a valuable role in business. Analog computers are much used by scientists and engineers, as they enable them to work directly at the machine and develop solutions in an educated trial and error fashion, proceeding from one idea to the next without the need to have pre-planned all the steps required beforehand. They are very good devices for research and development work.

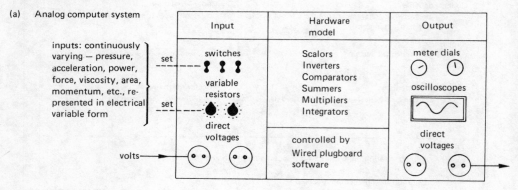

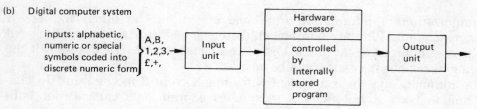

Figure 55　Computer types

Scientists also make use of digital computers. Although these have the disadvantage of requiring the processing steps to be preplanned, they are automatic and, therefore, work at machine speed which is very much faster than any human controlled device. Often scientists use a third kind of machine known as a hybrid computer which is, in effect, an analog computer controlled by a digital computer instead of by a human. This is to produce the flexibility of the analog device whilst gaining the advantage of the speed of the automatic digital machine. These hybrid machines are very special purpose devices and tend to be manufactured for specific applications which makes them very costly. Their main applications have been in the areas of aerospace and process control.

Digital computers

Data processing is concerned with facts and information which are already expressed in numeric and character representation and it is, therefore, the digital computer that is used for this purpose. A digital computer works by representing all the normal numeric, alphabetic and special symbol characters used by humans in terms of binary representations of electrical pulses. This is best understood by drawing a graph representing an electrical circuit being switched on and off over a period of time. The pattern produced is one of a series of pulses or no pulses, which can be represented in terms of binary digits 0 or 1. In this way all the requirements of human information can be inserted, processed and output from an electronic machine (Figure 56; see also Figure 29, Unit 6).

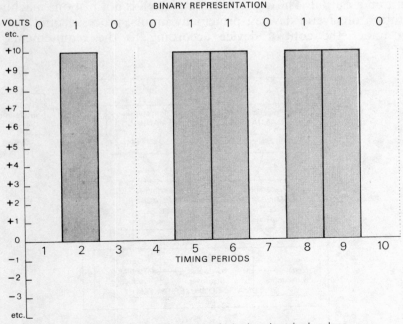

Figure 56   Representation of bits by electrical pulses

When digital computers are used for data processing they will be found as part of a larger data processing system consisting of interfaced manual, man-machine and automatic subsystems. This is an important point to remember for the most expensive and elaborate computerised system is only as good as its weakest link and the interfaces between the subsystems must receive as much attention as the rest of the system.

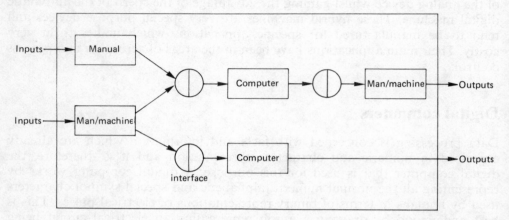

Figure 57   A data processing system

A typical computerised system will contain the elements found illustrated for a man-machine system: reception, decoding, processing, decoding and effecting, together with the additional requirements of preparation for input and presentation of output. The digital computer itself is not just one machine but a configuration of several devices, principally inputs, processor and outputs, all working under the control device according to the requirements of the software.

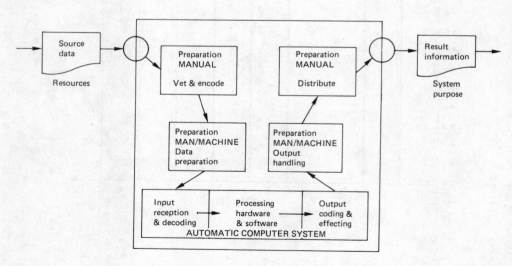

Figure 58   A typical computerised system

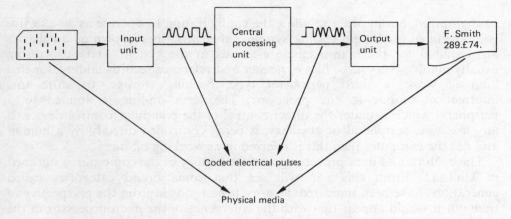

Figure 59   The essential computer configuration

Digital computer hardware falls under three broad categories:
    processors–micro, mini, mainframe
    peripherals–input, output, backing store
    ancillaries–communications, capture, preparation, presentation,
        miscellaneous.
The processor and its peripheral devices together make up the computer

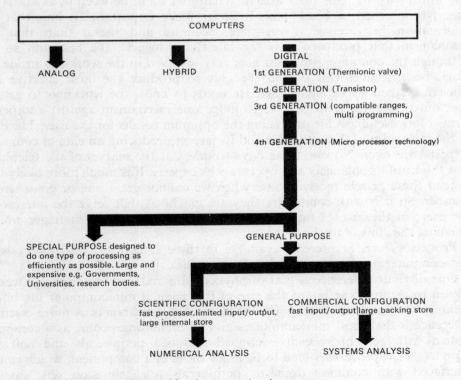

Figure 60   Computer hardware types

configuration, but in order to allow the configuration to operate as an effective component of a data processing system, other machines known as ancillaries are required for the man-machine elements in the system. Data processing usually involves very large files of master and reference records adding, for this kind of work, a third peripheral type, backing storage, to store this information on-line to the processor. The term on-line is applied to a peripheral which is under the direct control of the computer control device. If any machine, peripheral or ancillary, is being controlled directly by a human and not the computer then this is referred to as working off-line.

The evolution of data processing and the history of the computer is outlined in Unit 11. From this you will see that some broad categories called generations have been indicated. History is best judged from the perspective of time but it would appear that with the emergence of the microprocessor in the 1970s, we are now in the period of the fourth generation of digital computing.

Processors

In looking at computers and the detail of the processors themselves, it must never be forgotten that what we are really interested in is the flow of information through the system. Computerised data processing systems are man-made for man's purposes. Most systems start with humans (source areas) and finish with humans (user areas). What goes on in between is, as far as the user is concerned, a black box. It is far more important to him that the information he receives is on time, accurate and useful than that the mechanism that produced it is the latest, the biggest, the best and so on. Although the computer specialist gets very involved in the workings inside the black box, he does this only to be able to produce the most effective and efficient systems to serve the user. He needs to know the workings to get the best out of them and to be able to judge one mechanism against another in terms of its usefulness for producing the optimum results for the user. The days of the mysticism of the computer and its jargon producing an elite of computer 'experts' are over. No one these days wonders at the marvel of the telephone and thinks of its engineers and operators as experts. It is much more likely that instead these people receive abuse when we cannot get a line or get a wrong number. So it is with computers–they are machines that serve the interests of the user; in the case of business data processing this is the manager who is pursuing the aims of the business.

Processors are, at present, available in three categories: microprocessors; minicomputer processors; mainframe processors.

One obvious difference is that of physical size and cost; the microprocessor fits on to a mounting board the size of this page, a minicomputer fits into a desk size unit and mainframes fill one or more large cabinets. A more essential difference is that most minicomputers and all mainframes come as a computer system with sets of specially designed matched peripherals and software support. Microprocessors tend to be much more of a component, which can be interfaced with common domestic peripherals (e.g. television sets, cassette recorders) or original equipment manufacturer's hardware, although they can

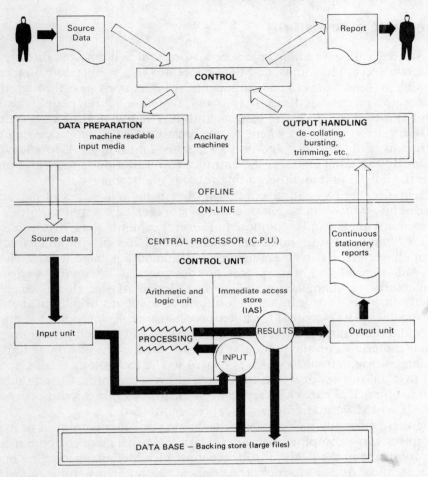

Figure 61   Processing source data for management information

also be purchased as complete desk-top machines. The main effect the arrival of microprocessors has had is to change our thinking of central processing units as being one device with three sections, immediate access store, arithmetic and logic unit and control unit, to regarding these as three separate components on a common mount and interconnected by a series of bus lines (electrical circuit signal connection paths). The microprocessor has brought the systems analyst's and programmer's perception of the machine much closer to that of the electronic engineer. By encapsulating these functions in chips that can be plugged into a mounting board, technology has actually simplified the analyst's perception of the machinery allowing him to concentrate on its suitability to application problem solutions.

The central processing unit (CPU) of a digital computer, whether it be a microprocessor, minicomputer or mainframe consists of an immediate access store (IAS), an arithmetic and logic unit (ALU) and a control unit (CU) with interconnecting data, control signal and store address paths and switches.

Immediate access stores

This store is called an immediate access store as it is connected directly to the arithmetic and control units, and data contained in it is, therefore, immediately accessible to (and from) these components. All data must pass through the IAS to get to the processing device (ALU) and, therefore, all the peripherals (input, output and backing store) are connected to it. The role of the IAS is rather like that of a railway platform where people must wait until the processing device, the train, is ready for them and on to which they must alight before leaving the station. By the same analogy, the entrance to the station is the input unit, the exit is the output unit and the waiting room is the backing store.

Essentially, the IAS can be conceived of as being a large set of pigeon holes or boxes into which can be put one unit of storage, the computer word. This, as was seen in Unit 6, can be composed of several subunits (bits, bytes, characters, etc.) enabling us to store numeric, alphabetic and special symbol characters or sets of characters, e.g. whole numbers and human language words. The word size will depend on the processor design and therefore varies from manufacturer to manufacturer. The overall size of the store, which is its capacity in bytes or words, varies and can be made up usually in units of 1k (approximately 1000 words) for microprocessors or 4k multiples for minicomputers and mainframes. The maximum store size will depend on the number of available interfaces on the particular processor or the size of storage unit (often very large for mainframes) which is related to the technology used. Capacity is rated in k (kilo) bytes or words or M (mega) bytes or words. Current minimum and maximum IAS capacities range from 1k to 256k for microprocessors and from 32k to 1M for mainframes (all expressed in words).

There are currently many different technologies being employed or explored for implementing computer memories. Until the 1970s magnetic core memories were dominant in the field but to these must be added magnetic film, magneto optics, semiconductor, ferroelectric, optical, cathode ray tube, planar film, plated wire, magnetic bubble, charged coupled devices, holographic and other memories.

IAS specification

To describe all these systems is unnecessary to all but electronics engineers. All of them work on the principle of being capable of storing the difference between one state and another, i.e. being able to change from one to the other of two states, and being able to read the current state of the device. If this can be done for one unit (one binary digit) it can be done for a group of units (a computer word) and thus for a whole store of words. On a human scale this can be done with a simple up or down switch, an East/West flag, a coin (heads or tails) or anything we can change two ways and see (read) the change.

What is important as far as these technologies is concerned is not how they work but their specification in terms of capacity, cost and speed of operation. Operation speeds are concerned with access time, which is the time to locate a particular part of the store, and transfer rate, which is the time to move data into and out of store. Access times are measured in ms (milliseconds = 1/1000s), μs   (microseconds = 1/1000000s)   and   ns   (nanoseconds = 1/1000000000s).

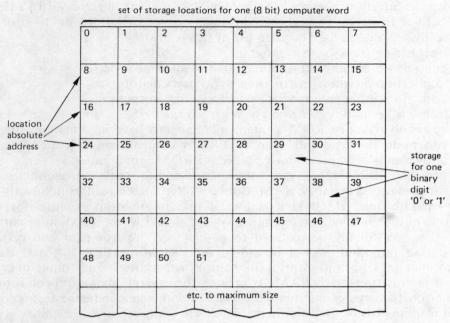

(a) Pigeon hole concept

Technology type	Maximum capacity	Access time	Transfer rate
e.g. core film semi conductor bubble	rated in kB (kilobytes) kW (kilowords) MB (megabytes) MW (megawords)	rated in ms (milliseconds) μs (microseconds) ns (nanoseconds)	rated in kB/S (kilobytes per sec) MB/S (megabytes per sec)

(b) Evaluation table

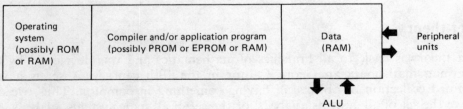

(c) IAS contents

Figure 62 Immediate access stores

Transfer rates are measured in k or M bytes/s.

With the advent of the newer technologies for the manufacture of IAS there has been a tendency to separate the functions of this store on to distinct physically separate units. The main use of IAS is to store

operating system–control program

compiler–program to translate human to machine code

application program–instructions to do particular job

data–from input, intermediate stage, awaiting output.

Regardless of technology, IAS can be regarded as

read only memory, ROM–contents permanently fixed in at manufacture

programmable read only memory, PROM–contents can be loaded by user
by means of a special device called a PROM programmer

erasable, EPROM–contents can be erased and the units reprogrammed

random access memory, RAM–can be written to and read from directly.

If separate units are used it is logical that information essential for the working of the machine, e.g. operating system, would be on ROM, information that may occasionally be required to be changed, e.g. compiler and certain application programs, would be stored on PROM or EPROM, and data, which changes constantly during its transitional journey from input data to output information, needs RAM. At present, the separate unit approach is only normal on the smaller microbased machines with semiconductor technology, but it is quite possible that future machines will contain a mix of memory types suiting cost and function for the most efficient approach to various application fields.

Arithmetic and logic unit

Having now stored our information in the form of binary coded digits, how can we perform the operations of arithmetic and logic? Obviously by various function circuits made up of normal electronic components such as resistors, transistors, printed or integrated circuits. You do not have to be an electronics engineer and know how all these function. However, a knowledge of the principles upon which these circuits are based is helpful both in understanding the action of the arithmetic unit and also in the tackling of other problems requiring a logical solution.

Set theory

Set theory is basic to all branches of mathematics and was developed by the German mathematician Georg Cantor in the 19th century. A set is a well defined collection of objects all having something in common. Thus, we can have the set of all systems analysts, or the set of all male systems analysts, etc. The set that nothing belongs to, e.g. the set of three legged systems analysts, is called the empty or null set.

A set may be defined in two ways. Either by listing every member of that set or by stating (as above) the property that is possessed only by every member of that set, in other words the common property. Set theory is concerned with the interaction of various sets, one with the other, and is sometimes called combinational logic. There are three ways in which combinational logic can be expressed: mapping; tables; algebra.

The most common technique for mapping is the **Venn diagram** named after its creator John Venn (1880). Tables used to represent logical operations are called **truth tables.** One form of mapping which you may come across concerning computer design is the Karnaugh map (not dealt with here). This is a combination of a Venn diagram and a truth table. Finally an algebraic method for working out logical problems was developed by George Boole (1847) and is known as **Boolean algebra.** Unfortunately the various connective symbols used in this algebra are not yet standardised (although the meanings are of course universal). Examples used here will be based on BS 3527.

Combinational logic

Let us first familiarise ourselves with the three techniques. We will do so by means of a simple example:

Problem: state by means of a Venn diagram, a truth table and a Boolean algebra expression, the situation given below:

I will buy a new car if
    (a) my present car breaks down *and* I have sufficient capital
or (b) a new model is introduced *and* I have sufficient capital
or (c) a new model is introduced *and* my present car breaks down

Venn diagram
I will buy a new car in (a) above is shown by the area where circle A and circle

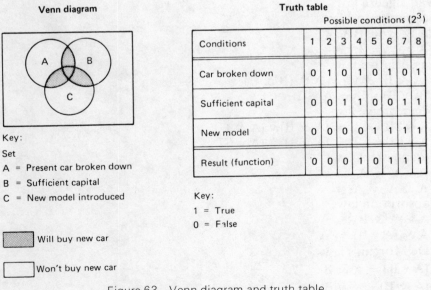

Venn diagram

Key:

Set

A = Present car broken down

B = Sufficient capital

C = New model introduced

    Will buy new car

    Won't buy new car

Truth table

Possible conditions (2^3)

Conditions	1	2	3	4	5	6	7	8
Car broken down	0	1	0	1	0	1	0	1
Sufficient capital	0	0	1	1	0	0	1	1
New model	0	0	0	0	1	1	1	1
Result (function)	0	0	0	1	0	1	1	1

Key:

1 = True

0 = False

Figure 63   Venn diagram and truth table

B overlap. In (b) above it is where circle C and circle B overlap and in (c) above where circle C and circle A overlap (Figure 63).

Truth table
Conditions can either be fulfilled or not (true or false) therefore the total possible is 2 (results) to the power of 3 (conditions) = 8. Each possible set of conditions is considered in the light of the problem statements above and the result determined (Figure 63).

Boolean expression
Let A be the set of 'car broken down'
Let B be the set of 'sufficient capital'
Let C be the set of 'new model introduced'
Let r be the result (buy a new car)
Let $\in$ (epsilon) mean 'belongs to the set of'
Let & mean 'and' (intersection)
Let v mean 'or' (union)
Then the problem statements can be expressed:
$$r = \in (A \; \& \; B) \; v \; (C \; \& \; B) \; v \; (C \; \& \; A)$$

Other Boolean connectives

A bar over set name (e.g. $\overline{A}$) or an expression (e.g. $\overline{A \; \& \; B}$) means the negation (inverse or complement) of that set or expression. In other words everything not belonging to that set.

The sign $\equiv$ means equivalence (giving a result of 1 when elements are alike) and $\not\equiv$ means nonequivalence (a result of 1 when elements differ).

Boolean algebra laws
(a)   commutative laws
      A & B = B & A
      A v B = B v A
(b)   associative laws
      (A & B) & C = A & (B & C)
      (A v B) v C = A v (B v C)
(c)   distributive laws
      A & (B v C) = (A & B) v (A & C)
      A v (B & C) = (A v B) & (A v C)
(d)   idempotent laws
      A v A = A
      A & A = A
(e)   absorption laws
      A v (A & B) = A
      A & (A v B) = A
(f)   De Morgan's laws
      $\overline{(A \; v \; B)} = \overline{A} \; \& \; \overline{B}$
      $\overline{(A \; \& \; B)} = \overline{A} \; v \; \overline{B}$

Boolean operations

Obviously then, many logical problems such as the worked example can be resolved by Boolean algebra, Venn diagrams and truth tables.

Boolean operations are logical operations on single binary digits, and as you have seen computers work in binary coded voltage pulses and arithmetic functions can be performed as variations of simple addition (complement addition, multiple addition, etc.).

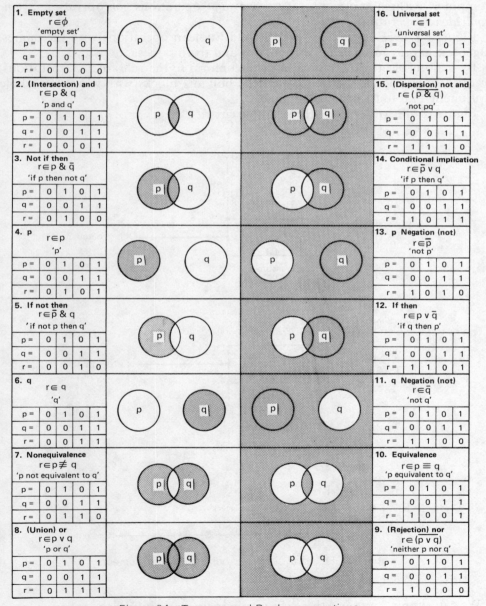

Figure 64   Two operand Boolean operations

The decisions that computers are supposed to be so good at are in reality just a simple two way decision and this again is based on comparison of numbers by subtraction (complementary addition). In summary then, basically all a computer has to be able to do is simple addition.

A simple addition operation involves the input and summation of two operands. There are sixteen possible Boolean operations on two operands. Of these only ten are **dyadic** operations, that is where the result is dependent on both operands. Of these ten operations, three have the greatest importance in computer arithmetic circuits. These are: *and* operations; *or* operations; *non-equivalence* operations.

Figure 64 gives all sixteen two operand Boolean operations with the names, algebraic expressions, verbal expressions and truth tables.

By making electrical circuits that will conform to the rules of *and* operations, *or* operations and inversion, we have the building blocks with which the whole arithmetic unit functions can be built.

Figure 65 illustrates these three simple circuits.

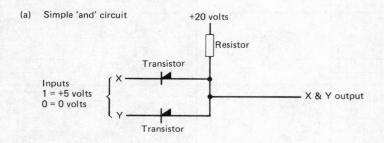

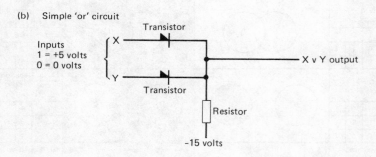

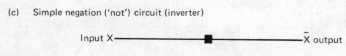

Figure 65   Electrical circuits of basic computer elements

We can simply represent these circuits in logic diagram form as follows:

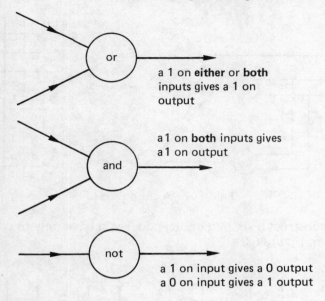

If we combine these elements as in Figure 66 we can build a non-equivalence circuit.

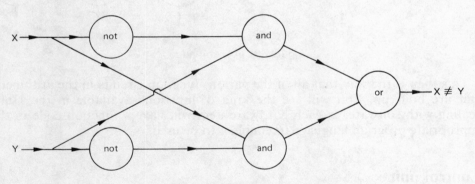

Figure 66   Nonequivalence circuit

Using the rules given above you will see that a non-equivalence circuit can be stated as:

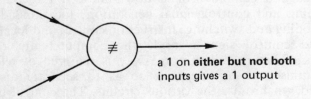

To make a one bit adder we can further connect the above elements (Figure 67). If you test the binary addition truth table you will see that in each of the eight possible positions the circuit will give the required results.

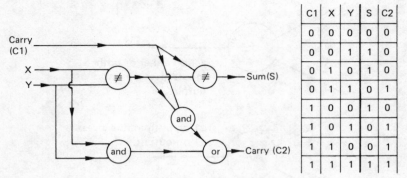

C1	X	Y	S	C2
0	0	0	0	0
0	0	1	1	0
0	1	0	1	0
0	1	1	0	1
1	0	0	1	0
1	0	1	0	1
1	1	0	0	1
1	1	1	1	1

Figure 67   A one bit adder

Finally to construct a six bit parallel adder you have only to connect six, one bit adders, as in Figure 68.

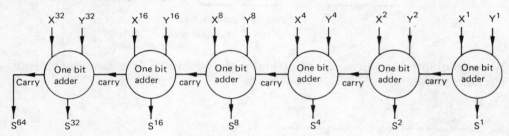

Figure 68   A six bit adder

This then is the way that all of the various function circuits in the arithmetic unit are built up. You will see the kind of functions available in the Units dealing with software, as each hardware item will have a function code in the appropriate program language to enable it to be used.

Control unit

The overall function of the control unit (CU) is to control and actuate the whole computer on-line configuration (IAS addressess, ALU functions, input, output and backing store peripherals) in accordance with the software step by step instructions and can be broken down into: timing pulse generation; function decoding and control signal generation; location address (IAS or peripheral) decoding and switching; instruction control and location registers.

As data and control signals inside the computer are represented by continuous sets of binary pulses, some way is required of referencing these pulses, or no pulses, to a time scale so as to separate discrete units of information and synchronise the various circuits. The control unit contains a clock (mill or timing pulse generator) which sends out a sequence of equal duration voltage pulses and intervals (no pulses), in an on/off/on/off/etc. manner. This signal is fed into and utilised by the other circuits of the machine as the overall referencing signal.

To help understand the use of the instruction control and function and address decoding aspects of the CU, a simple example may be useful. To do this it is necessary to have some concept of computer programs. A program is simply a list of the processing steps required in the sequence necessary to produce an answer from some raw input.

A PROGRAM—list of instructions (statements)

1. Print out headings.
2. Read in first number.
3. Read in second number.
4. Multiply first number by second.
5. Print out answer.
6. If there is more data go back to step 2.
7. If no more data, stop.

(What to do and the sequence of doing it)

Figure 69   A simple program

Each instruction (statement) contains two aspects: what to do (function) and where to get or put the data processed (address).

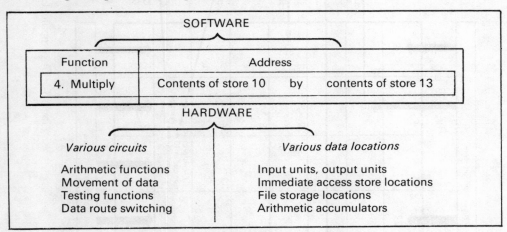

Figure 70   Program statement function and address

The computer cycle

The processor works in cycles of: read one program instruction–from IAS to CU; obey the instruction–decode and generate function and address control signals; update next instruction address register; repeat cycle until stop function instruction.

The sequence of events in our example is as follows

(1) The instruction control 'reads' the location of the next instruction from the 'next instruction address' register.

(2) Control signals are sent out from the instruction control causing a copy of the instruction (stored in location 39) to be moved to the CU, one part to the

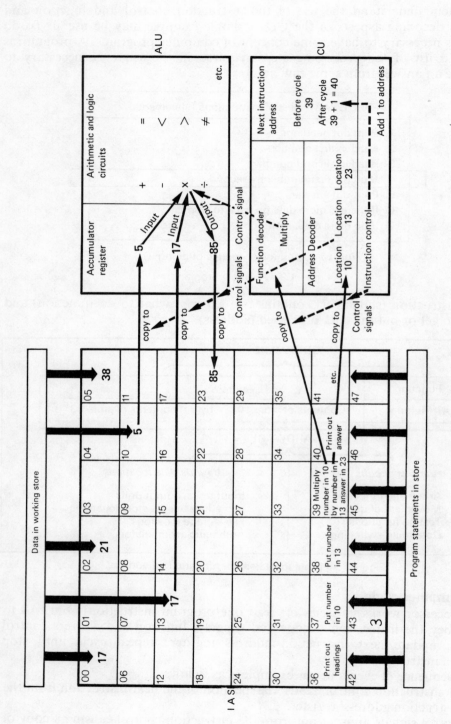

Figure 71 A computer CU cycle

function decoder and the other part to the address decoder. This ends the 'read' part of the cycle.

(3) The address decoder sends control signals which cause a copy of the data in the IAS to be moved to the accumulator register(s). The function decoder sends control signals which switch the accumulator to the multiply circuit and the output of this circuit to the accumulator. The address decoder signal routes the answer from the accumulator to the result location (23).

(4) Having obeyed the instruction, the instruction controller updates the next instruction address by adding 1 to the previous address.

There are two basic types of instruction–the **simple process** (illustrated here) and the **branching instruction**. In the case of a branching instruction, the address given is not that of data but that of the next instruction to be obeyed. In this case the instruction controller does not add 1 to the previous address. Instead the address given in the branch instruction is copied into the next instruction address register.

Alternative structures

The type of CPU described so far is the normal standard von Neuman architecture, so called after its inventor (see Unit 10). Recently, a different approach has been developed, still using the elements of control, storage and arithmetic and logic but put together in a rather different way. Instead of keeping the store and logic unit separate, **array processor** architecture merges these so that each store location has a small ALU function associated with it. These combined store/arithmetic units are known as processing elements and they are joined up in the form of an array, so that each one has four other elements as neighbours. These arrays of processing elements can be built up to large size units (e.g. 32k × 32k) with each element capable of carrying out a small part of the overall processing unit. Because of the linking of neighbours, rows and/or columns of processing elements can join forces on common problems. The advantage of this is rather like getting many hands working on a job all at the same time instead of one man doing all the work. The total man hours for the work remains the same but the job is completed much sooner.

In the same way as the employment of many people to do a job requires a supervisor to organise and control the work, so the use of distributed array processing elements requires an additional unit, a master control unit, to organise them. This type of CPU architecture is very good for certain types of work such as matrix calculation and image and pattern recognition. Now that the break away from the traditional CPU structure has been made, no doubt many new forms will evolve, each with its own area of application.

The latest microprocessor technology is already producing whole processors: control units, ALUs and up to 256k ROM and 256k RAM all on one 40 pin chip. Other developments include semiconductor material that will enable full power battery driven microprocessors and fully stable (nonvolatile) memories that do not lose their information when the power is switched off. This latter is very important in the development of RAM for use both as IAS and backing store and may well foreshadow the replacement of rotating devices (disks and tapes).

Peripherals

The CPU processes data that is entered into its IAS from the input units and backing stores. The resultant information is passed either as a report to the output units or as updated master or reference information back to the backing stores. These machines are the on-line peripherals of the CPU.

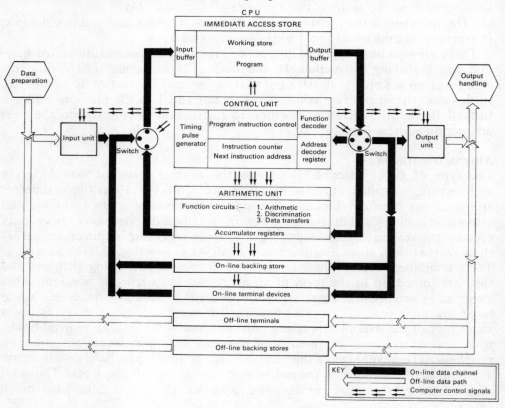

Figure 72   The central processor in relation to peripherals

Input units

Input units are essentially devices for translating a physical medium which is encoded with data into that same data in the form of sets (characters or words) of binary pulses. For some devices the physical medium must be specially prepared (intermediate devices) and for others, normal human media or activities provide the input (direct entry devices).

Current technology includes the following:

Intermediate devices

    Punched card readers–becoming obsolete

    Paper tape readers–being replaced by cassette tape, etc.

    Magnetic ink character readers (MICR)

    Optical character readers (OCR)

    Optical mark readers (OMR)

Perforated character readers
Perforated hole tag readers, e.g. Kimball
Edge punched card readers—punched tape coding

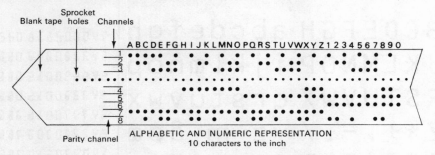

Figure 73   Eight-channel paper tape

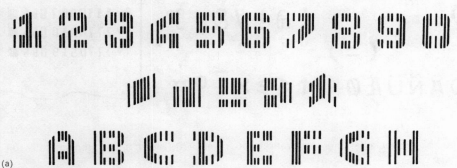

(a)

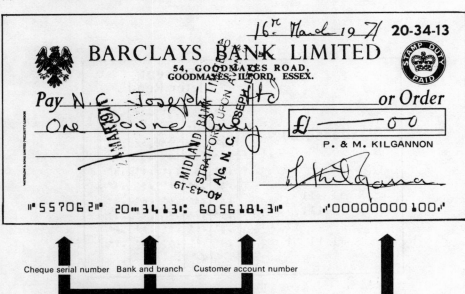

(b)

Figure 74   Magnetic ink character recognition (MICR): a, CMC7 MICR font; b, E13B font

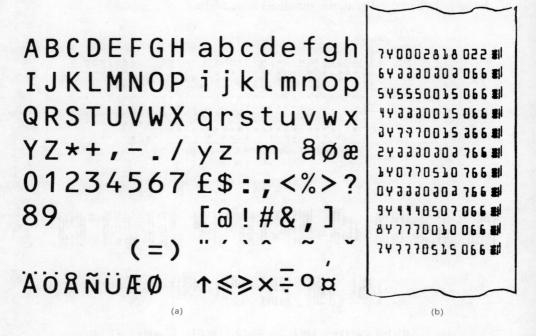

ABCDEFGH abcdefgh
IJKLMNOP ijklmnop
QRSTUVWX qrstuvwx
YZ*+,-./ yz m åøæ
01234567 £$:;<%>?
89   [@!#&,]
     (=) "´`^ ~ ˇ
ÄÖÅÑÜÆØ ↑≤≥×÷°¤

(a)   (b)

Figure 75   Optical character recognition (OCR): a, OCR B font; b, cash register tally roll

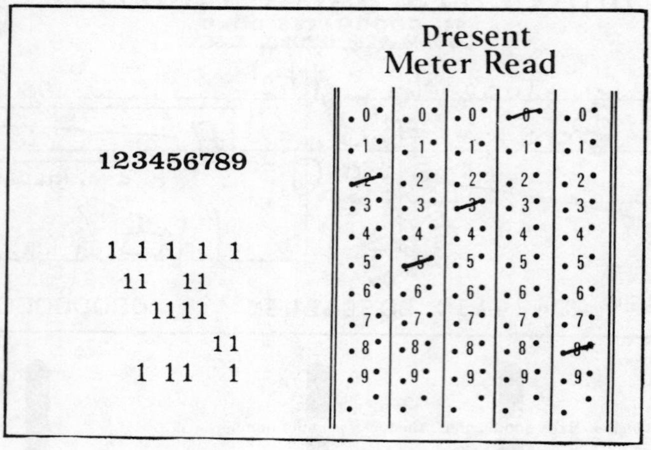

**Present
Meter Read**

123456789

1 1 1 1 1
11   11
    1111
         11
 1 11   1

Figure 76   Optical mark scan document (OMR)

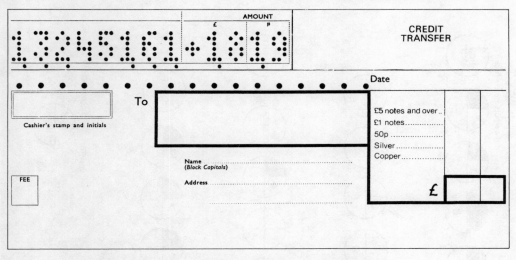

Figure 77   Optical perforated character document

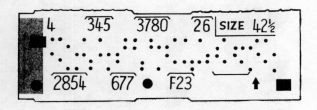

Figure 78   A Kimball tag

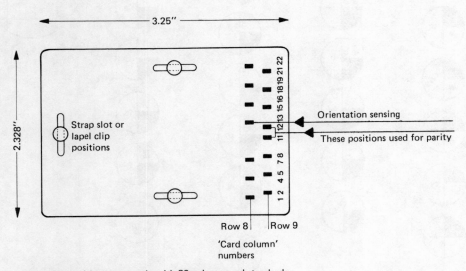

Figure 79   Punched hole badge

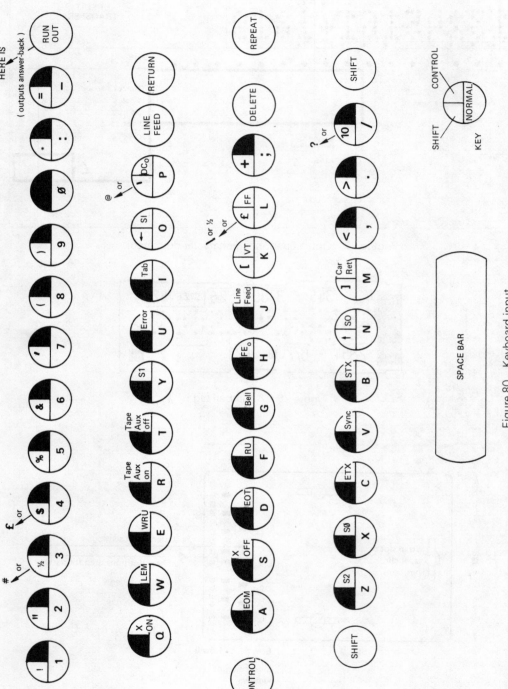

Figure 80   Keyboard input

Direct entry devices
> Keyboards
> Embossed, punched hole and magnetic stripe badge readers
> OCR/A and other wand readers
> VDU light pens and joysticks
> Voice recognition devices
> Direct point of sale devices
> Dial, button and lever selection
> Analog to digital converters

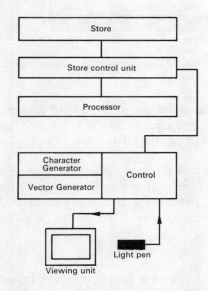

Figure 81   VDU system with light pen

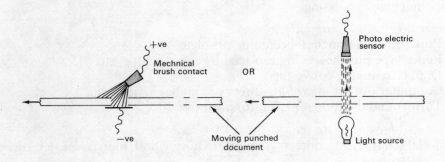

Figure 82   Reading punched holes

In addition to the above, various magnetic storage devices can be considered as input devices but these will be found under backing stores.

The major difference between the two main types of input is that the direct entry devices save costs in terms of the time and media saved in not having to prepare and verify an intermediate medium, in addition to the time delay in

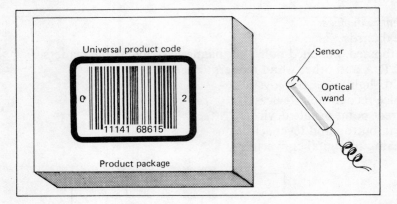

Figure 83   Optical wand reading universal product code

data entry and the dangers of an intermediate process adding errors to the data. However, intermediate devices are much faster than the manual method of direct entry and therefore the CPU time is not wasted waiting at human speeds.

The choice of device will depend upon the requirement of the application involved (batch or real-time, remote or in-house, etc.) and the relative speeds and costs (preparation, machine and media) involved. Examples of some of these methods are given in the illustrations which should be fairly self explanatory.

Output units

The output unit serves the reverse function to the input device. It receives the result information in the form of sets of binary pulses and it must translate these into a physical medium for either human sensory perception or for further machine processing.

Machine processable output devices
    Punched card punches–becoming obsolete
    Paper tape punches–being replaced by cassette tape, etc.
    Digital to analog converters
    Computer output microfilm–direct or via magnetic media
    Turn-round document perforators/printers

Human sensible output devices
    Serial (character) printers–typewriter, daisy wheel, matrix, ink-jet, thermal, electrosensitive
    Line printers–barrel, chain, xerox, laser
    Visual display–alphanumeric
    Visual display–full graphic–black and white, colour
    Graph plotters–digital incremental, electrostatic, drum
    Voice and sound synthesisers

Again, various backing storage devices can also be used as output units. The choice of device is dependent upon application criteria.

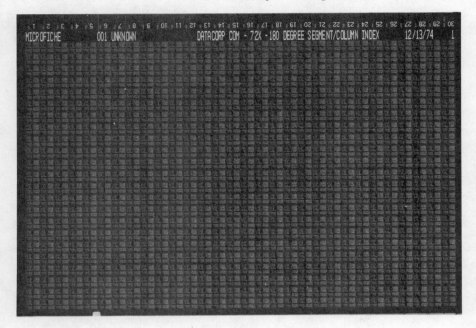

Figure 84   COM microfiche

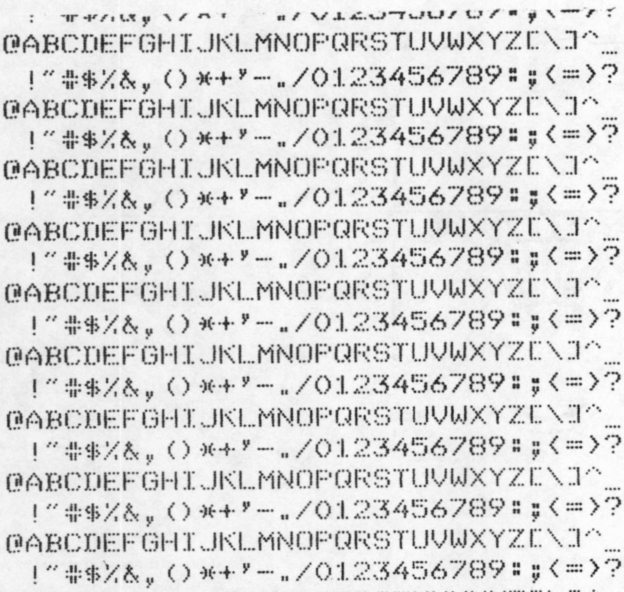

@ABCDEFGHIJKLMNOPQRSTUVWXYZ[\]^_
!"#$%&,()*+'-.,/0123456789:;<=>?
@ABCDEFGHIJKLMNOPQRSTUVWXYZ[\]^_
!"#$%&,()*+'-.,/0123456789:;<=>?
@ABCDEFGHIJKLMNOPQRSTUVWXYZ[\]^_
!"#$%&,()*+'-.,/0123456789:;<=>?
@ABCDEFGHIJKLMNOPQRSTUVWXYZ[\]^_
!"#$%&,()*+'-.,/0123456789:;<=>?
@ABCDEFGHIJKLMNOPQRSTUVWXYZ[\]^_
!"#$%&,()*+'-.,/0123456789:;<=>?
@ABCDEFGHIJKLMNOPQRSTUVWXYZ[\]^_
!"#$%&,()*+'-.,/0123456789:;<=>?
@ABCDEFGHIJKLMNOPQRSTUVWXYZ[\]^_
!"#$%&,()*+'-.,/0123456789:;<=>?
@ABCDEFGHIJKLMNOPQRSTUVWXYZ[\]^_
!"#$%&,()*+'-.,/0123456789:;<=>?
@ABCDEFGHIJKLMNOPQRSTUVWXYZ[\]^_
!"#$%&,()*+'-.,/0123456789:;<=>?
@ABCDEFGHIJKLMNOPQRSTUVWXYZ[\]^_
!"#$%&,()*+'-.,/0123456789:;<=>?

Figure 85   Dot matrix character printing

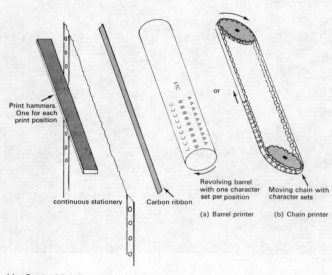

Print hammers.
One for each
print position

continuous stationery

Carbon ribbon

ETC

AAAAAAAAAA
BBBBBBBBB
CCCCCCCCCC

or

Revolving barrel
with one character
set per position

Moving chain with
character sets

(a) Barrel printer

(b) Chain printer

(a)   Barrel and chain line printers

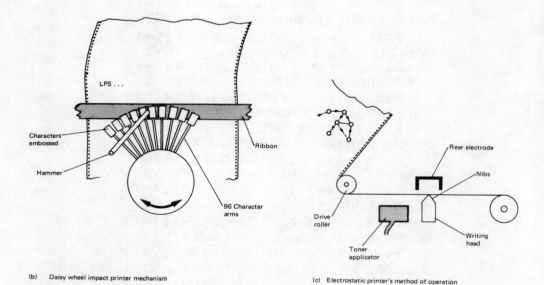

LPS . . .

Characters
embossed

Hammer

Ribbon

96 Character
arms

Rear electrode

Nibs

Drive
roller

Toner
applicator

Writing
head

(b)   Daisy wheel impact printer mechanism

(c)   Electrostatic printer's method of operation

Figure 86   Printer mechanisms

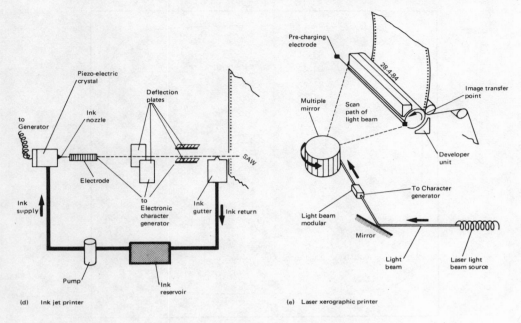

Piezo-electric crystal

Deflection plates

to Generator

Ink nozzle

Electrode

SAW

to Electronic character generator

Ink gutter

Ink return

Ink supply

Pump

Ink reservoir

(d)   Ink jet printer

Pre-charging electrode

28-4-84

Multiple mirror

Scan path of light beam

Image transfer point

Developer unit

To Character generator

Light beam modular

Mirror

Light beam

Laser light beam source

(e)   Laser xerographic printer

Figure 86   Printer mechanisms (continued)

720 SPECIFICATIONS

MAX. CHARACTERS/DISPLAY:	1024 STANDARD
MAX. CHARACTERS/LINE:	64
MAX. LINES/PAGE:	40
CHARACTER REPERTOIRE:	64
SPECIAL FUNCTION KEYS:	32
CHARACTER FUNCTION CODE:	ASCII
DISPLAY AREA:	7 1/2 X 9 1/2
BRIGHTNESS:	50 FOOT-LAMBERTS
SPOT SIZE:	.015 INCH
PHOSPHOR:	P4
RESOLUTION:	80 LINES/INCH
REFRESH RATE:	46.5 CPS
CHARACTER HEIGHT:	.12 INCH
CHARACTER WIDTH:	.09 INCH
CHARACTER SPACING:	.05 INCH
LINE SPACING:	.08 INCH
CHARACTER GENERATION:	STROKE
DEFLECTION:	MAGNETIC
STORAGE:	DELAY LINE
INPUT DATA RATE:	46.5 KC
OUTPUT DATA RATE:	46.5 KC
COMMUNICATIONS:	
CONTROL UNIT-DISPLAY:	UP TO 1000 FT.
KEYBOARD TO DISPLAY:	UP TO 10 FT.
COMMUNICATION CODE:	ASCII
CONTROL UNIT TO COMPUTER:	VIA DATA-PHONE OR DIRECT WIRE
MANUFACTURER:	SANDERS ASSOCIATES, INC.
ADDRESS:	NASHUA, N.H.

Figure 87   An alphanumeric VDU display

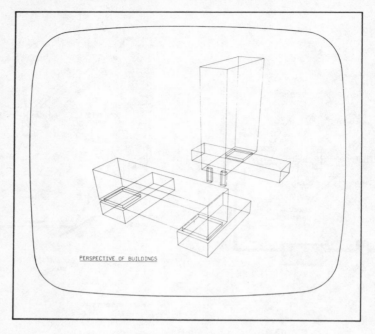

Figure 88 A full graphic VDU display

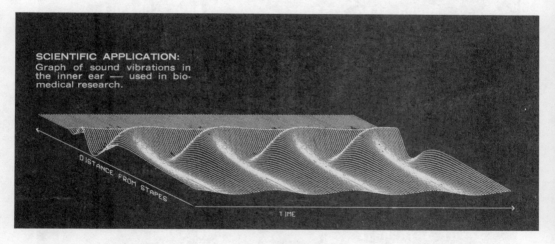

Figure 89 Output from digital plotter

Backing stores

Backing (or auxiliary) stores are required as an intermediate stage between the human environment and the CPU. The physical size limitations of the IAS prevent storage of all the application and control software together with all the relevant master and reference data used by an installation at the same time. This information could be stored off-line in the human environment but then the speed limitations of data input would waste much processor time as well as adding unnecessary cost to the input operation. Backing storage provides a compromise solution by having software and data available on-line to be input under computer control at relatively high speeds. The available devices can be analysed into the following physically different types:

Magnetic card
    Magnetic stripe (VRCs, badges) units
    Fully coated cards–now obsolete
Magnetic tape
    Cassette devices–individual, stack loading
    Cartridge devices
    Reel to reel $\frac{1}{2}''$ ($7''$–600', $8\frac{1}{2}''$–1200', $10\frac{1}{2}''$–2400')
Magnetic disc
    Fixed disc units–large special purpose or job dedicated
Exchangeable disc units
    Flexible disc units–$5\frac{1}{4}''$ minifloppy, $8''$ floppy
    Single rigid disc drives
    Disc pack drives
    Mixed fixed and exchangeable units
Magnetic drum
    Fixed head drum units–now military and special purpose
Solid state
    Add-on core units
    Semiconductor memories
    Bubble technology memories

At present, the various technologies producing auxiliary storage have produced a confusion of physically different, nonstandardised products. The choice offered to the user is often limited to processor manufacturer or manufacturer compatible units within a range of devices which are application oriented. In broad terms, reel to reel tape tends to be used for high volume, serial applications such as payroll, stock etc. or as a high speed input medium. Cassette and cartridge tape and flexible discs are best suited to desk-top and microcomputing file storage, and rigid discs are mainly employed for high capacity direct access and information retrieval applications.

A much more relevant method of differentiation for backing storage is, therefore, the split between serial devices (magnetic tape) and direct access devices (all other physical types). This is the essential difference between a record player and a tape recorder. For continuous background music a tape is ideal. It runs from start to finish reproducing each item, it has a long duration and uses a cheap, high capacity medium. However, if you want to select individual items and, furthermore, if these can be located anywhere on the tape, you can get involved in complex and tedious forward, rewind, stop and start operations. With a record player, you can either let each disc run through serially or you can select and play a passage directly without having either to play all the rest or forward and rewind the medium.

Figure 90   Cassette tape unit

Figure 91   Tape cartridge unit

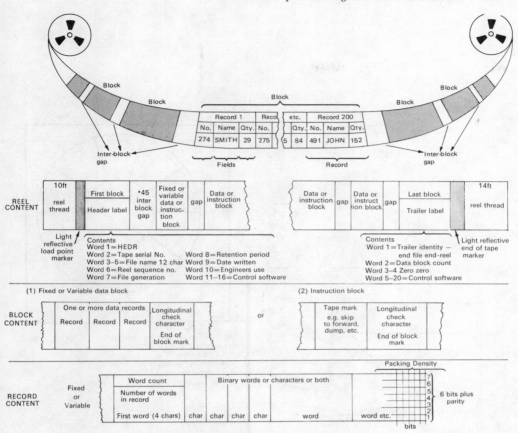

Figure 92   Magnetic tape data organisation

Figure 93   Flexible disc unit

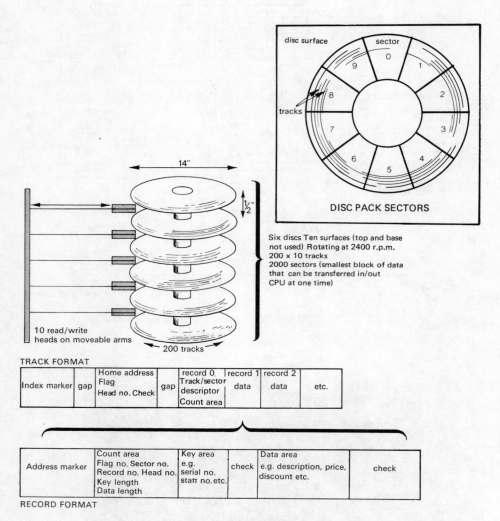

TRACK FORMAT

Index marker	gap	Home address Flag Head no. Check	gap	record 0 Track/sector descriptor Count area	record 1 data	record 2 data	etc.

Address marker	Count area Flag no. Sector no. Record no. Head no. Key length Data length	Key area e.g. serial no. staff no. etc.	check	Data area e.g. description, price, discount etc.	check

RECORD FORMAT

Figure 94   Magnetic disc data organisation

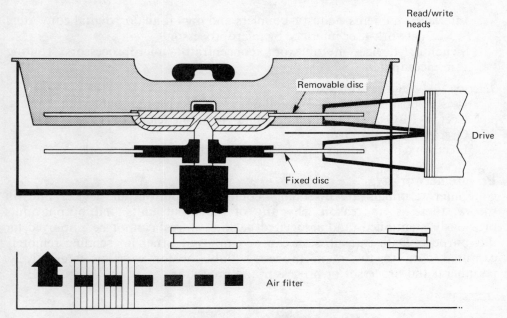

Figure 95   Mixed fixed and exchangeable disc unit

Communications peripherals and ancillaries

The distinction between a peripheral and an ancillary device is that a peripheral is under the control of the processor (on-line). Input, output and backing storage devices obviously come under this heading but communications devices can be operated in both modes. With the great increase in remote access applications the field of data transmission is an expanding one. There are two main areas of interest involved; that of sending remote data to the processor or of working interactively with the processor, both sending data and receiving information, and that of receiving information only direct from a processor or via some other agency. Both fields fall within the realm of data transmission but only the first is direct computer usage, the second being a communications application often employing computer technology to facilitate it. The hardware includes:

Computer terminals (input and output devices)
> Teletype terminals–keyboard or paper tape input and serial printer or paper tape output
> Visual display units–keyboard, joystick, light pen, magnetic media input and video display, magnetic media output
> Intelligent terminals–input/output as above plus built-in microprocessor for data checking and formatting
> Remote batch terminals–punched, optical, magnetic media input and line printer, magnetic media output
> Point of sale terminals–application oriented data capture

Communications devices
> Transmission lines–telephone, telegraph, private, public, networks

Interfaces–modems, acoustic couplers and digital-analog-digital converters
   X25 network-user interface by microprocessor
Switching devices–multiplexors, concentrator microprocessors, routing
   minicomputers

Teletext and viewdata systems
   Prestel–post office telephone and domestic television to public databank
   Ceefax–BBC electronic decoded data via public television
   Oracle–ITA (as above)
   Electronic mail–domestic processors linked via public network

Private networks

Computer terminals are essentially combined input/output devices and, in
theory, there is no reason why any of the input units and output units
previously mentioned (and associated backing stores) cannot be employed for
this purpose. Data transmission can be employed either for sending remotely
captured data to the main processor only, or for working interactively,
peripheral and processor or processor and processor.

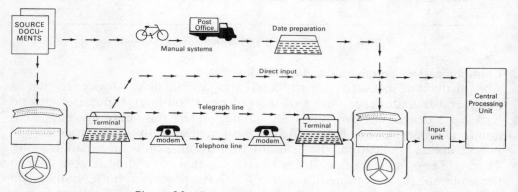

Figure 96   Data transmission for data capture

Data transmission

Transmission lines can be private or public, telegraph or telephone, single
line or networks. They are rated in bauds which is a measure of the maximum
speed that they can transmit data at a guaranteed reliability, e.g. 1 bit error in
a million bits. Lines can be used either asynchronously or synchronously. In
the first method, each character is transmitted separately as it is not known
when the message will start or end, e.g. working interactively at a terminal. For
this reason it is necessary for each character, normally of eight bits, to have an
additional one bit start indication and one bit stop marker. For synchronous
transmission, the message is prepared in advance and it is only necessary to
add a start and stop indicator plus a check character once to each message.
The check character is calculated by both the sender and receiver to determine
if the message was received without error or if it must be retransmitted.

   A baud is a rating of 1 bit per second. If the message is transmitted
asynchronously then the effective speed is the baud rating, typically
110,300,600,1200 baud, divided by the bits per character (8) plus the start and

stop bits (2) giving the formula: transmission rate in characters/second = baud rate ÷ 10. For synchronous working, given a reasonable size message, the start, stop, check indicators can be ignored and the character/second speed is the baud rate (typically 2400-9600) divided by 8.

There are three types of line that can be employed: simplex, half duplex and full duplex. In simplex working, the transmission can be one way only and is useful for remote data collection, terminal to processor only. Half duplex enables two way communication but not at the same time. This is the mode of working of the public telegraph (telex) system. Full duplex enables both parties to transmit simultaneously, e.g. the public telephone system where both parties can speak at once, and is often used for echo working where the data keyed by the sender is first sent to the processor, verified and then echoed back to the sender's output device. This is a useful security aspect as, for example, passwords can be print suppressed.

Data from input devices is in the form of digital pulses. Telephone lines work on acoustic, analog signals. In order to send data along telephone lines it is necessary to convert the digital pulses to analog signals (modulate) and then to reconvert these to digital pulses after transmission (demodulate). This conversion is accomplished by modems (modulator/demodulator) or acoustic couplers which can be hired from the public network or purchased from equipment manufacturers. Often, computer terminals are manufactured with inbuilt couplers.

With the expansion in telecommunications processing, the world's telephone networks are likely to be switching over from analog to digital transmission. This is going to mean that digital devices will interface with the system, adopting certain standard protocols, i.e. X25 (see below), but analog devices such as the normal telephone handset will not. This is leading to the development of microbased codecs (coder/decoders) to be fitted into the handset to convert the analog signals to digital ones.

Distributed processing

With the growth of communications technology, many variations of the standard input, processor, output in-house computer are now possible: users can be remote from the processor; many users can access the same machine; processors can be linked to other processors (side-by-side or remote); etc. The overall term for this kind of working is distributed processing. In distributed processing the computer, or more precisely, the computer configuration, can consist of many processors and many peripherals located all over the world (or even in space) all connected by some form of communications network. It is not necessary to have one communications line for each connection as this would be a wasteful and expensive solution. By the introduction of a device called a multiplexor, many users can use the same line simultaneously, or at least apparently so. The multiplexor makes use of the differing speeds of devices and line capacities and switches between the line and its users so swiftly that the disconnected time is not noticed. Multiplexors also give the opportunity for establishing user priorities or enabling fast devices to jump the queue. The only reservation with multiplexors is that the total baud capacity of all the units connected should not exceed the baud capacity of the line.

Where a line is not being utilised to its capacity, idle time occurs and to avoid this wastage it is possible to add a concentrator (micro or miniprocessor) to the communications network to organise and store and then transmit concentrated blocks of data. Another idea based on blocks of data is that of package switching networks. Normal communications are based on physical connection of two locations, the sender and receiver device. This in itself is wasteful and a solution is seen in constructing data packets which contain their destination address which are then transmitted into a network containing switching points (micro or miniprocessors) which route them to the receiver. In 1976, an international standard network (X25) was proposed and to this end, manufacturers and users are concentrating on a user-network interface system and devices (microprocessor) to implement it.

Peripheral specifications

With hardware technology changing so rapidly, it is not useful to try and include very detailed specifications for the various machines. The reader should always bring himself up to date by reading the computing press and contacting the various manufacturers for brochures, etc. There are also many hardware exhibitions where you may not only ask questions but often get the opportunity of looking at and sometimes using the latest computing equipment. As a guide, the following details (current 1979) are given:

(a) card readers—up to 2000 cards per minute (cpm)
(b) paper tape readers—up to 2000 characters per second (cps)
(c) MICR and OCR—up to 2400 documents per minute (DPM) or 500 inches per second (ips)
(d) tag and document readers—up to 1000 documents per minute (dpm)
(e) card punches—up to 1000 cards per minute (cpm)
(f) paper tape punches—up to 1500 characters per second (cps)
(g) computer output microfilm—usually off-line from magnetic tape at on-line tape speeds, off-line up to 500 pages per minute
(h) serial printers—up to 300 lines per minute (lpm) of 132 characters
(i) line printers —up to 2400 lines per minute (lpm) of 160 characters

	capacity	access time	transfer rate
(j) cassette tape	700 kB	20 s	24 kB/s
(k) cartridge tape	5 MB	35 s	48 kB/s
(l) $\frac{1}{2}''$ magnetic tape $(10\frac{1}{2}'')$	180 MB	100 s	780 kB/s
(m) flexible disc (8″)	250 kB	200 ms	500 kB/s
(n) single rigid disc	20 MB	100 ms	600 kB/s
(o) disc packs	320 MB	28 ms	1200 kB/s

Note: Theoretical transfer rates are given: to find effective speed for formatted work use formula (block size × theoretical rate) ÷ (block size + gap size)

Ancillary machines

In order to utilise computerised data processing effectively it is necessary to present the system with valid input that is well organised and on the correct

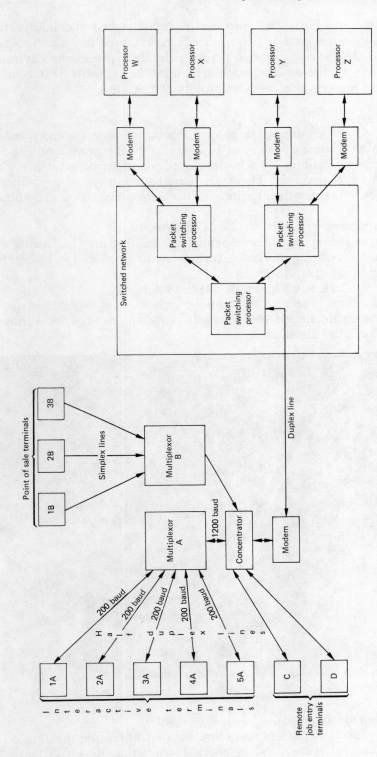

Figure 97   Distributed processing

medium for the machines that process it. Again, when the information is produced for human appraisal, it needs to be reorganised to human standards. In addition to this, various jobs to do with the data processing environment and the running of the on-line machinery must be performed. It is in these three areas that man employs ancillary (off-line) machines.

Data capture devices

The simplest way to capture data is for a human to note the facts and write (record) these on a piece of paper or business form. If this method is adopted either optical mark readers must be employed for input or a further stage of data preparation is required. There are some other ways of capturing data using machines, some of which require further data preparation and some that do not.

Clock punches–on to punched cards for direct input

Gang (reproducing) punches–copying from existing punched media

By-product producing machines–various media produced as by-product of some existing operation

Direct input devices, e.g. point of sale terminals, etc.

Data recorders/loggers–either as pure recorder on to medium for later input or as intelligent (microbased) portable terminal for verification, formatting and direct entry

Figure 98   Data recorder/portable terminal

Data preparation machines

There are two aspects to data preparation, the first to encode the data on to a suitable medium and the second to check (verify) that no errors have been introduced at the encoding stage. The machines used line up with those mentioned under input devices and should need no further explanation. One aspect is significant, however, and that is the movement away from individual item preparation for use on the slower pure input devices towards whole key-processing systems which lead to large batches of data on the faster auxiliary storage media. These systems are often based round micro and miniprocessors which incorporate verification routines.

Card and tape punches
Card and tape verifiers
Card and document sorters and collators
MICR and OCR printers
Badge embossers and other pre use encoders
Key-processing systems–key to tape, key to disc, etc.

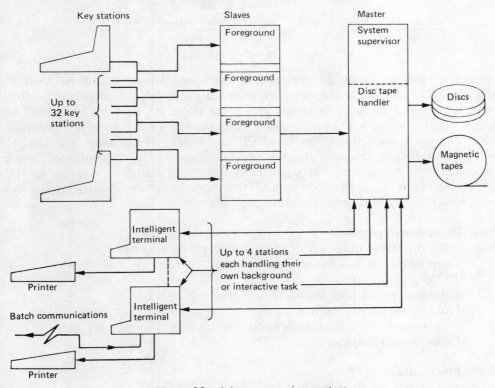

Figure 99   A key processing system

Output handling machines

Paper handling devices–guillotines, bursters, decollators
COM machinery–recorders, processors, duplicators, readers, mounters, etc.
Card sorters and collators
Tape spoolers and winders, etc.

Guillotines are used to trim the continuous stationery sprocket holes and to cut the paper into separate sheets. The available machines range from small,

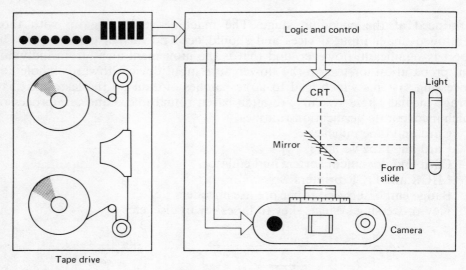

Figure 100   COM recorder

simple devices to large, programmable machines. Bursters can be used to separate the continuous sheets where presentation is not so important as they work by impact tearing the sheets along the perforation folds. They may be fitted with trimming knives for cutting away the sprocket hole edges, although often these are used for filing the sheets in binders. Decollators are used to separate multicopy sets and remove carbons if used. They range from simple machines which separate one copy at a time, and therefore require several passes for more than two copies and the more expensive multicopy devices which may be justified on application grounds.

Miscellaneous equipment

Among the other machines involved with data processing are
Magnetic media cleaners and erasers
PROM programmers
Media converters (any media to any other) and shredders
Media storage equipment
Environmental equipment–air conditioning, cleaning, security, etc.
Maintenance equipment

Word processors

Word processors are not strictly a peripheral but more an offshoot of the main line of computing work. They are complete microbased work stations or linked sets of work stations which replace the traditional typing function. When a letter or form is required, the key operator keys in certain parameters, and text which is stored in the processor is retrieved, formatted, justified and displayed on a video screen for the operator to validate and modify if necessary. The cursor can be moved around to shift, delete, change, add to or otherwise process the display and when this is satisfactory the operator can cause this to be high speed printed (at the station or remotely) and other functions such as indexing, archiving and document statistics can be performed.

Assessment tasks

1 Obtain a selection of the brochures for current processors and peripherals. Put together a suitable configuration for an application of your choice using peripherals not supplied by the processor manufacturer.

2 Produce an audiovisual presentation on the various advantages and disadvantages of the forms of data capture, preparation, input. Support your case with up-to-date costs, speeds, etc.

3 Write an essay on 'The computer in the year 2000'. This should be an educated forecast and not a science fiction story. Support your arguments with facts.

4 Demonstrate to an audience analogies between

(a) serial and direct access

(b) analog and digital methods.

5 Produce a wallchart in which the human body is represented in computer hardware terms.

6 Best of all–if you can finance it–build a personal computer and make it work. You will learn more this way than by reading any book.

Unit 9
Software and programming

Learning objective

To be able to understand the need for software and the different types of software required. To know enough about the types of software to appreciate the limitations and advantages of each. To be able to evaluate software options available with hardware to enable a suitable choice to be made for any application field. To be able to write simple, effective and efficient programs in a high level language both as an aid to work and as an appreciation of the capabilities and limitations of computer processing.

Software

A data processing system consists of raw data being subjected to a regulated activity to produce information output. The regulated activity is performed by a processing device (**hardware**) operating under the activity rules (**software**). We have seen (Unit 8) how these activity rules are, in fact, a list of job instructions containing the operations to be performed in the required sequence to produce the desired result. This list of job instructions for use by a computer is called a **computer program**. Unit 8, in particular Figures 69-71, showed how each program instruction contains a function part (what process is involved) and an address part (the location of the operands to be processed), and also gave a step by step account of how the processor obeys the rules of the program via the control unit's decoding and actuating mechanisms. The program illustrated was a simple **application program** but there are other kinds of program as well. In fact, although the term software can generally be equated with computer programs, it can, in a wider sense, be used to include other things as well. When used in the more general sense, software can be thought of as including computing support services and computer programs.

Software is available from several sources: computer and peripheral manufacturers; commercial consultants; educational and standards bodies; user groups and in-house provision.

Computing support services

This aspect of software enables programs to be written and moreover, if properly used, to be written effectively and efficiently. The field includes

     programming codes and languages–documentation
     programming conventions and standards–documentation
     training and technical advice.

Computers are machines that operate on binary organised pulses of electricity. To use these machines humans need to build into them the set of instructions to carry out a job. It would be a very arduous task to have to define these instructions in terms of binary pulses, so sets of simple codes, called programming languages, have been invented for the convenience of humans, to enable them to write their lists of instructions more easily. These programs, once written in the programming language, still need to be translated into binary pulses before the computer can be actuated (see page 188). Just as we need books and training to learn and use a human language or code so we require documentation and manuals to explain and define programming languages. Without these we would not be able to write our programs. There are different kinds of computer codes and languages, including

general purpose (machine oriented) languages

problem oriented languages for application programs

special purpose languages–job control and command languages, data description and manipulation languages, decision table languages, etc.

Having a suitable language available enables programs to be written but does not ensure that these will be good programs or that they will be written in the most efficient manner. For this we need the guidance of good practice in the form of methods and performance standards and the help of training and education to enable us to understand and use them. Support services may appear to be less glamorous than the programming itself but without them computerised data processing would not be possible.

Computer programs

Computer programming software can be likened to the analysis of human difference characteristics (Unit 4). We have seen that a person can be regarded as having a certain temperament, certain mental abilities and certain work experience abilities. Similarly, programming software can be defined under three headings: control software; skills software; applications software.

To understand this breakdown, it may help to consider an analogy. If I wish to perform a certain job, let us say getting invoices typed, I can look around for a suitable processing device to achieve this. I advertise and applicants for the post arrive at my door. First I must check the hardware. Can the applicant see (input device)? Does he have two hands (output devices)? Is he intelligent enough for the job (ALU functions)? Assuming the hardware is suitable, I must now make sure that the applicant has the correct software. A person can have all the physical attributes necessary to type invoices but due to disease, emotional disturbance or some other factor, may not be able to control his actions. His eyes, fingers or even his whole body may not receive or respond to signals from his brain or if they do, his actions may not be coordinated. He does not have the control software.

If my applicant does have control of his body and limbs it is still quite possible that he may not have learned to type. This is a skill which requires additional training (software). Lastly, if my applicant is a fully controlled typist, he may never have learned how to type invoices or, at least, my special kind of invoice. To do this requires the particular job instructions that we call an application program. We do not often think of ourselves, humans, as being programmed. And yet, that is what happens to us every moment of the day. A baby does not have the control software to stand up on two legs or to manipulate its fingers; he is programmed to do so by experience. Other abilities are programmed into us deliberately when we go to school, when we obey our parents, when we go on courses, etc.

A computer is a much more simple device than a baby. It also needs programs to control its configuration, to be able to perform simple skills and to achieve job results by following sets of instruction steps.

Program libraries

A program is a list of instructions. Some instructions when written in a programming language translate into a single instruction in binary pulse machine code. Others will generate more than one instruction in machine code. This kind of instruction is known as a macro. Macros are not hard to understand, we use them all the time. If I say to you 'open the window', you will stand up, push back your chair, walk over to the window, undo the catch, push the window open and return and sit down. One instruction has generated a whole series of operations. You have decoded the macro. Another name for a computer program is a routine. A subroutine or subprogram is a small part of the program with a special purpose (see page 160).

In most modern computers, it is normal to keep all the control, skills and application programs together in a library, usually held on a direct access backing store device. A means of entering at least part of this library is required after the machine has been shut down. This is called bootstrapping and is achieved in a number of ways; either by a series of switches at the operator's console, or by feeding in a binary coded card by manual operation of an input device, or some other manual operation. The bootstrap will cause the computer to load a program which will then take over the loading of all other programs from the library automatically.

The contents of a program library will consist of the following programs:

Control–resident supervisor (executive or monitor)
         resident IOCS (input/output control system)
Skills–operating system macros, subroutines and programs
      support software
Applications–application programs

Operating systems

The operating system (OS) of the computer is a machine oriented mix of macros, subroutines and programs which take over the running and internal organisation of the computer once the human operator has passed over control. Although considered as one system, the OS is often divided into two parts, the most frequently used part being resident in the IAS (supervisor and IOCS) and the other called as required from the backing store device (OS skills software).

The reasons for using a software rather than a human operator are: faster job throughput and response time; efficient utilisation of processor; automatic job accounting; ease of user interface; privacy and security aspects.

Against this is the cost of using additional software in terms of IAS space required for resident programs; peripheral devices required for program library storage and processor time overhead in processing OS instruction routines.

Present day computing has evolved into a series of operating method options depending on the hardware available and the application criteria. Each of these methods will require different facilities from an operating system. A list of methods would include:

serial processing–one program at a time–becoming rare

multi-programming–running several programs concurrently

batch processing–batched, therefore out-of-date sets of data processed

real-time processing–events processed as they occur, e.g. enquiries, process control, data collection

remote access processing–input/output connected to processor via telecommunications link

multiprocessing–use of several processors linked in various ways

multiaccess processing–several users, either local or remote

memory mapping, virtual storage and database processing–various methods of implementing and organising storage space

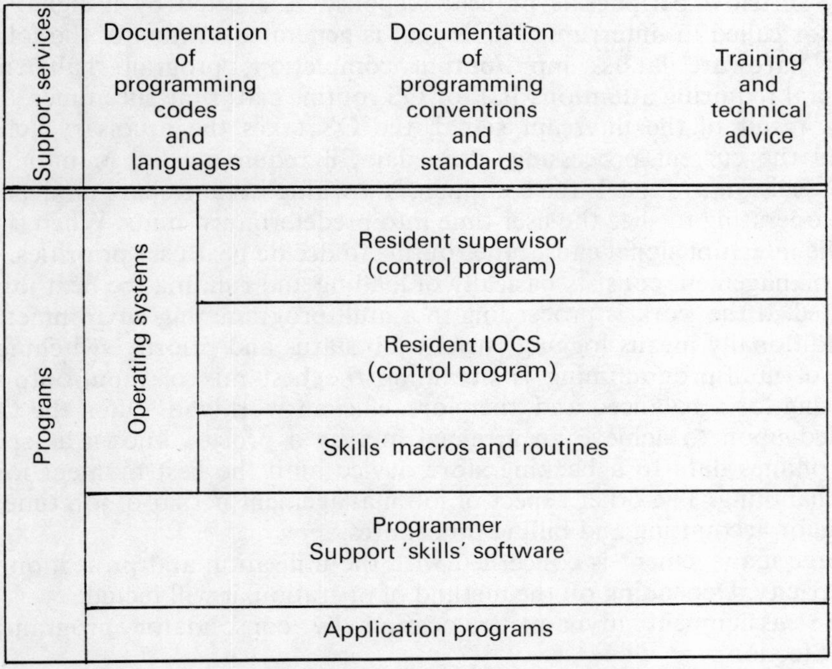

Support services	Documentation of programming codes and languages	Documentation of programming conventions and standards		Training and technical advice
Programs	Operating systems	Resident supervisor (control program)		
		Resident IOCS (control program)		
		'Skills' macros and routines		
	Programmer Support 'skills' software			
	Application programs			

Figure 101   Software

The operating system description (Figure 101) includes facilities for handling all of these methods. Obviously which facilities are implemented will depend on the particular application method in use.

Resident supervisor programs

Normally both the supervisor and the IOCS programs will be held resident in the IAS. Once they have been bootstrapped in by the operator, they will be required to carry out a series of functions including

> job control language and command language communications
> program library management–librarian program
> interrupt handling
> job management
> storage management
> channel control.

The job control language (JCL) or command language (used in interactive systems) is the interface between the operating system and the application program. It is used to indicate the requirements (peripherals, routines, entry points, event actions, etc.) of the user as operating instructions to the OS which, therefore, must have facilities to respond to these instructions.

The program library must be organised and have facilities for routine linkage and access to the various programs required. This is generally effected by a special librarian routine.

The ability of the processor to turn its attention to any of a series of possible activities and thus maximise utilisation at times when it would otherwise be waiting on slow peripherals or user response, is effected by a signal to the processor called an interrupt. This signal is generated on one of the following events: hardware faults; input/output completion; program halts/ends; a peripheral requiring attention; JCL or OS routine call; time slice timer.

As a result of the interrupt signal, the OS takes the necessary action to suspend the current processing, store data, if required, and go into a 'next action' decision routine. If the computer is working in time-share mode, a timer will be operating to slice the user time into predetermined units. When the time is up the interrupt signal causes the routine to decide next user priorities.

Job management consists basically of loading and running the next job to be processed. If the work is proceeding in a multiprogramming environment then this additionally means logging current job status and priority switching. One aspect of multiprogramming is obtaining the best mix of input/output and processing for a balanced and, therefore, efficient workload. Often the OS will be called upon to achieve an artificial mix by a process known as spooling which offlines data to a backing store device until the best moment for slow device handling. The other aspect of job management is that of job time/space logging for accounting and billing procedures.

Storage management is concerned with the utilisation and protection of the IAS capacity. Depending on the method of operation, it will include

> IAS assignment (dynamic relocation by consolidator program) and protection
> memory mapping–address table organisation for page segments of store

virtual storage control–data on backing store to be overlayed to IAS index organisation-access-swapping

program swapping–data and program IAS backing store swapping for dedicated multiaccess systems

security dumping–copying of IAS to other media for security during run.

Channel control allows various devices to access the IAS simultaneously by time-sharing the physical IAS to device connections. It is through these channels that the other resident control program operates.

Resident IOCS

The input/output control system is a general name for a set of control programs managing the handling of data records and files between the IAS and its peripherals. The main work of these programs includes file management; file processing; teleprocessing; multiprocessor slave control.

File management consists of the organisation and formatting of files into records or blocks of records and the opening and closing of files by the processing of header and trailer labels.

File processing is concerned with the use of the records or blocks including the accessing, reading and writing of these between the peripherals and IAS buffers. Included in this work would be the checking and correcting of read and write errors and the repeat of read and write operations upon error detection. Finally file processing covers the provision of checkpoint records for restarts after dumps.

If teleprocessing is used, the IOCS must handle line control interfaces with communications processors as well as any time slice processing requirements. In addition, it will handle message input/output control, namely text editing, routing, queuing and access security.

Operating system skills macros and routines

In addition to the control programs used in the operating system, there is a mix of available skills routines which enhance the capabilities of the computer. These include

standard functions–arithmetic functions (%, logs, etc.)

mathematics and statistics routines, e.g. floating point arithmetic, metric converters

listing routines–program listings, file listings, etc.

media conversion–copy and print any medium to any other

program diagnostics–error list, trace routine, test monitor, core dump

assemblers and compilers

Assemblers and compilers are often regarded as a separate category in their own right. These are the translating programs that turn a program written in a programming language (source program) into a set of binary pulse instructions in machine code (object program). If the chosen program language is a general purpose, machine oriented one (low level) which, for the most part, generates one machine code instruction for one program language instruction, then the translating program is called an assembler. If the program is written in a high level, problem oriented language where every instruction is a macro then the translating program is called a compiler.

Assemblers and compilers are obviously machine dependent programs a
they translate to the machine code of the processor involved. They are writtei
to operate with the OS of the machine and there are different programs fo
different program languages. It is also possible that the OS will contain severa
compilers for the same language, written for different application purposes o
environments.

Programmer support skills software

There are other programs in the field of skills software that do not, generally
form a part of the operating system but nevertheless play a large part in the
working environment of the computer programmer. Amongst these are
merge and sort programs
editing and validity check programs
simulator programs–line by line translation of machine dependent
language A on machine B, effectively simulating machine A
language/code converters–translation of whole program, source or object
in language A to machine code B
documentation generators–flowcharts, decision tables, critical path networks, etc.
program generators–report program generators, decision table programs,
etc.
test data generators

Application Programs

When most people think of computer programs they think of application
programs. These are the sets of instructions that produce information from raw
business data. They are available in two broad categories–package programs,
e.g. payroll, production control, and tailor-made programs.

The package program is useful where the user organisation does not have
the expertise, the time or the programmer effort to produce their own
programs. Against these advantages must be weighed the modifications
necessary, either to the package or the user's system, to make the program fit
the job or, if this is not done, the inefficiency of the program or system due to
the poor fit.

Most programs used in data processing are specially written to fit the job
they have to do. This is initially expensive but the savings obtained for
frequently run jobs will pay off in the long run. Figure 69 showed a simple
program for the purpose of demonstrating how the control unit works. This
was, of course, nothing like as large or involved as a real data processing
program. The programmer does not just write programs in isolation, they must
be related to the business job that they are required to achieve. The computer
part is only one subsystem in the whole data processing system and this in turn
is just one part of the business. It is the systems analyst who designs the
systems, both manual and computer processed, to achieve the business aims.

When he has designed the computerised subsystem he will document his design in the form of a systems specification. This detailed specification of all the computer programs (suite) required by his system design will be passed on to the programmer and it is from this basis that the programmer starts work.

The systems specification will be illustrated in detail in Unit 15. It will help us at this stage to know that it will include systems scope; hardware specification; systems outline; computer run charts; media formats, volumes and statistics; control requirements; test data specification.

Given this information, the programmer will know what programs are required, what data will be input, what data will be on backing store, what output is required and what hardware, software and control restrictions he must work within. It is the business of the programmer to design, test and produce these required programs to work as effectively and efficiently as possible at the least cost to his employer. There is no better way to understand how he achieves this than by learning to write at least simple programs yourself.

Writing computer programs

The steps to be followed when writing computer programs are
(1) Problem definition–systems specification familiarisation
(2) Workload planning–program progress schedule estimates
(3) Program structure planning–macro flowcharting
(4) Module problem solution–manual simulation with test data, analysis and sequenced synthesis
(5) Incorporating control requirements
(6) Micro flowcharting or decision tables
(7) Trace table check on micro flowchart solutions
(8) Evaluation of alternative solutions
(9) Module coding in appropriate language
(10) Desk check on coding
(11) Preparation of testing log and operations request
(12) Assembly and compilation–language error debugging
(13) Correct and error data testing–logic error debugging
(14) Module interfacing and linkage testing and debugging
(15) Program documentation

Figure 102 shows that the programmer will liaise with the systems analyst during the design stages of the system and, therefore, the contents of the systems specification should not come as any great surprise to him. In fact, it is quite probable that he has influenced the design by advising the analyst on the software capabilities and limitations of the installation. When the job is handed over to him, the programmer should spend some time familiarising himself with the system, its aims and purpose, so as to understand the role of his required programs. By looking in particular at the media formats, and statistics and control requirements in relation to the run charts and hardware specified he will be able to use his experience to evaluate the work load involved.

The next stage in a well-organised installation will be for the programmer,

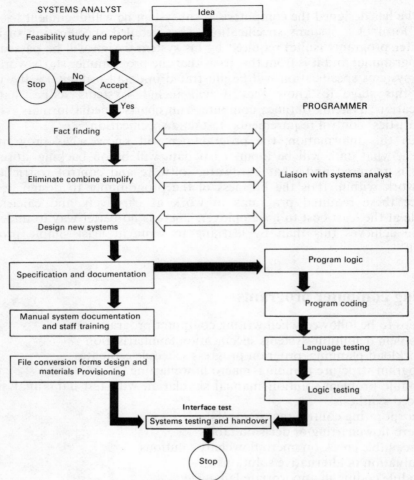

Figure 102   Programmer/analyst liaison

possibly in cooperation with his senior, to plan how he will tackle the job and produce target estimates for job stage completion. This provides a brake on the tendency to get carried away by elegant as opposed to efficient programming, gives an incentive towards progress and, over a period of time, helps to build up a body of knowledge in the installation to be used towards the establishment of programming performance standards. The program progress schedule acts as a checklist for the programmer and can be incorporated in the documentation set.

Program structure

The first step in tackling the problem, in program design, is the development of an overall program structure for each required run. For a start, the programmer will consider if there is already in existence, in the program library, a program or utility routine that can achieve the required result either directly or with minor modification. There is no point in writing a program if one already exists. If, however, there is no suitable alternative, the programmer

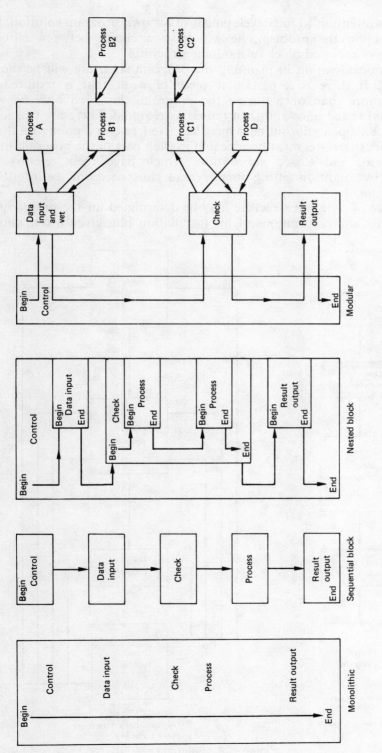

Figure 103   Program structures

will turn his attention to the development of his own program solution. In this, depending upon the problem, he will have a choice between monolithic, sequential block, nested block or modular structures.

Another consideration in planning the program structure will be the use of subroutines. If there is a particular piece of work that is required to be performed more than once during the program, this need only be written, compiled and tested once and then reused as required. There are two forms of subroutine, an open subroutine which has fixed re-entry points to the main program and, therefore, must be repeated in each part of the program in which it is required, and closed subroutines which have their re-entry points determined by condition setting on entry and, thus, need only be inserted once in the program.

The choice of program structure may be determined for the programmer by the standards and conventions of his installation but, given a free choice, he

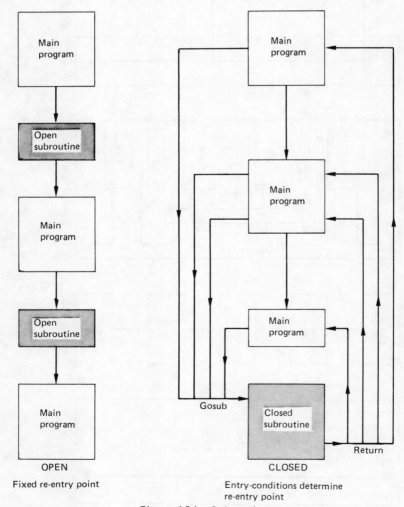

Figure 104   Subroutines

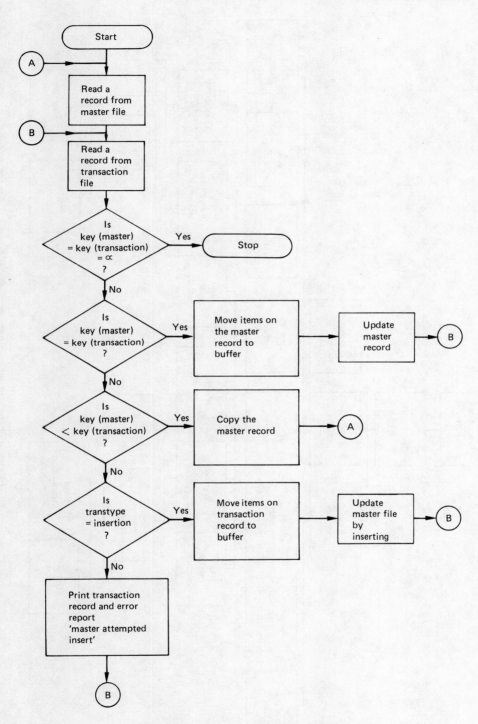

Figure 105 (a) Program macro flowchart

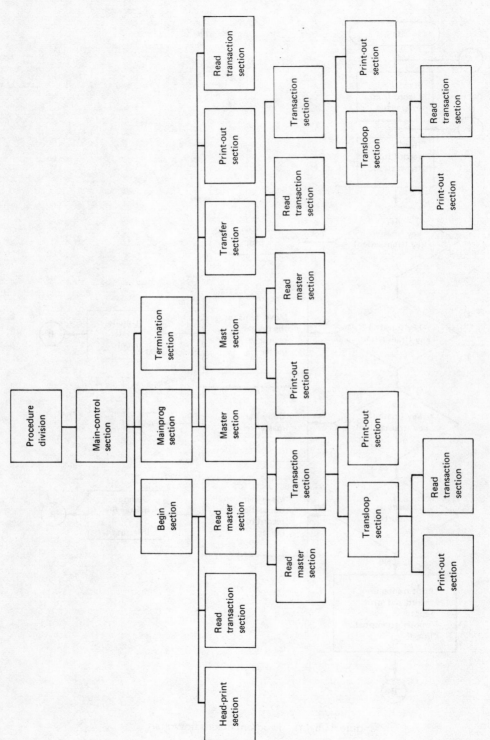

Figure 105 (b)   Program structure chart

should consider the advantages of the modular approach, or the stricter adaptation structured programming. The modules that the program is broken into are self-contained sets of instructions similar to closed subroutines. These can be written, compiled and data tested independently and then interfaced by a control or driver module. In this way, the program workload can be spread over a team of programmers for faster results and the program is very flexible and easy to amend or update. If necessary, each module can be written in different programming languages and then the whole can be put together after compilation by a consolidator program. Structured programming allows only three program control structures; simple sequences, loops and alternative procedures. The structure is built up from segment pages of instructions which makes for simple documentation and facilitates overlay in virtual storage machines. To achieve a modular structure it is necessary for each module to avoid having its own local storage and the modules may not be modified in any way during processing.

Having decided on the type of structure he will use, the next task is for the programmer to proceed to evolve his macro logic. He will start from the system outline which, if it is not already in that form, he should summarise in such a way as to help him identify the main functional processing areas. Most data processing problems contain similar elements such as: initialise and print headings; set up control loops; input transaction and master data; validity and other checks; process decisions and operations; credibility checks, etc.; output results; closing procedures.

It is helpful if the system outline is expressed in the form

to produce......................result output

and......................error control output

and......................operator message output

from......................transaction data

and......................master data

and......................program literals and constants

Working from rough pencilled notes, via scribbled alterations, the programmer will then identify the main control, input, processing and output blocks and the sequence in which they should be carried out. He can identify those processes that will be sequential and those that are alternatives and indicate how and where his control requirements will be met. He is now in the position to draw his macro program structure flowchart.

Program error checks

The first set of checks that the programmer can build into his program are concerned with the validity of the data that will be processed. This data can come either from the input units as transaction or enquiry data or from the backing stores as master or reference data. Validity checks can be

completeness checks–control and hash totals, counts, etc.; serial number completeness, duplication

sequence checks–check, resort and merge routines

item validity–check digits, range limits, code credibility; current date checks, authorisation, interactive confirmation

Control totals can be either value, count or hash (meaningless totals used solely for checking). These totals which have previously been calculated offline or by some other part of the computer system can be recalculated and cross-checked. Check digits (selfchecking numbers) have been explained in Unit 6. Range limits can be used to specify minimum and maximum values, and any item falling outside this expected range can be automatically queried. Code credibility checks can also be for codes outside a given range, or the item can be checked for sign (+ or −), picture (size and alpha/numeric) format and inter-relationships. Authorisation checks can be performed by checking the item against tables of authorised items. With the advent of interactive working it is often desirable to ask the user to confirm any input entered at the keyboard before processing.

Once the data has been processed it can be further scrutinised before it is output by means of credibility checks. These include most of the above input checks with the addition of others such as balance control checks–old balance + transactions = new balance; suspense account checks–data processed + data suspended = total; subtotals–all subtotals = total.

There may also be a requirement for inbuilt audit routines which will print out details during processing to form an audit trail and which are brought into use during audit spot checks by use of data switches.

Micro flowchart programming

For each block or module on the macro flowchart, a micro flowchart must be prepared. This micro chart is a diagrammatic representation of the program solution and, therefore, in order to draw the final micro charts the programmer has to solve the problem of what instructions are required in which sequence. In other words, he must produce his program and then chart it. As an alternative, if the problem is one which contains many decisions and alternative actions he may choose to use a decision table to represent his solution, with the possibility of using one of the special decision table coding languages for his coded machine instructions.

Whichever method, or mix of methods, he may adopt, the process of programming will be a sequence of trial and error, thinking, scribbling, crossing out and charting, based on experience and logical, creative abilities. Charts and tables help in this process and there are some guidelines that can be adopted which should speed up the process and give a better chance of a correct solution being arrived at. Modular or structured programming is one such aid to program writing. It is easier to program a small simple module or segment than to attempt to produce the whole integrated set of instructions in one go.

One of the most frequently used methods is for the programmer to attempt a manual solution using the test data provided in the systems specification, or simplifications of this, and then note down the operations he had to perform to achieve his manual result. These notes can be drawn as blocks on a rough chart and then juggled until a suitable sequence is found. It should be remembered, however, that computers are different from humans and, therefore, some manual methods may well be tackled in a different manner by the machine.

There are various flowcharting conventions that have been found to help in the problem solution of certain kinds of application or for various program languages. These tend to be useful only in a particular environment and are best explained by a person concerned in that environment. One way of getting experience and building up a set of useful techniques is to analyse the various program structure types and see these as building blocks for larger programs.

(A) **Straight line structures**

    (1) printing literals

    (2) calculation of constants and numeric output

    (3) as (2) using standard functions

    (4) input variables, calculation and output

    (5) input transaction and master data, calculation and output

    (6) interrogation for input, calculation and output

    (7) input string and numeric data, calculation and output

    (8) summary of straight line programs plus 'remarks'

(B) **Branching structures**

    (9) fixed by-pass decision branch forward

    (10) variable by-pass decision branch forward

    (11) as (10) using logical operators 'and' and 'or'

    (12) alternative procedures branching–fixed variable and Boolean

    (13) error check using (12)

    (14) switch branching–$\emptyset$ = off, 1 = on

    (15) summary of branching structures

(C) **Loops**

    (16) fixed counted loops and total accumulating

    (17) variable counted loops

    (18) loops terminated by dummy input

    (19) variable and fixed 'for' or 'do' loops

    (20) file loops, end of file markers and switches

    (21) iterative loops

    (22) nested loops

(D) **Arrays and matrices**

    (23) one-dimensional arrays (lists)

    (24) multidimensional arrays and matrices (tables)

    (25) matrix arithmetic (see Unit 7)

(E) **Subroutines**

    (26) open and closed subroutines (Figure 104)

(F) **Structures and control**

    (27) program control–initialisation: setting values (Figure 108, No. 22, blocks 10, 20); zeroise (Figure 108, No. 18, block 100); open files (Figure 108, No. 20, block 5); dimension (Figure 109, No. 24, block 10); set switches (Figure 108, No. 20, blocks 130, 170); reset switches (Figure 108, No. 20, block 150); close files (Figure 108, No. 20, block 220)

    (28) tracing–selective or full (Figure 107, No. 15, block 200)

    (29) modular structures–call routine links and interfaces

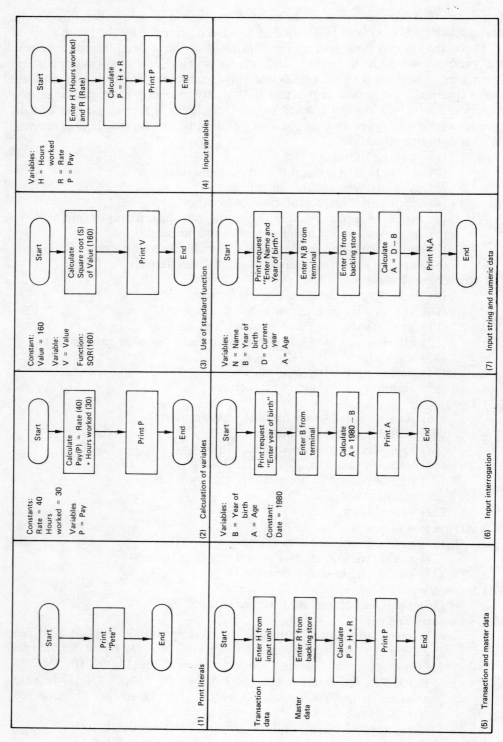

Figure 106   Straight line structures

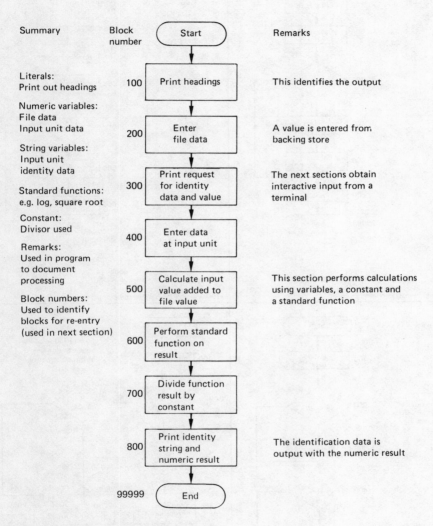

Summary

Literals:
Print out headings

Numeric variables:
File data
Input unit data

String variables:
Input unit
identity data

Standard functions:
e.g. log, square root

Constant:
Divisor used

Remarks:
Used in program
to document
processing

Block numbers:
Used to identify
blocks for re-entry
(used in next section)

Block
number

Start

100   Print headings

200   Enter
      file data

300   Print request
      for identity
      data and value

400   Enter data
      at input unit

500   Calculate input
      value added to
      file value

600   Perform standard
      function on
      result

700   Divide function
      result by
      constant

800   Print identity
      string and
      numeric result

99999   End

Remarks

This identifies the output

A value is entered from
backing store

The next sections obtain
interactive input from a
terminal

This section performs calculations
using variables, a constant and
a standard function

The identification data is
output with the numeric result

(8)   Summary of straight line structures

Figure 106   Straight line structures

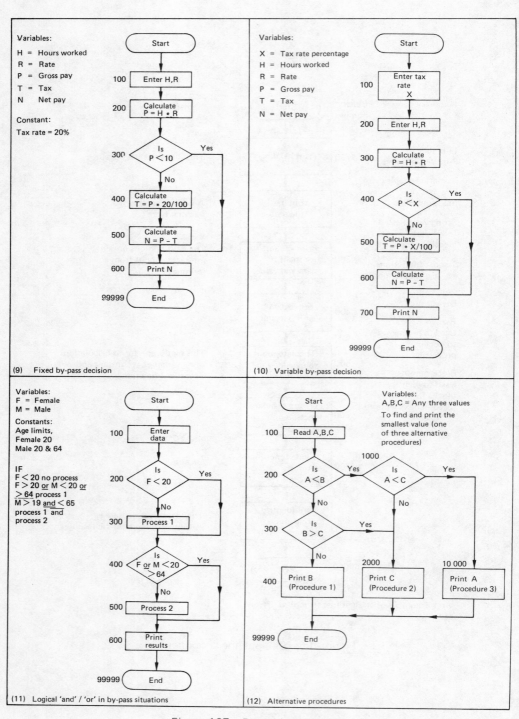

Figure 107   Branching structures

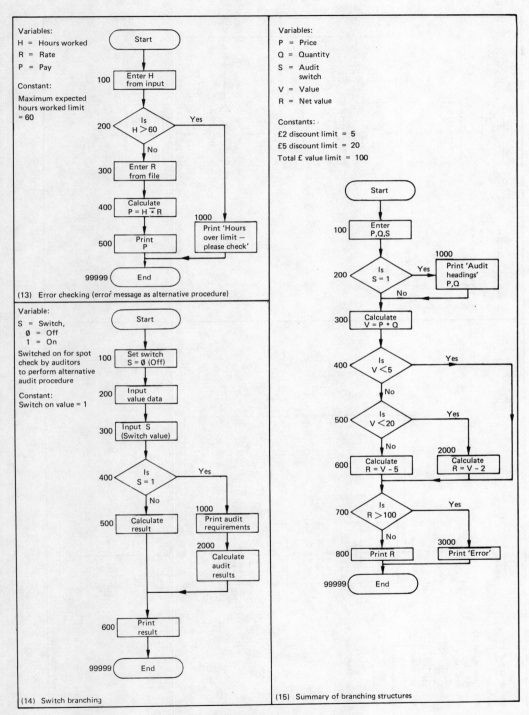

Figure 107   Branching structures

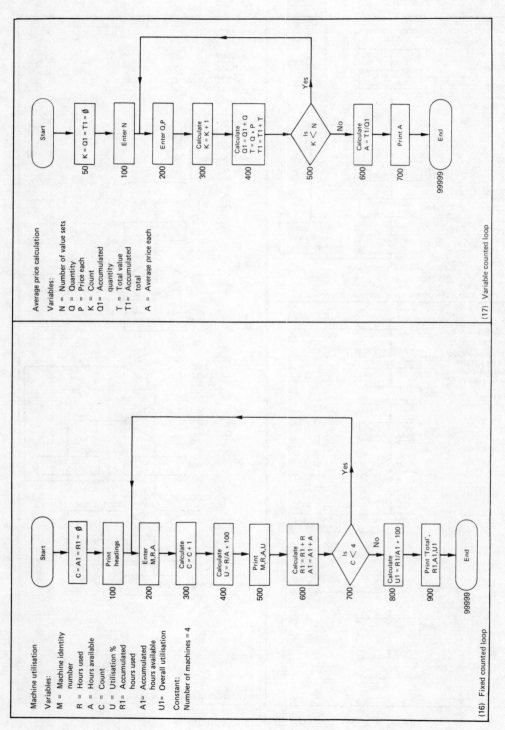

Figure 108 Loops

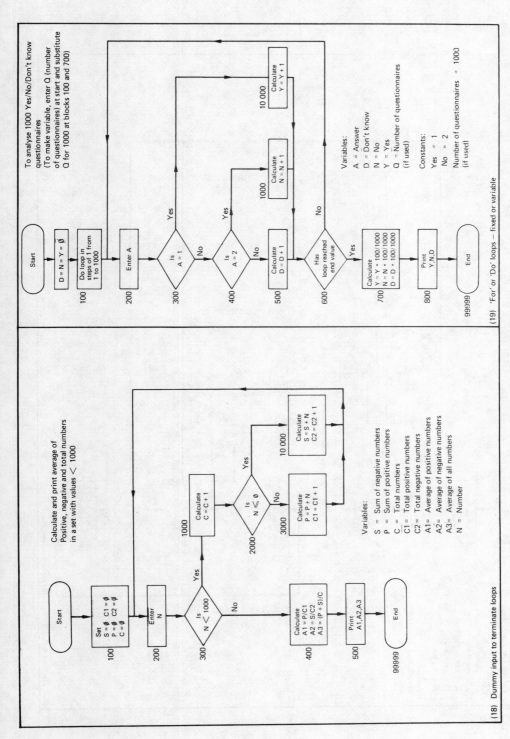

Figure 108   Loops

(18) Dummy input to terminate loops

(19) 'For' or 'Do' loops – fixed or variable

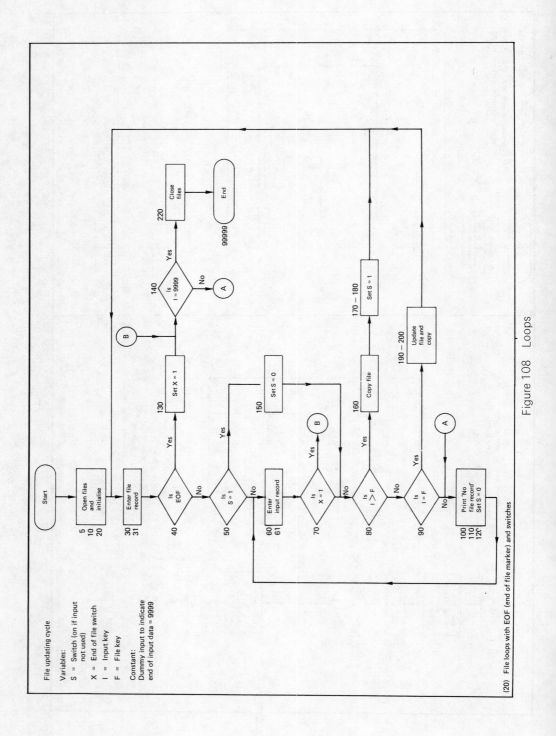

File updating cycle

Variables:

S = Switch (on if input
       not used)

X = End of file switch

I = Input key

F = File key

Constant:
Dummy input to indicate
end of input data = 9999

(20)   File loops with EOF (end of file marker) and switches

Figure 108   Loops

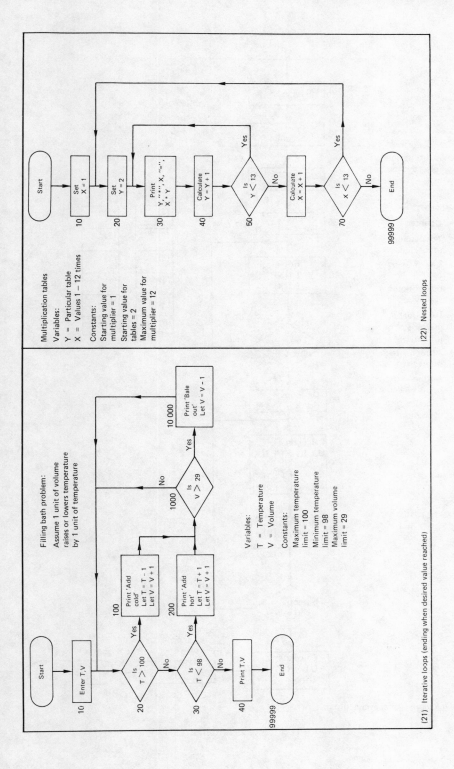

Figure 108 Loops

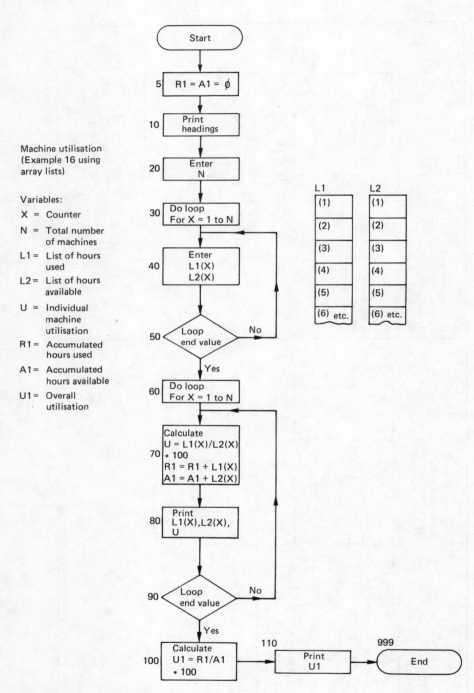

Machine utilisation
(Example 16 using
array lists)

Variables:

X = Counter

N = Total number
       of machines

L1 = List of hours
       used

L2 = List of hours
       available

U = Individual
       machine
       utilisation

R1 = Accumulated
       hours used

A1 = Accumulated
       hours available

U1 = Overall
       utilisation

(23) One dimensional arrays (lists)

Figure 109   Arrays and matrices

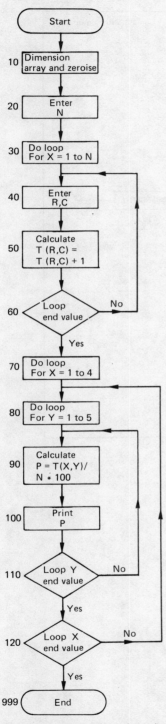

Survey of moviegoers' preferences
by type of film and age

Table T(4,5)

	Age < 19	Age 19–25	Age 26–35	Age 36–45	Age > 45
Love stories	(1,1)	(1,2)	(1,3)	(1,4)	(1,5)
Musicals	(2,1)	(2,2)	(2,3)	(2,4)	(2,5)
Westerns	(3,1)	(3,2)	(3,3)	(3,4)	(3,5)
Thrillers	(4,1)	(4,2)	(4,3)	(4,4)	(4,5)

Variables:

N = Number of persons interviewed
R = Type of film preferred
C = Age of interviewee
X = Loop counter
Y = Loop counter
P = Percentage of survey

Constants:
Number of film types (rows) = 4
Age groups (columns) = 5

(24) Multidimension arrays (tables)

Figure 109   Arrays and matrices

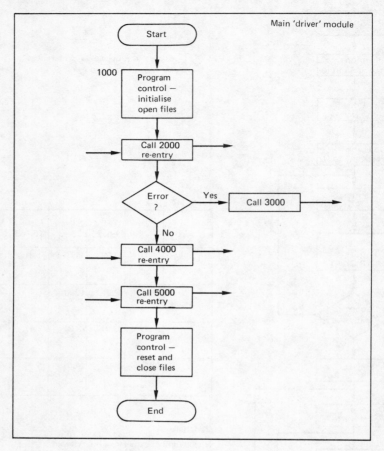

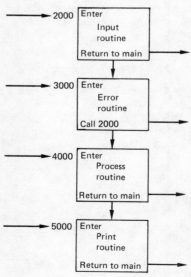

Figure 110   Modular structures

Study the diagrams and then attempt (under guidance) to use the various structures to solve as many of the problem programs (p. 199) as you can. In this way you will slowly build up experience of simple programming. The following notes should help you to develop your solutions.

Drawing flowcharts

(1) Use these symbols:

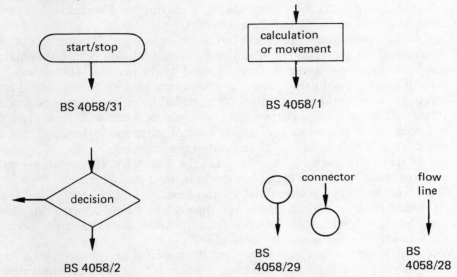

(2) All the outputs required from this run must be identified and dummy sample results, with the exact format dimensions and units, must be prepared from the given test data.

(3) Any item on the output can only come from
   (a) direct input or input from file–variables
   (b) constants built into the program–alphabetic literals or numeric constants
   (c) calculations based on the above variables and constants
   (d) direct input, constants or calculations arrived at by following alternative paths or repetitions based on decisions taken.

(4) The programmer must visualise how he himself would arrive at the output results from the given inputs and in doing so prepare lists of the outputs, inputs, file data, literals, constants, calculations, repetitions and alternative path decisions.

(5) Together with the lists, the programmer should keep a glossary of variable names used and their meanings.

(6) The lists produced in (4) must be reviewed and you should decide which should be logically processed first, which next and so on, numbering the processes and decisions as you go along.

(7) The first rough freehand flowchart can now be commenced with the start symbol and the appropriate symbol for the chosen statement. These are joined by flowlines and then the next logical statement chosen from the lists and

drawn on the chart until all the listed statements are exhausted. In developing the chart the programmer must bear in mind the following rules:

(a) The aim of the chart is to be completely comprehensive whilst at the same time being simple and clear.

(b) The string of symbols is accompanied by brief notes or mathematical signs in each box or diamond indicating the processing involved.

(c) Each symbol may only have one flowline entering it and with the exception of the decision diamond, one leaving it. The decision symbol must have two and only two flowlines leaving it.

(d) Avoid too many process boxes by putting all statements not interrupted by a decision or a return flowline into one box. Boxes should not be duplicated but one box used, joined by the necessary flowlines.

(e) All symbols requiring program statements should be numbered from top to bottom working in vertical columns left to right, in time sequence.

(f) If a decision is to be carried out only once then this will normally come before a set of processes but if it is part of a repetitive sequence then it will normally be best placed at the end of the sequence.

(g) If there are many decisions then the one with the most probable positive result will come first, then the next most probable, etc.

(h) All connectors are sequentially numbered.

(i) One branch at a time is followed through to a final conclusion. This is usually the 'down' path (decision 'no'). After this the 'right' branch (decision 'yes') is followed through.

(8) When all branches have been brought to conclusion, the original lists of probable statements should be checked to ensure all have been incorporated or eliminated.

(9) The first rough draft should now be tidied up, checked for charting conventions and redrawn until the programmer is satisfied it is complete.

Decision tables

Another program development and design technique that can be used as an alternative or supplement to program logic flowcharts is the decision table. Where the programmer is faced with a complex set of conditions which can result in one of a number of alternate actions being taken depending upon which conditions are fulfilled at any one time, he will find the use of a decision table will help in a number of ways.

Firstly, in the definition of the problem itself, as the very act of setting out the table will clarify the position. Secondly, he is able to check by reference to the table that all possible combinations have been covered. Thirdly, he will, in completing the action entry part of the table, be designing the problem solution.

In addition to the above, a decision table is a good, concise method of communicating both problem and solution to anyone, regardless of any knowledge of computer techniques. For computer personnel it has further advantages in that it provides an alternative to logic charts in situations where the number of decisions makes the flowchart unwieldy. Also special

TABLE NAME Selection procedure	SIZE	C	A	R
		6	4	4
AUTHOR F. Smith + M. Marchant	DATE 18.1.1985			

RULES

Conditions	1 IF	2 IF	3 IF	4 IF	5 IF	6 IF	7 IF	8 IF	9 IF	10 IF	ELSE
1 IS Preliminary interview suitable	Y	Y	Y								
2 IS Applicants education qualifications o.k.	Y	N	Y								
3 IS Aptitude test score exceptional	Y	Y	N								
4 IS " " " average	N	N	Y								
5 IS " " " fail	N	N	N								
6 IS Medical report satisfactory	Y	Y	Y								
7 IS											
8 IS											
9 IS											
10 IS											

Actions	1 THEN	2 THEN	3 THEN	4 THEN	5 THEN	6 THEN	7 THEN	8 THEN	9 THEN	10 THEN	ELSE
1 Apply for references	X										
2 Employment procedure 'A'			X								
3 Employment procedure 'B'		X									
4 Employment procedure 'C'			X								
5											
6											
7											
8											
9											
10 Reject letter procedure											X

Figure 111   A decision table

programming languages (DETAB–65, FORTAB) have been developed which allow direct coding from decision table to program.

There are three variations of decision tables: extended entry tables; limited entry tables; tables using the ELSE rule. All rely on the same basic format

Condition stub List of conditions	*Condition entries* Indication of which conditions apply in particular cases
Action stub List of all possible actions	*Action entries* Indication of which actions apply under particular conditions

Extended entry

Usually the table will be initially built up as an extended entry table even if later this is changed to limited entry format. In extended entry the main conditions topic is entered in the condition stub and this is qualified in the condition entry, e.g.

Age	21–25	26–30	31–35	36–40
Value	£10	£50	£100	£200
Etc.	etc.	etc.	etc.	etc.

In the action part of the table again only the main topic is entered in the action stub and this qualified in the action entries section, e.g.

Write cheque for	£1	£5	£20	£30
Direct to department	sales	despatch	queries	security
Etc.	etc.	etc.	etc.	etc.

Limited entry

When the extended entry table has been developed, it may be that, whilst it saves space by compressing the data, this form is not suitable either for checking completeness or direct program coding. It can however easily be converted to limited entry format using the same structure. The only difference is that the condition and action stubs will now be filled in with all the detailed conditions and actions and the entry sections will contain only a Y for yes, N for no, X for act or—for not applicable. Figure 111 illustrates this together with the ELSE option.

The ELSE rule

If certain combinations of conditions do not lead to one of the sets of actions listed or if the majority of cases all lead to the same action it is convenient to omit these from the detailed table and list only the specific cases.

To cater for those omitted, one final rule column is added. This is the ELSE rule which is obeyed if none of the specified combinations is found. This is illustrated in Figure 111.

Where limited entry tables become large and unwieldy then the problem should be broken down into a set of tables with action entries cross referring to the next table. In the illustration the employment procedures A, B and C could be examples of this.

Desk checking flowcharts and decision tables

It is very important to thoroughly check all program logic before it is coded into a program language and tested on the computer. Imagine what could happen if the design of a supersonic airliner were not tested until its maiden flight. The programmer must prepare his sets of **test data** based on the information in his systems specification. One set must be prepared for every path through the logic, taking both branches at every decision. The test data will include not only **correct data** but also **bad data**, that is data that will be rejected by the error checks in the program. For each set of data, the result must be known so the programmer should choose simple examples to simplify his manual calculations.

A **trace table** can now be drawn up using one ruled column for each variable in the program, representing the subsequent values in the computer storage locations. The programmer works through his program, blindly obeying his logic instructions as if he were the machine and noting each change in variable value in the appropriate columns. At the end of each program path sequence he will be able to compare his final variable values with those he had previously calculted and thus know if his logic is correct or not. If it is not, he will have a valuable trace of variable values to enable him to locate where the logic went wrong.

When he has corrected all his mistakes and the logic of his program appears to be in order, it is sensible to ask someone else to recheck the logic. It is possible that they will spot an error that the programmer has not seen or, if they are more experienced, they may be able to show methods of achieving the same results more efficiently. In fact, several solutions may be arrived at as there is never just one way of doing something. The programmer should, within reasonable time limitations, attempt to find several alternative logic solutions and then evaluate these in terms of effectiveness, which is the value of the information produced in that format to the user; IAS and peripheral usage; throughput time and processor time consumed and accuracy of results. Each installation and application will bring their own weightings to bear on these factors but the programmer should always make the user requirements top priority.

Program coding languages

For the most part the program logic chart will be independent of the programming language to be used, depending more on the problem to be solved. There may be minor variations on this, mainly in the way that work and decision symbols are presented, due to the programmer's knowledge of the advantages and limitations of the programming language involved.

From this you will have gathered that there is a choice of programming

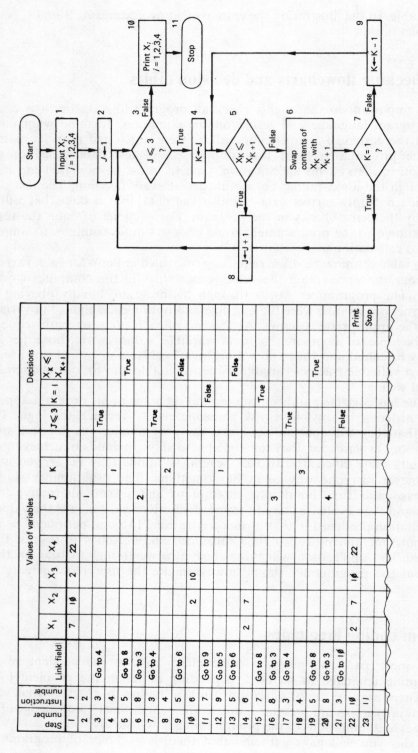

Figure 112　A trace table

languages available. These fall into several types or level of languages.

(1)	machine code	'low level'
(2)	symbolic address system	computer
(3)	assembly language	oriented
(4)	autocodes	
(5)	standard languages	'high level'
(6)	special purpose languages	problem oriented

Machine code

So far we have spoken only of machine code in our examples. This is where the handwritten program statements have to be written in a pure binary form, e.g.

FUNCTION   ADDRESS
101   1011

You can imagine that writing a typical 3000 statement program in this way can be rather tedious. To make matters worse the addresses referred to are absolute addresses which means that the programmer must keep track of which locations he has used for which data items, etc. This was how the first programs had to be written and it was soon realised that something should be done to make program writing easier.

Symbolic address systems (SAS)

The idea of making the computer itself take some of the work out of programming was introduced in the form of symbolic address system languages. Two innovations were made. The first one was a simple idea. Instead of writing say, 101, meaning copy into the accumulator register, the programmer was allowed to write a simple mnemonic (easy to remember) instruction such as **CPA**. Copy into the store would be **CPS** and so on. What this meant was that before putting the program into the computer direct (as he could before) the programmer must now enter his written (source) program as data to be run against a translating program so that the computer could produce an object program in machine code. This object program would then be used as the machine code program had been used previously.

The other more important change was (as the name suggests) in the use of a **symbolic** rather than an absolute address in the program statement. This enabled the programmer to use a name (variable) in place of the absolute address and meant that the computer translating program had the additional task of keeping a cross reference table so that when it came to a variable in the source program it could recognise that this meant a certain absolute address that it had previously allocated, and translate it as such in the object program.

Program statements in a symbolic address system would therefore look rather like this:

(mnemonic)   (symbolic)
FUNCTION   ADDRESS
CPA   wage

Assembly languages

Each instruction in machine code was obeyed by the computer as one step of the program. When programs were written in symbolic address languages they

Data Processing

1900 Series PLAN coding sheet

Programmer: S HEAM AW

Title: REVERSE

Sheet 1 of 1

Date 2·11·1984

Identity/Page: [   ]   73

Label	Operation	Acc.	Operand	Comment
#PROGRAM	PROGRAM		REVERSE	
#LOWER			A(12),B,C	[DECLARES AN ARRAY SIZED (1×12)
				[AND TWO VARIABLES]
#PROGRAM	PROGRAM			
#ENTRY	ENTRY			
	PREP		0	
	LDN	2	11	[COPY INTO ACCUMULATOR (ACC) 2
				[CONSTANT −11 INTO ACC 2
	READ	3	'12',A	[READ ARRAY,12 NUMBERS *A
LOOP	LDCT	7	12	[THIS SETS THE COUNT PART OF ACC 7
				[−12 EQUAL TO 2
	LDX	7	A(3)	[COPY INTO ACC 7 THE CONTENT OF A(3)
	STO	7	B	[COPY INTO STORAGE LOCATION B, THE
	LDX	6	A(2)	[COPY INTO ACC 6 THE CONTENT OF A(2)
	SBN	2	1	[SUBTRACT FROM ACC 2, THE CONSTANT 1
	STO	6	C	[COPY INTO STORAGE LOCATION C, THE
				[CONTENT OF ACC 6
	WRITE		B	[WRITE NUMBERS FROM B, B+1 *
	LINES		'2'	[WRITE ONE NEW LINE
				[THIS DECREASES THE COUNT IN ACC 3
LOOP	BUX	3	LOOP	[BY 1, TRANSFERRING CONTROL TO
				[PROGRAM ADDRESS LOOP UNLESS COUNT
				[REACHES ZERO WHEN IT WILL PASS
				[CONTROL TO NEXT INSTRUCTION
	SUSWT		2HAW	[*THESE INSTRUCTIONS ARE BEGINNERS
#END				[I/O SUBROUTINES

Figure 113   An assembly language coding sheet

were first translated into machine code, each SAS statement producing one machine code statement. The next step was to recognise that in all programs written in SAS certain commonly used combinations of statements kept cropping up over and over again. It was logical that to ease the task of program writing these combinations should be recognised by one name and the programmer wishing to use them should merely write this name in the function part of his program statement leaving the 'translation' program to recognise this and generate the necessary set of instructions rather than a single instruction as it had previously had to do.

These single instructions that generate sets of instructions in machine code are known as macro instructions. Because the translating program had now not only to translate from a mnemonic/symbolic statement to machine code but had also to put together all the required sets of instructions, the new languages consisting of some single and some macro instructions were called **assembly languages** and the translating program the **assembler**.

The language structure is still far closer to machine code than it is to normal written English and therefore each make and model of computer needs an individual assembly language which is not compatible with that of any other make.

Statements in programming languages have eventually to be stored in a computer word and each language will have its own field formats within that word. An example of part of a program written in an assembly language is given in Figure 113. A typical assembly language may have 100–150 program function commands, about a quarter of which are macros. Possible function types are illustrated by the simple City and Guilds code, Figure 114.

Autocodes
All of the languages previously described were **computer oriented**. The next stage in the development of programming languages was to provide a language that was **problem oriented**, that is one structured to accept statements with a layout very similar to that of the problem solution steps stated verbally.

This was done by an expansion of the use of macros so that all the autocode statements generated sets of machine code instructions either directly or through an intermediate language. Many different autocodes were developed by various manufacturers for specific jobs. There were autocodes for scientific problems, for commercial data processing, even for military applications. The problem was that although autocodes made program coding easier it was still not possible to be completely machine independent as each manufacturer had his own language which again was noncompatible with any other.

Standard languages
From 1959 onwards manufacturers and users came together to agree on standard languages which would be completely machine independent and problem oriented. At present there are five or six standard languages accepted by the majority of manufacturers. This acceptance means that the manufacturers have written programs that will accept source programs written in these languages and convert them into the particular machine code programs required by their machines. The programs that do this are known as **compilers** and the act of converting is called **compilation**.

Instruction set

Numeric function	Mnemonic instruction		Operation	Remarks
00	LDA	n, m	$(n+(m)) \to A$	Load operand into cleared accumulator.
01	ADD	n, m	$(A)+(n+(m)) \to A$	Add operand.
02	SUB	n, m	$(A)-(n+(m)) \to A$	Subtract operand.
03	MLT	n, m	$(A) \times (n+(m)) \to A$	Multiply by operand.
04	DIV	n, m	$(A)/(n+(m)) \to A$	Divide by operand.
10	LDAN	n, m	$n+(m) \to A$	Load integer $n+(m)$ into cleared accumulator.
11	ADDN	n, m	$(A)+n+(m) \to A$	Add integer.
12	SUBN	n, m	$(A)-n+(m) \to A$	Subtract integer.
13	MLTN	n, m	$(A) \times n+(m) \to A$	Multiply by integer.
14	DIVN	n, m	$(A)/n+(m) \to A$	Divide by integer.
20	STA	n, m	$(A) \to n+(m)$	Store (A) without clearing the accumulator.
30	JUN	n, m	$n+(m) \to C$	Jump unconditionally.
31	JEQ	n, m	If $(A)=0$ $n+(m) \to C$	Jump if $(A)=0$.
32	JNE	n, m	If $(A) \neq 0$ $n+(m) \to C$	Jump if $(A) \neq 0$.
33	JLE	n, m	If $(A) \leqslant 0$ $n+(m) \to C$	Jump if $(A) \leqslant 0$.
34	JGE	n, m	If $(A) \geqslant 0$ $n+(m) \to C$	Jump if $(A) \geqslant 0$.
35	JLT	n, m	If $(A) < 0$ $n+(m) \to C$	Jump if $(A) < 0$.
36	JGR	n, m	If $(A) > 0$ $n+(m) \to C$	Jump if $(A) > 0$.
37	JSR	n, m	Link $\to$ 4; $n+(m) \to C$	Set link and jump.
			(Link is the address of the next instruction to be obeyed on return i.e. that immediately following JSR.)	
38	JST	n, m	Wait; $n+(m) \to C$	Wait, jump when start button operated.
39	LOP	n, m	If $(5) > 0$ after $(5)-1$, $n+(m) \to C$	Jump if after subtracting 1 from location 5, $(5) > 0$.
40	SQT	n, m	$\sqrt{(A)} \to A$	If $(A) < 0$, jump to $n+(m)$.
41	EXP	n, m	$\exp(A) \to A$	If (A) too large, jump to $n+(m)$.
42	LGN	n, m	$\ln(A) \to A$	If $(A) < 0$, jump to $n+(m)$.
43	SIN		$\sin(A) \to A$	(A) in radians.
44	COS		$\cos(A) \to A$	(A) in radians.
45	ARC		$\arctan(A) \to A$	
46	ENT		$\text{entier}(A) \to A$	Integral part of $(A) \to A$.
50	ARD	n, m	Allocate input device $n+(m)$ to program	
51	AWD	n, m	Allocate output device $n+(m)$ to program	

Device code	Device
0–9	Typewriters
10–19	Paper tape readers
20–29	Paper tape punches
30–39	Card readers
40–49	Card punches
50–59	Magnetic tape units
60–69	Disc drives
70–79	Drums
80–89	Line printers
90–999	etc. etc.

52	RNA	n, m	Read number to accumulator. Jump to n+ (m) if error in number.
53	WNA	n, m	Write number from accumulator, with n integral, and m fractional digits, if n and m are zero, floating point output is implied.
60	RCH	n, m	Read 1 character to store at location n+ (m).
61	RCH	n, m	Write 1 character from store at location n +(m).
62	RNB	n, m	Read next block of characters to store beginning at location n+ (m).
63	WNB	n, m	Write block of characters from store beginning at location n+ (m).
64	WNL	n, m	Write n+ (m) new line characters.
65	WSS	n, m	Write n+ (m) spaces.
66	CNN	n, m	Convert character string beginning at location n+ (m) to number in accumulator.
67	CNC	n, m	Convert number in accumulator to character string beginning at location n+ (m). Location 6 contains number of places before point. Location 7 contains number of places after point. If. both locations are zero floating point representation is implied.
70	ACB	n, m	Access block n+ (m). For direct access devices n+ (m) defines the sector address. On other devices the instruction has the effect of skipping n+ (m) blocks.
71	BSP	n, m	Backspace device by n+ (m) blocks and stop ready to read or write.
72	RWD		Rewind device and stop ready to read or write first block.
99	STOP		Return control to operating system.

Input directives

(STORE n')	Commence storing program sequentially from location n'.
(WAIT)	Temporary stop during input for change of tapes.
(EXECUTE n')	Commence execution of program at instruction in location n'.
(TITLE) "String"	The alpha-numeric string immediately following the right bracket will be copied on to output tape.

Notes concerning instructions

The written form of each instruction will be, in general, as follows: LDA n, m where L is the opening symbol of the instruction, n is the address and m the modifier address. In the description (m) denotes "the contents of location m".

If there is no modification necessary, the ",m" may be omitted and modification by location 0 will then be implied. Specimen instructions are:

LDA 100   (100) unmodified→ A
MLT 200,3   (A) × (200 modified by (3))→ A

Figure 114   City and Guilds code

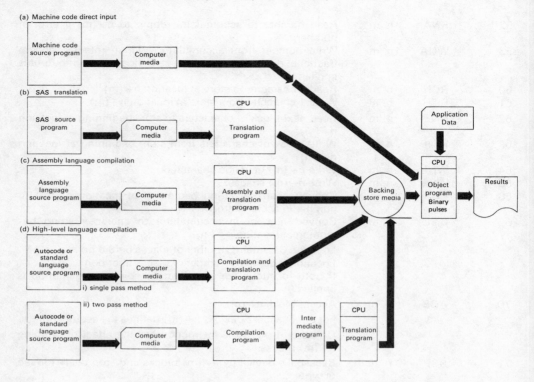

Figure 115   Methods of producing an object program

The way compilation is achieved varies from manufacturer to manufacturer as does the efficiency of compilation and the minimum configuration requirements needed. Figure 115 illustrates the processes of assembly and compilation.

The standard high level languages at the present time are ALGOL, FORTRAN, PL/1, COBOL, PASCAL and BASIC.

An **algorithm** is a rule for the solution of a problem in a finite number of steps. The name ALGOL stands for **Algo**rithmic **L**anguage and is the accepted European programming language for scientific and mathematical problems. FORTRAN is the American equivalent of ALGOL and the name stands for **For**mula **Tran**slation. Both languages are similar in instruction content but differ as to format and language rules. Both languages are quite old now and are tending to be replaced by BASIC, which is under constant development and enhancement, as the method of computing is changing to remote access time sharing or the use of local microprocessors with built in BASIC compilers.

COBOL is another language that has been in use for some time. There was a movement to replace this rather cumbersome language with PL/1 (Programming Language 1) which was intended to be a universal language suitable for both commercial and scientific applications. This now looks less likely to happen and PL/1 may remain a rather minor standard language in terms of universal acceptance. What is more likely is that COBOL will be replaced by a language

```
11/11/13    12/04/78         COMPILED BY XALE MK    5E
STATEMENT
    0        ´LIST´ (LP)
    0        ´SENDTO´(FD,GEN-WORKFILE(6),.PROGRAM XXXX)
    0        ´WORK´(ED,GEN-WORKFILE(7))
    0        ´PROGRAM´(LUCK)
    0        ´INPUT´0,1=CR0
    0        ´OUTPUT´0,2=LP7
    0        ´INPUT´3=TR0
    0        ´OUTPUT´4=TP7
    0          ´BEGIN´
    1            ´PROCEDURE´MILLION (X); ´VALUE´X; ´INTEGER´X;
    4                ´BEGIN´  ´INTEGER´N,REMAINDER;
    4                      N:=X´/´1000000;
    6                ´IF´ N<1 ´THEN´
    6                    THOUSANDS (X)
    6                    ´ELSE´
    6                    ´BEGIN´
    6                       DIGITS (N):
    8                       WRITETEXT (´(´%MILLION´)´);
    9                       REMAINDER :=X-N*1000000;
   10                ´IF´ REMAINDER<100 ´AND´ REMAINDER ≠0 ´THEN´
   10                       WRITETEXT (´(´%AND´)´);
   11                       THOUSANDS (REMAINDER)
   11                     ´END´
   11                ´END´;
   11
   11
   11
   11            ´PROCEDURE´ THOUSANDS(P); ´VALUE´P; ´INTEGER´P;
   15                ´BEGIN´ ´INTEGER´ Q,A;
   15                    ´IF´ P<1000 ´THEN´
   16                    HUNDREDS (P)
   16                    ´ELSE´
   16                    ´BEGIN´
   16                       Q:=P´/´1000;
   18                       ´IF´ Q>100 ´THEN´
   18                       HUNDREDS (Q)
   18                       ´ELSE´
   18                       TENS (Q);
   19                       WRITETEXT (´(´%THOUSAND´)´);
   20                       A:=P-Q*1000;
   21                ´IF´ A<100 ´AND´ A≠0 ´THEN´
   21                       WRITETEXT (´(´%AND´)´);
   22                       HUNDREDS (A)
   22                     ´END´
   22                ´END´;
   22
   22
   22
   22            ´PROCEDURE´ HUNDREDS (K): ´VALUE´K; ´INTEGER´K;
   26                ´BEGIN´ ´INTEGER´ Z,D;
   26                    ´IF´ K<100 ´THEN´
   27                    TENS (K)
   27                    ´ELSE´
   27                    ´BEGIN´
   27                       Z:=K´/´100;
   29                       DIGITS (Z);
   30                       WRITETEXT (´(´%HUNDRED´)´);
```

Figure 116   Algol program statements

```
        MASTER EXAMUP
C
C       THIS PROGRAM UPDATES A MASTER FILE CONTAINING EXAMINATION
C       MARKS HELD ON MAGNETIC TAPE WITH INPUT FROM CARDS.
C       MARKS RANGE FROM 0 TO 10 AND A MARK OF -3 IS A DELETION OF
C       A RECORD AND -1 IS A CODE WHEN EXAMINATION NOT TAKEN
C
        INTEGER ID,TESTS,EXAMSAT,MARKS,STUDNO,SCORE,LASTIN
        REAL AVERAGE
        WRITE (3,800)
        WRITE (3,850)
        WRITE (4,900)
        STUDNO = 0
        ID = 0
        LASTIN = 0
1       CALL READMASTER (ID,TESTS,EXAMSAT,MARKS,AVERAGE)
2       CALL READCARD (STUDNO,SCORE)
C
C       IF BOTH FILES ARE EXHAUSTED, THE PROGRAM STOPS.
C
3       IF(ID .EQ. 999 .AND. STUDNO .EQ. 999) GO TO 999
C
C       LASTIN IS THE NUMBER OF LAST-IN-SEQUENCE RECORD.
C       USED FOR THE CHECKING OF AN OUT OF SEQUENCE RECORD.
C
        IF (STUDNO .LT. LASTIN) GO TO 4
C
C       THE FOLLOWING COMPARES THE TWO NUMBERS AND DEPENDING
C       ON THE RESULTS THE CORRECT COURSE OF ACTION IS TAKEN
C       TO UPDATE THE MASTERFILE.
        IF (STUDNO .EQ. ID) GO TO 5
        IF (STUDNO .LT. ID) GO TO 6
        WRITE (3,300) ID, TESTS, EXAMSAT, MARKS, AVERAGE
        CALL READMASTER (ID, TESTS, EXAMSAT, MARKS, AVERAGE)
        GO TO 3
4       WRITE (4,100) STUDNO
        WRITE (4,200) LASTIN
        GO TO 2
5       CALL SAMEREC (ID, TESTS, EXAMSAT, MARKS, AVERAGE, SCORE, LASTIN)
        GO TO 1
6       CALL NOMASTER (STUDNO, SCORE, LASTIN)
        GO TO 2
100     FORMAT (1H0,20X,13HRECORD NUMBER,I6,3X,15HOUT OF SEQUENCE)
200     FORMAT (1H ,20X,26HLAST IN-SEQUENCE RECORD   ,I6)
300     FORMAT (1H0,20X,I6,9X,I6,10X,I6,10X,I6,10X,F8.2)
800     FORMAT (1H1,50X,17HEXAMINATION MARKS)
850     FORMAT (1H0,23X,9HID NUMBER,6X,8HTEST SAT,6X,11HTESTS TAKEN,5X,11H
       1TOTAL MARKS,5X,12HAVERAGE MARK)
900     FORMAT (1H1,50X,12HERROR REPORT)
999     STOP
        END


END OF SEGMENT, LENGTH   171, NAME  EXAMUP
```

Figure 117   Fortran program statements

```
1900 COBOL COMPILER #XEKB MK.7C/2    COBOL SOURCE FILE DATE 02/05/78
COMPILER SEQUENCING
      000100 IDENTIFICATION DIVISION.
      000200 PROGRAM-ID.      GROUP1.
      000300 AUTHOR.          SHEAM
      000400*    THIS MASTER PROGRAM READS 2 INPUT FILES, BOTH SEQUENTIAL:
      000500*    A MASTER ON DISC AND A TRANSACTION FILE ON CARDS.
      000600*    AND CATERING FOR DELETION OR AMENDMENTS FOR A NON-
      000700*    EXISTING RECORD.
      000800*    OUTPUT ERROR MESSAGE WHEN EXAMPLE INSERTION FOR
      000900*    EXISTING MASTER RECORD.
      001000 ENVIRONMENT DIVISION.
      001100 CONFIGURATION SECTION.
      001200 SOURCE-COMPUTER.  ICL-1902.
      001300 OBJECT-COMPUTER.  ICL-1902.
      001400               MEMORY 10000 WORDS.
      001500 SPECIAL-NAMES.    CHANNEL-1 IS NEWPAGE.
      001600 INPUT-OUTPUT SECTION.
      001700 FILE-CONTROL.
      001800     SELECT MASTERFILE ASSIGN TO EDS 1,
      001900     ACCESS MODE IS SEQUENTIAL,
      002000     ORGANISATION IS INDEXED.
      002100     SELECT TRANSFILE ASSIGN TO CARD-READER 0.
      002200     SELECT PRINTFILE ASSIGN TO PRINTER 1.
      002300 DATA DIVISION.
      002400 FILE SECTION.
      002500 FD  MASTERFILE BLOCK CONTAINS 512 CHARACTERS,
      002600     LABEL RECORDS ARE STANDARD
      002700     VALUE OF IDENTIFICATION IS "DFC-FDXC1-01"
      002800     DATA RECORDS IS MASTFI.
      002900 01  MASTFI.
             02  FIL
      011
      012000        LER            PIC X          SPACES.
      012100 01  UNLINE.
      012200     02  FILLER             PIC X(120) VALUE ALL "*".
      012300 PROCEDURE DIVISION.
      012400 MAIN-CONTROL SECTION.
      012500 CONTROL-10.
      012600*    THIS SECTION CONTROLS THE OVERALL PROCESSING OF DATA
      012700*    THROUGH THE PROGRAM.
      012800     PERFORM BEGIN.
      012900     PERFORM MAINPROG UNTIL CUST-NO = INFINITY
      013000                 AND TRANS-NO = INFINITY.
      013100     PERFORM TERMINATION.
      013200     STOP RUN.
      013300 BEGIN SECTION.
      013400*    OPENS ALL INPUT FILES AND THE OUTPUT FILE
      013500*    PRINTS THE NECESSARY HEADINGS FOR THE OUTPUT
      013600*    READS A CARD IE TRANSACTION AND A RECORD ON MASTER.
      013700 BEGIN-10.
      013800     OPEN INPUT MASTERFILE,TRANSFILE, OUTPUT PRINTFILE.
      013900     PERFORM HEAD-PRINT.
      014000     PERFORM READ-TRANSACTION.
      014100     PERFORM READ-MASTER.
      014200 BEGIN-999.
      014300     EXIT.
      014400 MAINPROG SECTION.
      014500*    DETERMINE THE RELATIONSHIP OF THE TRANSACTION AND THE
      014600*    MASTER RECORD AND THEN DETERMINE THE CORRECT ACTION
      014700 PROG-10.
      014800     MOVE SPACES TO OUTLINE-1.
      014900     MOVE SPACES TO OUTLINE-2.
      015000     MOVE SPACES TO OUTLINE-3.
      015100     IF CUST-NO EQUAL TO TRANS-NO THEN
      015200     PERFORM MASTER ELSE
```

Figure 118　Cobol program statements

more suitable for use by the newer machine architecture whilst still being commercially oriented. The addition of data description and data manipulation language facilities to COBOL for database applications may be a step in this direction. The name COBOL stands for **C**ommon **B**usiness **O**riented **L**anguage.

COBOL *structure*

A COBOL program is comprised of four **divisions**: identification division; environment division; data division; procedure division. Each division consists of **statements** constructed from either specified words or phrases laid down in the language (reserved words) or names made up by the programmer according to certain rules of the language. These statements contain symbols (+ − = etc.) and punctuation (,.' etc.).

Some divisions are broken down by sections and others by paragraphs. Normally all letters are capitals but in the following examples the reserved words are given in capitals and the programmer supplied names in small letters.

Identification division—The purpose of this division is to give identifying information about the program. It must contain the program name and may contain other information, such as the date written, the author, remarks, etc.

```
e.g.  IDENTIFICATION DIVISION
      PROGRAM–ID
        'payroll'
```

Environment division—There are two sections in this division. The configuration section specifies the computers used to compile the program and to run it, and the input–output section assigns data files to particular peripheral devices.

```
e.g.  ENVIRONMENT DIVISION
      CONFIGURATION SECTION
      SOURCE–COMPUTER
        IBM–360
      OBJECT–COMPUTER
        IBM–360
      INPUT–OUTPUT SECTION
      FILE–CONTROL
        SELECT pay ASSIGN TO 'SYS001'
```

Data division—This is used to specify all the data files, records and fields processed by the program. It does this by indicating file and record structure together with field levels and pictures. There are two sections; the file section and the working-storage section.

```
e.g.  DATA DIVISION
      FILE SECTION
      FD    pay
            DATA RECORD IS pa
      01    pa
            02    number              PICTURE 9999
            02    name                PICTURE A(15)
      WORKING-STORAGE SECTION
      77    switch                    PICTURE 9
```

Procedure division—This division contains the sequenced set of statements that instruct the computer to process and make decisions on the data specified in the data section. This is the part of the program that corresponds to the logic flow chart prepared by the programmer. As in English, the statements contain verbs (action, commands, e.g. READ, ADD, GO TO) and nouns (data names, e.g. pay, pa, slip) and are grouped into paragraphs each with its own paragraph heading.

```
e.g.   PROCEDURE DIVISION
       first
           OPEN INPUT pa, OUTPUT slip
       next
           READ pay AT END GO TO last
           MULTIPLY hours BY rate GIVING total
           WRITE slip
       last
           IF total = 30 GO TO next
           CLOSE, pay
           STOP, RUN
```

BASIC

BASIC stands for **B**eginners **A**ll-purpose **S**ymbolic **I**nstruction **C**ode because it started its life as a simple language designed to introduce college students to program coding. The method being used for student training was remote access time sharing and the language quickly became adopted as the standard language for this form of computing. As more and more users and manufacturers became involved, the language became richer in the facilities offered and it became available in two forms–standard BASIC and advanced BASIC. With all the advanced facilities, BASIC is now a very powerful language and becoming increasingly more popular than ALGOL and FORTRAN. It has also been developed to handle data files and may often be found in commercial data processing, although usually on the smaller machines, in time sharing environments and for program development prior to implementation on larger machines in other codes.

Its popularity is due to the fact that BASIC is easy to learn, easy to teach, less tedious to write and, in its advanced form, just as powerful as other languages. In certain circumstances, another language may have a structure or facility that can do a particular job much better but, in general terms, BASIC has begun the process that can lead eventually to simple program writing by anyone on their personal microprocessor. As an example of how easy BASIC can be, the following statements are all that are needed to code most of the simple example flowcharts found in Figures 107 and 108. Read the rules and attempt to code some of the programs.

Rule 1 BASIC statements take the following form:

	Statement number	Function word(s)	Variable name or constant
Example	10	Input	A, V3, J

Rule 2 You may choose any variable name from the 286 possibilities formed by using any single letter of the alphabet (A–Z) or a single alphabetic letter followed by a single numeric digit Ø-9 (e.g. A7, H3, M9). Variables are used to

name IAS store locations designated to hold data. The above applies if the data is purely numeric. If it contains non-numeric characters then the variable must be a single alphabetic character followed by the dollar sign (e.g. B$, K$).

Rule 3 To put data into the computer you use the function word INPUT followed by the variable name of the location where your data will be stored. If you wish to store more than one data item, use additional variables separated by commas (see example in Rule 1).

Rule 4 To perform calculations you use the function word LET followed by the name of a variable location where your answer will be put after the operation has been performed. You follow this variable by the = sign and then put your arithmetic formula made up of variables, arithmetic operators and constants.

Examples   20 LET G = A + V3/J
                  30 LET L4 = G * 24 (note / means divide, * means multiply)

Rule 5 To make the computer produce an answer you use the function word PRINT followed by the names of the store variables containing your answer.

Example   40 PRINT L4

You can also print out messages (literals) by enclosing your message in quotation marks.

Example   50 PRINT "THE ANSWER IS", L4

Rule 6 To code a decision box for a branch you use the function word IF followed by some comparison of variables, or variables and constants, using the relational operators, =, <, >. This comparison is followed by another function word THEN and a statement number.

Examples   60 IF L4 < 200 THEN 10
                  70 IF L4 = B THEN 30

Rule 7 To set up 'do' or 'for' loops you need two statements, one at the start of the loop and one at the end. The function word for the first statement is FOR followed by a counter variable name, the = sign, the start value of the count, the function word TO and then the end value of the count. The statement at the end of the loop uses the function word NEXT followed by the counter variable.

Example   20 FOR C = 1 TO 20   (causes a loop of twenty times)
                 statement
                 statement
                   etc.
            60 NEXT C   (loops back to statement 20)

Rule 8 To conclude a program you write the function word END on its own.

Example   999 END

There are, of course other BASIC function words (facilities) but you will be surprised at the number of quite sizeable programs that you can write with just these seven. A close examination of the sample program given in Figure 119 will give you an idea of how to put your programs together.

```
10 DIM A(25,2)
20 DIM B(25,2)
30 READ N
40 FOR I= l TO N
50 READ A(I,1)
60 LET A(I,2)=I
70 NEXT I
80 PRINT " THE ORIGINAL LIST "
90 FOR I= l TO N
100 PRINT A(I,1)
110 NEXT I
120 PRINT
130 FOR M=N TO 2 STEP -1
140 LET S=0
150 FOR I=1 TO M-1
160 IF A(I,1)<=A(I+1,1) THEN 240
170 LET B(I,1)=A(I,1)
180 LET A(I,1)=A(I+1,1)
190 LET A(I+1,1)=B(I,1)
200 LET B(I,2)=A(I,2)
210 LET A(I,2)=A(I+1,2)
220 LET A(I+1,2)=B(I,2)
230 LET S=1
240 IF I>M-1 THEN 270
260 NEXT I
270 IF S=0 THEN 290
280 NEXT M
290 PRINT " THE SORTED LIST IN ASCENDING ORDER "
300 PRINT "WITH THE POSITIONS OF THE VALUES IN THE ORIGINAL LIST"
310 PRINT
320 PRINT "VALUES          THE POSITIONS"
330 FOR I=l TO N
340 PRINT A(I,1), A(I,2),
350 IF A(I,1)= A(I+1,I) THEN 380
360 PRINT
370 GOTO 420
380 IF N<I+1 THEN 430
390 PRINT A(I+1,2),
400 LET I=I+1
410 GOTO 350
420 NEXT I
425 DATA 10,45,-4,76,34,99,-89,56,12,57,34
430 END
RUN

BUBSRT        12:45        03-MAY-78
  THE ORIGINAL LIST
  45
-4
  76
  34
  99
-89
  56
  12
  57
  34

  THE SORTED LIST IN ASCENDING ORDER
WITH THE POSITIONS OF THE VALUES IN THE ORIGINAL LIST

VALUES        THE POSITIONS
-89           6
-4            2
 12           8
 34           4          10
 45           1
 56           7
 57           9
 76           3
 99           5
TIME:  0.48 SECS.
```

Figure 119   A program coded in Basic

Coding the flowchart or decision table

The choice of program language that the programmer will use is often determined for him by his installation standards. These will be based on several factors such as which compilers are available on his machine, if the program must be portable to other machines, how efficient, in terms of IAS space required and processor time used, the program is and how frequently it is to be run, the level of training of the programmers, how soon the program is required to be ready and so on.

Language type evaluation (comparative data i.e. not actual or average data)		
Criteria	Low level	High level
Efficiency (100%)	75%–90%	50%–85%
Programmer training	200 hours	30 hours
Program writing time	50 man days	30 man days
Compilation and testing	20 hours	15 hours
Object program run time	2 hours	3 hours
Immediate access store	4000 words	6000 words
Configuration required	Basic	Large IAS+backing store
Machine compatibility	Same only	Most manufacturers

Figure 120   Factors in choice of program language

It is normal for the programmer to write his coding onto **coding sheets** which are designed for the structure of the language concerned and are part of the documentation standards for the installation. The main reason for these sheets is to provide clarity for the data preparation operators who will prepare the program for entry into the computer. Programmers who punch their own programs have been known to write them on cigarette packets but they usually suffer later from legibility and punching errors.

Once the program is coded, it should be desk checked for language errors. Again this is best done by a second party if you can find someone patient enough to work through your efforts. This is another reason for clarity and legibility.

Special purpose languages

In addition to the machine oriented and problem oriented standard languages there are many programming languages which are non-standard problem oriented for special purposes. Job Control Languages are an example of these. Each JCL will be particular to the range of machines using that operating system. If a database management system is in use then a special data description and data manipulation language (or modification to an existing language) will be required. There are special languages for coding decision tables, special languages for distributed array processing and many other applications. These need not concern the beginner as often these are very simple and user oriented and are picked up quite rapidly if the job for which they are designed is understood.

Compilation

Having worked out the logic and shown this in diagrammatic form, then checked the logic with a trace and coded it into a suitable programming language and checked this coding, the programmer must now submit his work for testing on the computer. In most well run installations, this means filling in some form of operating request documentation if the testing is to be performed by the operating staff. Some installations allow the programmers to test their own programs and, of course, this is normal in remote access time sharing situations. In most cases, if all the proper desk checking has been carried out, it is preferable to submit the program for test by the operating staff. In this way, the operating instructions can be tested at the same time. It may be that, at this stage, the program is just going to be tested for language errors. This is done at the compilation stage. As the compiler translates the program, it will obviously not be able to translate something that is not in the correct code in the first place. It is to be hoped, however, that fully trained and experienced programmers will not make many language errors and the process of compilation and data testing can be carried out in sequence at the same time.

The operating instructions will vary from installation to installation but are likely to include the following:

(1) Instructions to prepare the run:
    JCL instructions
    input data and media required
    backing store files and media required
    output media required
    program details–language, size, priority
(2) Instructions during run:
    program initiation
    messages and operator action required in sequence
    errors and halts expected and action
    unexpected halts action
    media changes
(3) Instructions after run:
    storage or distribution of run data media
    distribution of results

At the time of sending his program for testing, the programmer will raise an entry in a **program testing log**. If his program is returned and he finds either language or logic errors he will have to locate and correct these (debugging) and resubmit his program for retesting. This procedure is repeated until the program is error free and his testing log becomes part of the documentation giving a testing history that is valuable for efficiency evaluation and the development of installation performance standards.

In order to data test the program it is necessary to have test packs of input and backing store data. These test packs must contain data that will be used to produce results which can be checked against the manually prepared expectations, and also deliberate errors which are designed to test that the error control parts of the program achieve their objectives. As with the program coding sheets, these test data items must be written out and submitted to the operations department for preparation on the appropriate media. In the case of master file data, this can be a large operation and it is possible that the whole backing store file may be changed over to computer media in anticipation of the success of the program, as the workload involved may take many clerical and data preparation man hours to complete and much time would be lost if this was not commenced until the program works.

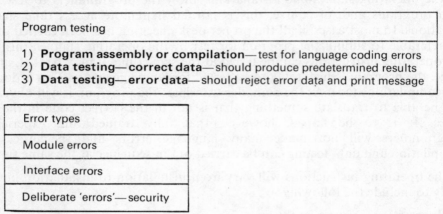

Figure 121   Program testing

Debugging

If the program is returned with logic errors then the task of locating these may not be an easy one. The programmer will have been reasonably sure that his program was going to work because he had thoroughly desk checked this beforehand. His first natural suspicion is that the operating staff have introduced some error at the data preparation stage and that this has not been discovered at the verification stage following. In this he is sometimes correct. Keying errors are made and even the simple mistake of omitting a full stop can make the difference between a program producing good results or rubbish. Sometimes this kind of mistake is due to poor operating and sometimes to illegibility of the programmer's handwriting. In either case, this kind of error shows up the need for high installation standards.

If the error has not been introduced at this stage, it must have been overlooked at the desk checking stage and will therefore not be too obvious, although it can be very simple. This is when the programmer may utilise the diagnostic facilities of the software available. By printing out the intermediate results as the program goes along or giving a listing of the contents of the storage devices used, the programmer is able to follow the processing as he did (or should have done) with his trace table and so locate the sector where things started to go wrong. With patience, perseverance and often some help from his friends, the program fault(s) will be located and rectified and in time the results will be satisfactory.

If a modular approach has been adopted rather than a monolithic one, the module testing will be simpler but there will be the added stage of putting all the working modules together, writing the linkage, driver program and then testing the whole package, debugging if necessary, until the complete program works. There will later come the problem of testing a complete suite of programs together with the manual procedures but, as long as the individual programs work, this will fall into the sphere of the systems analyst.

Program documentation

The programmer will have started on his work from the basis of the systems specification passed to him by the systems analyst. As he has proceeded, he has raised documentation of his own and, at the completion of his work, he himself will have the responsibility of preparing a **program specification** for passing on to the next stage in the system, the operating department. Once his work has finished, the program will be the responsibility of the operating department for the day-to-day data processing work of the company. From time to time, the program will need modification and updating and then a programmer, probably not the program author, will be assigned to make the amendments. He will need to find out what exists and what the program aims are in order to do his work and he will turn to the program documentation for this information.

The programmer must, therefore, put together a program specification pack consisting of the documents shown in Figure 122.

```
Program documentation

1) Program narrative and authorisation
2) Logic flow charts or decision tables
3) Coding sheets and glossary of symbolic address names
4) Sample input and file data in format (test data)
5) Test data results—correct and error data
6) Program progress and testing history
7) Operating instructions
8) Amendment log
```

Figure 122   Program documentation

Assessment tasks

1 Write an essay on the analogy between computer and human software.
2 Submit a report to your manager recommending the software necessary for your proposed distributed database system installation.
3 Write and document programs (in Basic or any language you know) to

(a) produce some invoices
(b) produce some payslips
(c) calculate mortgage interest
(d) sort ten numbers to sequence
(e) update a master file

Unit 10
Data processing evolution

Learning objective

By understanding the various methods man has employed to calculate and record data to provide him with information as a basis for action, to be able to recognise the relative value and application of present day methods and, further, to be able to project and evalute future developments in the light of past experience. To place current research in perspective.

Early processing needs

If we go back to prehistoric man we find the basis of all information processing. In his simple life, man needed to do two things with information: to record it and to calculate with it.

In keeping track of the seasons or the years, early man looked for an aid to his simple memory. In working out an exchange rate for barter deals or just plain simple counting he needed some physical system to supplement his limited capacity for mental arithmetic.

Recording information

Early forms of recording information were by cutting notches on trees, tying knots in string or making simple tally marks (e.g. I, II, III,) in the earth or on cave walls. Note that all of these methods are digital, that is they represent the information discretely in terms of numbers. As man progressed the writing method became more and more popular and writing materials were developed to make the records formed more portable. Writing involves the use of symbols to express ideas. Let us exclude for the moment the use of symbols to convey ideas other than numeric ideas (cave animal drawings, etc.). So far only one symbol (I) has been used. This expresses unity. To show multiples of this more than one unity symbol is written. If our primitive man wanted to record many items he would be faced with the prospect of repeating his one symbol many times. To overcome this other symbols representing other amounts were devised.

Symbols

In 3400 BC the Egyptians had a separate symbol for ten units, another for a hundred units and yet another for a thousand. The Etruscans had symbols for

200

five and for fifty. The Greeks of 300 BC had a system of symbols which used nine alphabetic symbols for the numbers one to nine, the next nine alphabetic symbols for ten, twenty etc. up to ninety and a further nine for the numbers one hundred (in hundreds) to nine hundred. This system was in use until the fifteenth century.

The best known early set of symbols representing numbers is of course the Roman numeral system. This was based on finger signs and was used for all recording of numeric information in the western world until about 1600 AD.

Positional notation

The point about the above number systems is that they were all non-positional. It did not matter if a number was expressed by the Roman symbols (IV) or (VI). In the times of the Romans both meant six units.

There were however some systems in which the position of the symbols relative to each other did matter. In 3000 BC the Babylonians had a system with a **radix** of 60. This means that the symbol used on its own had one value whereas if that same symbol was placed in a position one space removed from its original position it had a value 60 times that of its previous value. In 200 BC the Mayan Indians had systems with radices of 5, 20 and 360. The radix chosen for any number system (our own decimal system radix is 10) has no importance in itself and was usually chosen more by accident than design.

Working with numbers

If we now return to our second basic need, to calculate, we find that a completely separate system evolved to do this. Man found that he could not manipulate the numbers he had recorded cut on trees or scratched on boulders. Even when he had evolved the written systems using symbols he still could not directly calculate with these without the use of mental arithmetic. To prove this try to multiply two large numbers directly in Roman numerals without first turning them into our own decimal number system.

Early obvious ways for man to count were the use of fingers (one hand-radix 5; two hands-radix 10), and fingers and toes (radix 20). Our word for a single number, digit comes from the Latin for finger. The main problem with these systems was that if the number was greater than ten (or twenty) you needed a second man with a new supply of fingers to 'hold' your tens for you.

This gave rise to the development of the cheap, portable and convenient method of using little piles of stones arranged in groups according to the radix used. These could be added to and subtracted from and the result determined by counting. For multiplication, multiple addition was performed $(4 \times 2 = 2 + 2 + 2 + 2)$ and for division, multiple subtraction.

The abacus

As man became more organised, he began to carry around trays with grooves representing his radix positions into which the stones were placed. Again our word calculation comes from the Latin calculus, meaning a pebble. As stones had a habit of getting lost from the trays the next logical step was to use beads threaded on string and put on a frame. Adding to or taking away was then simulated by pushing the beads to the top or bottom of the strings. Thus the abacus evolved. It evolved and was not invented as examples have been found in China (2600 BC), Egypt (600 BC), South America (pre-Columbian) and ancient Greece.

Several types of abacus were introduced to the Roman empire from sources as distant as India and China. As you probably know this instrument is still in use today in Asian countries and in the hands of a skilled operator is a very fast calculating machine indeed.

Numbers today

The position then in Europe by the twelfth century was that there were two systems for dealing with numeric information.
(1) for recording–the Roman numeral system
(2) for calculating–the abacus
We have now to go back in time to about 100 AD to see the development of a number system that changed our whole way of thinking about numbers, greatly contributing to our world as we know it today.

This was a period known as the golden age of Hindu mathematics when there developed in India a number system that combined positional notation, with the decimal scale (radix 10) and first introduced into the system the concept of zero with a separate symbol of its own. This system is now known to all of us. It is the system we use today. We call them Arabic numbers as this is the route by which they became known to us.

Computing history to 1600 AD

773 AD   The Arabs who had been trading with India naturally found it an advantage to learn the number system used there. This proved so successful that by about 770 AD Arabic astronomical tables were translated into the new system.

830   The Arab mathematician Alkarismi wrote a maths book entitled *Algebr we'l mukabala* from which we derive the words algebra and algorism (written calculations in arabic numerals).

1120   At the time of the Crusades, Adelard of Bath disguised himself as a Muslim and studied the new number system, at Cordova. As a result of this he translated Alkarismi into Latin thus introducing Arabic numbers into Europe.

1202   Fibonacci of Pisa produced his book *Liber Abaci* which popularised the use of this number system for scientific problems. By 1400 AD all important scientific work was done by this method.

1478   This year produced the publication of the first printed arithmetic book in Venice. This caused the 'new' number system to be available to all and not just scientists. Its popularity grew slowly.

The turning point

By the year 1600 AD the 'new' algorismic method of both recording and calculating with arabic numerals had been fully accepted in the Western hemisphere replacing the traditional Roman numerals for recording and the abacus for calculation.

Even so, only a few learned men, scholars and scientists, could actually use this system with any degree of competence. As late as 1662 Samuel Pepys who was at that time responsible for the placing of Admiralty contracts wrote in his famous diary that he was learning his arithmetic multiplication tables.

There followed many experiments and inventions of machines and devices to assist people in using this new numbering system:

1614   John Napier, a Scot, published the first logarithm tables, which he had been working on for about twenty years.

1617   Napier produced an embryonic slide rule (**Napier's Bones**) consisting of a set of rods for each digit 0–9 marked off in squares with the results of multiplying by digits 2–9 engraved on them.

1618   Henry Briggs produced common logarithms (to base 10), the same logs that we use today.

1621   An Englishman, John Gunter, combined Napier's two ideas to produce the first real slide rule, a pair of sliding rods marked off in logarithmic scale. This was the first analog computing device of the algorismic system.

The first adding machine–Pascal

1642   If the slide rule was the first analog computer, the first algorismic digital computer was the adding machine invented by Blaise Pascal. In order to aid his father (a French customs officer) to calculate taxes, Pascal, a mathematician, produced a device of geared cog wheels which when moved with a stylus forwards or backwards performed addition or subtraction and indicated the result in a series of windows. Multiplication and division were performed by multiple addition and subtraction.

1671   To simplify multiplication and division Baron Gottfried Von Leibniz improved upon Pascal's machine and incorporated a stepped drum with varying length teeth into a separate multiplication section of the machine. By operating a set of push rods automatic multiplication and division could be performed. Variations and improvements for speed and accuracy were produced by Leibniz up to 1694 and machines of this type were used for astronomy calculations by Newton.

1719   An idea that had nothing directly to do with calculation but was to have great influence later on was developed by Basile Bouchon in this year. To mechanise the production of weaving looms he proposed to regulate the threads (and therefore the pattern) by a series of rods actuated by a series of holes in a paper roll.

1728   Bouchon together with another Frenchman, Falcon, improved the original idea by substituting cards with holes which allowed for easier changes in the weaving 'program'.

The Jacquard loom–punched card automation

1804   The final refinement of the above automated weaving came when Joseph Jacquard produced his famous loom incorporating the punched card program technique in a reliable, accurate design.

1810   Meanwhile others had been at work developing the mechanical calculator. Hahn in Germany had incorporated some further refinements by 1774 and then in 1810, Thomas de Colmar, Alsace produced the first model to be made available in large numbers for the commercial market. Between 1810 and 1820 some 1500 machines were made and sold.

1812   A young Englishman Charles Babbage (later to become a professor of mathematics at Cambridge) had an idea for a large calculating machine which would automatically work out mathematical function tables, by the use of the difference method, and automatically print the results. Convinced of the need for such a machine, as the published tables of his time contained many inaccuracies, Babbage went ahead and built a small prototype model and by 1823 had persuaded the Admiralty of its potential to the extent of a £17 000 development grant. Babbage now commenced working on the full size machine which he called a **difference engine** but due largely to his growing interest in another project this machine was never completed and in 1842 government support was withdrawn and the project abandoned.

1823   In this year Babbage became interested in the application of the Jacquard loom principle of automatic control as applied to calculating machines. Whilst working on his full scale difference engine he began to devise ways of putting this idea into practice which caused him to lose interest in the original project. In 1828 he obtained his Professorship at Cambridge.

Babbage's computer theory

1832   Working now at Cambridge Babbage finalised his ideas for an automatic, mechanical, general-purpose calculator. This machine was known as the **analytical engine** and was to be program-controlled by packs of cards punched with holes in the manner of the Jacquard loom. He now began to design and develop the actual mechanisms needed to build this device and by 1840 the original design for the world's first automatic computer was complete.

He gave a series of lectures in Italy on his ideas which were translated for publication by a twenty-five year old mathematician Lady Lovelace (daughter of Lord Byron). She was so interested in this project that she began working with Babbage developing the program control theory for the machine. Lady Lovelace is acknowledged as the world's first programmer and much of the programming theory used today was developed by her. She was the first to propose changeable programs stored in the machine and before her death in 1852 the analytical engine had a software library of card puched mathematical function programs.

Babbage (the hardware man) designed his machine to store 1000 words of 50 decimal digits each. It was to have punched card (Jacquard style) input and output and online printing facilities. All of this had to be accomplished by mechanical methods (push-rods, gears and cogwheels) and therefore it is not surprising, if rather sad, that the manufacturing techniques of the period were not up to the job and the analytical engine was never built.

Babbage continued to work on the project until just before his death in 1871.

1836   This year saw the first demonstration of the telegraph, a discovery which is of great importance today in the field of data transmission.

1844   Samuel Morse produced his **Morse code** method of communicating information over telegraph lines by a standard set of coded signals.

1847   George Boole introduced a shorthand notation (**Boolean algebra**) for working out two state logic (true or false) as originated by Aristotle.

1851   A small calculating machine with keys replacing push rods was shown at the Great Exhibition at Crystal Palace. It was not taken seriously by the visitors, who considered it a toy.

1857   Sir Charles Wheatstone produced a punched paper tape recorder for transmitting and receiving coded messages by telegraph line.

1863   A Swedish engineer succeeded in making a machine based on Babbage's difference engine. Georg Scheutz's automatic printing calculator produced accurate life insurance tables and was the forerunner of the modern 'National' type accounting machine, in design principles.

1870   F. J. Baldwin patented a cog wheel with variable length teeth for use in Leibniz type calculators. This enabled Colonel W. T. Odhner (in 1875) to produce calculating machines which were reliable yet lighter and smaller than was previously possible. The present day version of this is the Brunsviga calculating machine.

1876   Alexander Graham Bell patented the telephone which is currently being used via signal modulators or acoustic couplers to provide a high speed, reliable means of computer online data transmission.

Kelvin's mechanical analog machine

1876   A Scot, James Thomson, invented a device called a mechanical integrator which allowed gearing ratios to be continuously variable. This is important when using mechanical devices (cogs etc.) to represent an analogy of a real situation. This is the basis of analog computing and in the same year Lord Kelvin (Thomson's brother) proposed a form of mechanical **analog computer** known as a differential analyser for calculating tidal variations. This device is acknowledged as the immediate forerunner of modern analog computers.

1876   Cash registers were first introduced in this year. Today, with modifications to produce printed details of transactions in a special type font, cash registers are used as an immediate source of data capture for processing via optical character readers.

1880   Boucher in France produced a ten-key keyboard version of a printing calculator. In 1885 Alex Burroughs in America produced a full keyboard version, the first in a long line of Burroughs calculating machines.

Hollerith's punched cards

1887   A German immigrant to America, Herman Hollerith, revived the **punched card** principle of the Jacquard loom but this time using a much smaller card. He devised a series of machines to process information punched into the card using electromechanical techniques. In 1887 he used his machines to process statistics for the city of Baltimore and this was such a success that his equipment was chosen to process the data for the 1890 US census. By 1911 Hollerith machines were employed for processing the UK census figures. During this period cards held between 35–40 columns of data digits.

1917   The American Computing, Tabulating and Recording Company started to sell calculating equipment outside the United States and therefore changed its name to International Business Machines Ltd. (IBM).

1919   W. H. Eccles and F. W. Jordan patented an electrical device known as a bistable trigger. This is also known as a flip-flop circuit and was to be of prime importance in two later electronic developments, radar and the automatic electronic computer.

1928   Eighty-column punched cards, later to become a standard input/output medium for computers, were first introduced in this year.

Bush's mechanical differential analyser

1930   Vannevar Bush at the Massachusetts Institute of Technology (MIT) constructed a working mechanical differential analyser based on Lord Kelvin's proposals of 1876. This was the first modern mechanical analog computer made and produced a renewed interest in automatic computing. Variations of this machine were pursued until about 1942.

Turing's computer proposition

1936   Alan M. Turing, a British mathematician, gave a paper to the London Mathematical Society on 18th May 1936 propounding the general proposition of the modern computer. His paper *On Computable Numbers* defined the theory of a universal machine to carry out arbitrary calculations. His paper was published and was read by leading mathematicians and scientists of the day and when Turing visited America he discussed his ideas with John von Neuman at Princeton. Both Turing and von Neuman began developing computer theory until their research was interrupted by the second world war.

1939   Professor Howard Aiken of Harvard and George Stibitz of Bell Telephone Laboratories developed an idea for putting Turing's proposition into practice by means of a large automatic electromechanical calculator. This in essence was to be an electrically driven version of Babbage's analytical engine controlled by electrical relay and switch techniques as developed for punched card machines. In 1940 they approached IBM for technical assistance and work on the project commenced.

1941–   It is claimed that in 1941 Zuse in Germany constructed a machine of
1943   the type proposed by Aiken and Stibitz but this was destroyed by allied bombing.

In general during the war years all the top mathematicians and scientists were engaged on secret war work such as radar, atomics and electronics. Electronic theory was being developed which was to be incorporated into the emerging generations of computers.

During this period several electronic versions of Bush's differential analyser (1930) were produced.

Cybernetics theory

1943   At the Moore school of electrical engineering, University of Pennsylvania, J. Presper Eckert and John Mauchly had worked out an idea for a large machine, similar to the one being developed at Harvard, which would automatically calculate and print ballistic tables for the US army. By the end of the year a small relay-operated prototype Mark I had been constructed.

This year also saw the publication of three papers on the emerging science of cybernetics. The first was by Norbert Wiener, Arturo Rosenblueth and Julian Bigelow of MIT, another was by K. J. W. Craik at Cambridge and the third came from Warren McCulloch at Illinois University and Walter Pitts from MIT.

The first working automatic computer

1944   At Harvard the Aiken-Stibitz-IBM machine was completed. It was called an automatic sequence controlled calculator (ASCC) and has the distinction of being the first working automatic computer. It was not a computer as we know them today because it was not electronic and therefore was comparatively slow (multiplication took 4 seconds). Also it did not have electronic storage or jump instructions but was controlled in strict sequence by a punched paper tape program. Nevertheless, the machine worked very well and went on printing tables up to 1959, some of which are still in use.

Eckert and Mauchly at Pennsylvania were joined in this year by John von Neuman who had been working on electronic logic circuits. Progressing from the success of the Mark I they commenced building a larger machine called the Electronic Numerical Integrater and Computer (ENIAC).

The EDVAC report

1945   By the summer of 1945 ENIAC was part complete but von Neuman had already seen its limitations and in June he published the draft report on EDVAC (electronic discrete variable automatic computer), in which he laid down the design for an internally stored program machine with 1000 words of 10 decimal digits capacity.

In England, Alan Turing, fresh from war work on electronics and now at the National Physical Laboratories (NPL), put forward in the autumn the theory and proposals for building a computer of the type described by von Neuman. In the USA work started on a large aircraft simulator at MIT. This specialised computer was not to be complete until 1951.

The first automatic electronic computer

1946   Summer 1946 saw the completion of ENIAC at Pennyslvania. It was the first automatic electronic computer containing 18 000 valves and weighing 30 tons and having a cycle time of 200 μs. It was not however a stored program machine of the type used today having storage for only twenty, ten decimal digit words. It had to be programmed by setting switches and making many wired plug-board connections which was a very tedious business. ENIAC was installed at Aberdeen proving ground, Maryland and was put to work calculating ballistic tables. It was finally scrapped in 1958. Work now commenced on making von Neuman's proposed EDVAC machine.

Dr M. V. Wilkes of the Mathematics Laboratory, Cambridge made a visit to see ENIAC having become interested in computers after reading von Neuman's EDVAC report. On his return he began to work in collaboration with Dr Hartree and S. Gill on a stored program computer.

At Manchester University, F. C. Williams and T. Kilburn started working on the design of a machine which would store information on a cathode ray tube. This work proceeded at Manchester in close contact with Ferranti Ltd.

IBM, progressing from their collaboration in the Harvard ASCC, brought out the IBM 604 plug-board programmed, punch card computer. Between 1946 and 1960, 4000 models were sold all over the world.

1947   At Harvard a Mark II version of ASCC was produced. This was a larger faster version of the Mark I but was still a relay controlled electromechanical machine.

Turing's proposal to the NPL was given the go-ahead and with a team comprising Woodger, Alway, Wilkinson and Newman, work commenced on a machine called Version H in cooperation with the GPO.

Early in 1947, the large catering firm J. Lyons sent two representatives, Thompson and Standingford to visit the ENIAC installation at Pennyslvania. On their return they also investigated the work being done at Cambridge by Hartree and Wilkes. The purpose of these visits was to ascertain the potential of computers as applied to office work and on 20th October 1947 they published their report which led to a decision to build a machine that could perform data processing.

1948   During 1948 Lyons approached office machinery manufacturers with a view to purchasing such a machine but no manufacturer at that time was prepared to undertake the development work required.

At the NPL experimental work on Version H (which was never completed) proved that a larger machine was feasible and English Electric were called in to provide technical and production assistance. Work commenced on a machine to be called Pilot ACE.

In June 1948 at Manchester the first baby computer was completed. Although only a tiny prototype, this was the first computer built and actually working in Britain. Work was immediately started on two larger versions.

Also in this year the point contact transistor was invented. This was not reliable or powerful enough to be of use in computer circuits; and Claude Shannon a mathematician at Bell Telephone Laboratories defined the universal unit of information for data transmission–the bit (binary digit).

The first automatic electronic stored program computer

1949   In January, Lyons decided to build a machine in collaboration with Dr. Wilkes at Cambridge. J. Pinkerton was put in charge of the project. On 14th September Lyons electronic office (LEO) was named and work commenced with components and a new storage medium, magnetic tape being developed by Wayne Kerr and STC.

On 6th May 1949 the Cambridge computer EDSAC (electronic

delay storage automatic computer) was completed. This was the world's first automatic electronic stored program computer. It had a mercury delay line store of 16, 35 bit words and contained 3800 valves. Input and output were achieved by 15 cps, 5 track paper tape. On 23rd June the machine made its debut at the first European computer conference. From then on work was concentrated on developing a large program library.

At Manchester full details of the larger machines developed there were, in August, passed over to Ferranti, who had the necessary resources, to actually build.

1950   At Pennsylvania EDVAC (proposed in 1945) was finally built one year after the Cambridge machine which was inspired by von Neuman's report.

An unusual computer, Maddida (magnetic drum digital differential analyser) was built for Northrop Aircraft Inc. by Floyd Steel. This was a large programmable, digital, version of the analog electronic differential analysers (EDA) built during the war years. Although a very special purpose machine it is of interest as an early development of the **time sharing** properties of computers.

In May 1950 the NPL–Turing computer, Pilot ACE (automatic computing engine) first worked. It was given a press showing in December and was one of the first machines to earn money being used amongst other things in the design of the Comet aircraft. This computer like EDSAC had mercury delay line storage and from this were later developed a larger ACE computer and the GPO Mosaic machine.

By March EDSAC at Cambridge was working full time for university customers and late in 1950 a report (published as a book in 1951) was issued by Wilkes, Wheeler and Gill entitled *The Preparation of Programs for Electronic Digital Computers*. This was the first book on modern computer programming.

British Tabulating Machines (Hollerith) the major British punched card company had in 1949 been working on large punched card calculators. In 1950 they were joined by J. R. Womersley who had been working at NPL on the Pilot ACE project. At Birbeck College, A. D. Booth working on a shoestring budget had constructed a small machine with magnetic drum storage. A deal was made for BTM to develop this machine into a commercial computer in exchange for financial support for the project.

The first data processing computer–LEO 1

1951   BTM (Hollerith) and Powers Samas joined forces to form ICT and a team comprising Davis, Cox, Townsend and Bird began working on the hardware with Ashforth as programmer of the proposed magnetic drum computer. In late 1951 HECI (Hollerith electronic computer) was completed.

In February LEO I was undergoing trials and was demonstrated to Princess (now Queen) Elizabeth. On 30th November the first full scale job, Bakeries Sales Evaluation, was run on the 7000 valve, magnetic tape machine. This job continued to be run on this computer for the next 13 years. The next two years' work was concentrated on ironing out teething troubles and program development.

The first Ferranti Mark I was delivered and installed at Manchester University in June. This was the first general purpose computer available on general sale.

In America, Eckert and Mauchly of ENIAC completed UNIVAC I (Universal Analog Computer). This machine was used, like Hollerith's early punched card equipment, by the US Bureau of Census. Altogether it gave 73 000 hours of service before being scrapped. It was the first computer to have a compiler.

This year saw the completion of the MIT Whirlwind Computer-simulator. It had a 2k store and contained 5000 valves and 11 000 semiconductor diodes. A special purpose machine, it provided new standards of speed and reliability.

The junction transistor first appeared in 1951 but like the point contact transistor of 1948 was not reliable enough to be of use in computers.

1952–
1953
A period of consolidation and hard practical work followed the first frantic period of research breakthroughs. Office machine, scientific instrument and electrical equipment manufacturers started to join forces and put into practice the techniques and theories developed at the universities. Much work had to be done on programming software and in 1952 Hopper produced an important text in this field–*Introduction to Automatic Programming Methods*. In 1953, J. Backus (IBM) wrote the first FORTRAN compiler. At the business efficiency exhibition of 1953 ICT's second machine HEC 2 was introduced. Altogether 7 modified HEC 2s were built and delivered from 1954 onwards at a cost of £18 000 each.

On Christmas eve 1953 LEO I was put to work on the Cadby Hall payroll (1700 staff) and from then on continued working until shut down in January 1965. Development work was now commenced on LEO II.

The second generation

1955–
1956
In America Autonetics-Verdan produced a military computer TRANSVAC with transistor circuitry.

English Electric, in England, followed up the ACE computer with DEUCE (digital electronic universal calculating engine). This had both mercury delay line and magnetic drum storage and was the forerunner of the KD (e.g. KDF) series computers for scientific work.

Ferranti started to work on Pegasus for the NRDC using a nickel delay line store. W. S. Elliott was responsible for hardware whilst Christopher Strachey was working on software.

In 1955, magnetic core storage, was invented (Harvard and MIT). This was to replace all other types of immediate access store until the late 1960s.

ICT's HEC 4 was made in two versions the 1201 (1k store) and the 1202 (4k store). Altogether 124 were built and delivered. Elliotts produced the 401–405 series for scientific work using nickel delay line store.

In 1956 IBM introduced with the IBM 700 series the FORTRAN language and Honeywell's 400 and 800 series computers appeared.

In 1956 also the **planar silicon transistor** was discovered and UNIVAC II, the first commercial transistor machine, heralded the second generation of computers.

In the cybernetics field there was a meeting at Dartmouth College on machine intelligence. Those present included Marvin Minsky (MIT), Arthur Samuel (IBM), Allen Newell, Clifford Shaw and Herbert Simon (Rand) and John McCarthy (MIT).

1957–
1958

In 1957 ICT joined with GEC to form a subsidiary Computer Developments Ltd., which produced the ICT 1300 series computers.

The British Computer Society was formed.

At Manchester Ferranti replaced the Mark I machine with a Mercury computer, one of the machines in the Pegasus, Orion, Aries series which reached its peak with the large Atlas computer. The first LEO II was installed in 1957 and a total of 11 were sold, one of which was used with Ferranti and Lyons cooperation as the world's first computer bureau.

In July 1958 at Cambridge the father of LEO, EDSAC I was switched off and EDSAC II took over until it was scrapped in 1965.

IBM's second generation machines, the IBM 1400 series which were to scoop the world's medium size computer market were introduced in 1958.

In Switzerland, a conference between the European Association for Applied Mathematics and Mechanics and the American Association for Computing Machinery was held in Zurich. This was an attempt to find a universal standard programming language which culminated in ALGOL 60.

COBOL and ALGOL

1959–
1960

In 1959 the USA government held a meeting with computer users and manufacturers with the purpose of defining a standard programming language for data processing. The result of this meeting was the publication of a report defining the COBOL language.

Christopher Strachey at Oxford University gave a paper at a UNESCO conference proposing for the first time the theory of a time sharing system. This idea was also evolving at MIT's computation centre and was put forward by John McCarthy. Practical research work was commenced here by a team led by Professor F. J. Corbato.

The ALGOL 60 report was published in Paris in January 1960. This same year saw the introduction of the highly successful Elliott 803 computer.

UNIVAC III was introduced with thin film memory.

Time sharing and real time

1961–
1963

In November 1962 MIT's first model of a compatible time sharing system was unveiled. This theory had been put into practice in collaboration with IBM using an IBM 709 machine with four time sharing console terminals. The system was known as Project MAC (multiple access computer).

Late in 1961 the first LEO III, one of 44 sold altogether, was installed. This was the first commercially available multiprogramming computer and was the forerunner of the LEO 326 and 360 models.

1962 saw the first demonstration of computer light-pen drawing by two brothers Ivan and William Sutherland at MIT. In September, Bolt, Beranek and Newman at Cambridge, Massachusetts brought out a **time sharing system** using a PDP 1 computer. Meanwhile the US government had adopted the Project MAC scheme and provided funds for large scale development of time sharing under Professor Robert Fano.

Virtual memory (paging) was implemented on Ferranti Atlas in 1963.

On the hardware scene the first integrated logic circuits were being used in military equipment such as the Autonetics–Monica, AC Spark Plug–Magic, General Electric A212 and Honeywell's Alert.

Minicomputers such as Hughes HCH 2 and Burroughs D210 were developed for aerospace applications.

Applications of computers were now increasing rapidly and the first large scale, real-time system was the Sabre reservation system for American Airlines, New York. Lockheed Missiles developed a large automatic data collection system with 25 terminals covering a 300 mile radius and Westinghouse installed the beginnings of a fully integrated system in the form of a giant automatic message switching complex.

In April 1963 a new company English Electric LEO Computers was formed and at Santa Monica (USA) SDC, an offshoot of the Rand organisation, started a time sharing system.

The third generation

1964–
1967

Digital Equipment Corporation introduced their first minicomputer, the PDP 6.

In May 1964 Dartmouth College (USA) commenced time sharing with a system based on General Electric computers.

By 1965 various universities in America including Stanford, Illinois and Florida were deep in research into computer aided instruction.

1965/6 saw the introduction of the third generation of computers comprising software compatible families of machines with interchangeable hardware options. Based on the Ferranti-Packard of Canada FP 6000 machine ICT brought out the ICT 1900 series.

National Computer Centre was set up in 1965.

The first commercial minicomputers, such as DEC PDPs appeared in 1966.

The first commercial machines with integrated circuits were introduced, including the IBM 360 series, RCA Spectra 70 (upon which the English Electric LEO Marconi System 4 was based) and the Honeywell 2200 series.

1968–1969	Following a process of rationalisation of the British computer industry, ICL was formed by a merger of ICT and English Electric with the government and the Plessey company taking part interest.

Database report group CODASYL was set up.

The fourth generation–micros

1970	Intel produced the 4004, a 4 bit word length silicon chip for a calculator manufacturer. This was later developed into the 8 bit 8008–the first **microprocessor** computer.
1972	Honeywell 2000 series marketed. This was a specifically communications oriented series. Intel produced a scaled up version of the 4004, the 4040, which is applied in the field of personal games.
1973	The Post Office started an experimental switched service network. General Automation Company introduced large scale integrated circuit versions of previously successful minicomputers. Intel brought out 8080, the basis of early personal computing hardware. This was closely followed by the Motorola 6800 and Zilog Z80.
	Floppy discs and cartridge tape storage introduced.
1974	ICL brought out 2900 series–a high level language, user oriented system.
1975	A Government White Paper on *Computers and Privacy* published. In the US personal computing really got underway with the publication in the magazine *Popular Electronics* of the design for Altair 8800 based on the Intel 8080.
1977	The arrival of computer chess in the UK. The start of the micro explosion. Introduction of the 16 bit word length micros. Expectations of the micro going into homes for the control of heating systems, model railways, cookers, etc. The computer comes to society in the same way that the electronic hand calculator has. A great impact expected for the small business–anyone who can afford a cash register or typewriter. Implications also in the fields of education and training. Mainframe manufacturers' sales diminishing.
1978	Only time can decide what is of historical interest but with the

computer scene changing almost daily, a subjective review of matters at the end of 1978 is offered as some indication of the future.

In general terms it is microprocessors and applications that are hitting the headlines. The 'big' names, IBM, ICL, etc. still crop up from time to time with the introduction of a new small business range or some university collaboration research (e.g. array processors) but on the whole it is the microprocessor manufacturers and the large software houses who have their names published alongside those of politicians and trades union bosses arguing over whether the micro will create mass redundancies or provide even more work. The general consensus seems to agree that even with the UK government entering the micro manufacturing field (INMOS and its proposed 64k RAM chip) the future for Britain lies in software expertise, leaving the hardware to the US and Japan. Both IBM and Phillips announced a laser disc storage system towards the end of the year.

1978 in the UK saw the introduction of the PET stand-alone 8k 'personal' computer (see Figure 90), the colour graphics APPLE, the NASCOM kit and the hi-fi shop TANDY TRS 80 amongst others. Development to date appears to have been as follows:

The 1970 Intel 4004 led to the Intel 8080 upon which the following 1978 available machines are based–SOL 20, ALTAIR, HEATH H8, EXTEL MICROFILE, LIMROSE MICROTUTOR, IMSAI.

The Intel 8080 led to the Zilog Z80 upon which the following are based–CROMEMCO Z2, MICROS, TANDY TRS 80, NASCOM 1, CASU SUPER C, RESEARCH MACHINES 380Z, VECTOR MZ, SORCERER, HORIZON, COMPUCORP MKII.

The 1973 Motorola 6800 provided the basis for–NEWBURY 77/68, MSI 6800, SWTPC 6800, CROFTON LMI.

A development from the Motorola 6800 was the MOS Technology 6500 series, the basis of–PET 2001, APPLE II, AIM 65, KIM, ITT 2020, SYM 1.

Based on the National Semiconductors SC/MP2 chip, two low priced kits the MK 14 and SCRUMPI are available.

Trends 1979 onwards

By the end of 1978, the following 16 bit microprocessors had been announced–Intel 8086, Zilog Z800, Motorola 68000, Fairchild 9440, Rockwell Super 65 (development of MOS 6502). National Semiconductors announced the single chip 8070 processor with 64k of RAM included. Although the 8 bit micros listed could have add-on memory, most had a limitation of around 32k due to the structural limits of addressing store locations. It is claimed that the 8086 can address 1 megabyte and the Z800 can address up to 8 megabytes.

In terms of memory chips, the following have announced the impending production of 64k RAMs–Inmos, Texas Instruments,

Fujitsu, ITT and GEC/Fairchild. The US Defence Department announced research into a 2 megabit RAM.

Problems of standardisation for interconnection of processor, store and peripherals had not been sorted out. Bus specifications included the Mostek 56 way, the E78 Europa, the S50 SWTPC and, probably the most sucessful, Altair/MITS S100. The very popular Commodore PET used an IEEE 488 interface whilst most printers, floppy disks and other terminals in the UK used the V24/RS232. The problems of interfacing to PRESTEL terminals looms on the horizon.

In the software field, most micros used BASIC with variations from 2k Tiny BASIC to 8k or even 16k Extended BASIC. The smaller kits were only available for hex machine code programming whilst at the other end of the scale Micro COBOL and versions of ALGOL and FORTRAN were being offered. However it seemed possible that PASCAL would eventually replace BASIC, particularly with the introduction of the 16 bit machines. A large market for programs, particularly games and small business software, had developed with many small suppliers offering listings or cassette tape versions at between £5 to £10 a time.

The reality at the end of 1978 would appear to be that for between £40 and £300 hobbyists and others can obtain a keyboard/processor which they can plug into their TV and cassette tape, program in hex or Basic or buy £5 taped programs and play games or learn programming. For between £500 and £1500 educationalists and owners of very small businesses can buy a ready-built computer system consisting of a video display, keyboard, 8–16k boxed processor and two cassette tape backing store capable of running fair sized and complex BASIC programs to do real, useful business work but lacking a print facility and running at tediously slow cassette tape speeds. To enable these systems to be really useful to the average small business (or to be used as a local processing facility in a distributed processing net of a larger company) an upgrade of at least £1000 is needed to add on floppy disk and printer. To be quite realistic a small business system with the above and add-on storage for other language and software requirements would cost between £3000 and £5000. Microprocessor based systems supporting BASIC, LISP, PASCAL, Assembler, FORTRAN, COBOL and other software with up to 256k memory and 40 megabyte hard disc storage and running up to 12 timesharing stations are available at a cost of about £25 000.

Apart from the ever increasing power and decreasing costs of both hardware and now even software, the other major feature dominating the end of 1978 is the impending impact of **videotext/viewdata/teletext**–the provision of information databanks and processing power via the public television and telephone networks. Apart from some rather ordinary public information (share prices, weather, etc.) transmitted by the television companies and some tantalising demonstrations by the Post Office Prestel service, little impact has yet been made by this mode of computer technology. Its promise is high and speculation even higher. If all these promises are fulfilled. . . . ?

Assessment tasks

1 Write a 1000 word essay on 'The use of computers in the year 2000 AD'.

2 Draw a diagram to illustrate the ten most significant developments in the field of computing to date. Give your reasons.

3 What advantages have computers brought to mankind in the period from 1946 to date? Support your answers by the results of a survey carried out on a representative sample of your local population.

Module 3
Systems analysis and design

Unit 11
The systems analysis environment

Learning objective

To be able to show how the discipline known as systems analysis is one of the many problem solving techniques which have been developed throughout history to improve the effectiveness of man's activities. To be able to define the role of the systems analyst in relation to the business as a whole and the other members of the EDP department. To understand the requirements imposed upon the analyst in terms of the methods and performance standards he is expected to attain and to be able to define the control standards he must build into the systems he designs. To be able to explain the projects an analyst may be called upon to perform and the areas of potential improvement in which he will work.

The historical environment

Man has an inbuilt curiosity which drives him to attempt new activities, in addition to those activities which he performs to fulfil his needs. As each need is satisfied, his curiosity invents new needs for him to pursue. Often, he will attempt to justify these activities in terms of progress or as a search for improvement of his living conditions. But, without a definitive explanation of what is and is not good for mankind, the improvements produced by these activities are open to question. Did the Industrial Revolution bring good or evil to mankind? What are the benefits of space travel? However much argument is generated by questions such as these, there is no denying that one of the basic drives of mankind is a quest for perfection. This is the basis of all religion, the need to be perfect and, thus, good and, hence, define a lifestyle for attaining goodness.

An offshoot of this drive for perfection, is the desire to define not only what activities man should be performing (the fields of philosophy, religion and politics) but also to describe how best to achieve these aims. Once an aim has been defined, then an activity can be designed to achieve it. Activities require resources, both prime resources to be manipulated and producer resources to do the work. Resources are usually hard to come by and even if they are not scarce they require work to obtain them. It is therefore considered wise to use resources efficiently. Throughout man's history there have been attempts to define how work should best be performed in the interests of effectiveness (achieving the required aims) and efficiency (economy of resources). In Plato's *Republic* there is a description of what we should now call the division of labour. Leonardo da Vinci spent much time designing ways of improving work with the help of machinery. From the middle of the 17th century, mechanisation began to play an increasing role in the extension of man's physical abilities. Science became respectable and in 1662 the Royal Society was formed. With the growth of the clock industry in the 1650s, through the inventions of the horse drawn hoe (1714), the weaving fly-shuttle (1733) and various mining engine pumps (early 18th century), the Industrial Revolution was underway. A major factor in bringing this about was the increasing use of the scientific approach to problems, that of analysing a situation and searching in a disciplined way for alternatives. Early examples of the application of this approach to the study of working methods were Diderot's *Encyclopedie* (1751), which contains a descriptive breakdown of a number of jobs, Perronet's glossary of terms used in the pin making industry (1762), and James Watt's studies of work flow and factory planning (1795). By the end of the 19th century, these early attempts to control and improve the industrial processes had evolved to the status of scientific management with the work of F. W. Taylor (1898, Bethlehem Steel), the pioneer of work measurement, Frank Gilbreth (motion study), Atkinson, Gantt and Bedaux. By the 1930s, work study, as applied to production, was a well-established productivity improvement technique.

During the second world war, the need for effectiveness and efficiency in administrative procedures and office work began to demand attention. It was found that much of the technology of work study, fact finding, charting, questioning, timing and so on, could also be applied to paperwork situations with good effect. In addition to these methods, new techniques, particularly in the fields of organisation theory, ergonomics and human relations, were being developed. This work study in the office, became known as **organisation and methods** and by the early 1950s was firmly established as an additional management tool.

The 1950s also saw the introduction of the electronic computer into the field of business data processing and the rise of a new breed of specialist called the **computer programmer**. At first, this was a person who knew the intricacies of the machinery and conducted the whole job of computerising the business procedures. With the spread of the machines and the simplification of the job of programming, it was found desirable to employ people with a good knowledge of business to design the systems to be computerised and then to pass the work over to a machine specialist programmer. During the same period, advances in other disciplines, particularly pure science and engineering, had given rise to a new area of interest, **systems theory**. This soon proved to be of such universal application that it began to be adopted in almost all fields of investigatory activity. It was found to be a particularly useful way of looking at the activities found in business data processing, especially as the computer itself epitomises the essential ingredients of a system—input, activity, rules and output. By the 1960s, the term **systems analysis** was well-established as meaning the job performed by the person investigating data processing procedures with a view to transferring the processing of these to the computer. The people doing this job made use of any of the techniques of work study, organisation study and method study that they found useful together with specialist techniques developed by the early computer programmers.

Today, systems analysis is applied in many spheres. Biology, economics, electronics, sociology, all have their own specialist systems analysts. Analysis is not the end-product of this endeavour but is only a means towards the design and installation of more effective and efficient systems. The data processing systems analyst is the latest in a long line of people attempting to do this.

A definition of a systems analyst employed in EDP might read as follows: 'A data processing systems analyst is a mature, ethical person who applies his abilities and experience of business systems analysis and design methodology and data processing to the scientific investigation, analysis and solution of business system problems. To do this he will design new systems and select optimum processing methods which are firstly the most effective and then the most efficient for the greatest possible overall business productivity.'

The organisational environment

Theoretically, there are two major parts of a computer department: the part concerned with processing data (the operating and control sections) and the part concerned with investigating potential computer work and converting it if justified (the systems and programming sections).

To be logical, these two parts should be located in separate places in an organisation, the processing part under the resource management function and the investigation and design part under the systems management function. However, in practice, it is normal to have both parts under one manager as one department, and as this should provide a general, unbiased service to the organisation as a whole, the best organisational location for the computer department is in the productivity improvement function, heading up directly to the management services director.

The following brief outlines should help put the work of the systems analyst into perspective in relation to his colleagues.

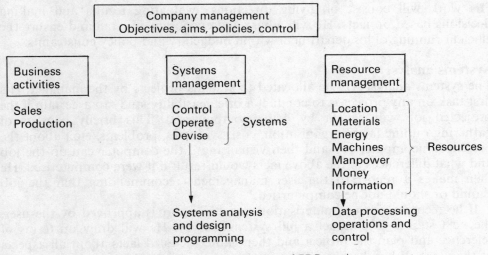

Figure 123   Logical location of EDP sections

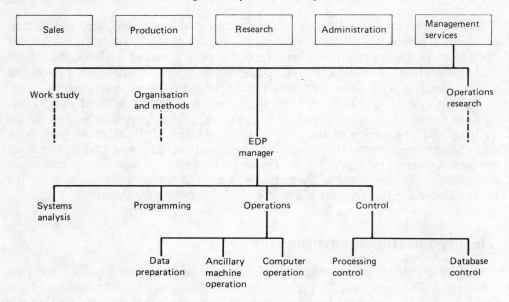

Figure 124   The EDP department

EDP manager

The EDP manager is responsible for the management of the electronic data processing department. He must plan, organise, coordinate, control and motivate the resources of his department to achieve the departmental aims of the business as a whole.

In practical terms the departmental aim is likely to be the employment of computing hardware and techniques to increase productivity by eliminating bottlenecks, solving problems, reducing costs and improving information wherever this is needed. The manager must select and evaluate potential computer work and deploy his staff and machines in the most productive way. His work will consist of giving directions, evaluating results and making decisions based on facts. He will advise and encourage his staff and ensure the efficient running of his department within budgetary and policy constraints.

Systems analyst

The systems analyst will be allocated to systems projects by the manager. His first task on any project is to conduct a brief feasibility study to ascertain if the projected job will benefit by being computerised. This briefly consists of gathering outline facts (organisation, costs, volumes, problems, etc.) about the present noncomputer job and then visualising if the computer can do the job and what differences in the above facts would result if it were computerised. He then makes a report to the user management recommending that the job should or should not be computerised.

If he recommends computerisation and his report is approved by the user, the next step is to conduct a full systems survey. He will draw up terms of reference and plan the project and then gather detailed facts about all aspects of the work. When he has all the facts he will analyse them to determine the minimum amount of processing required to obtain the necessary results. He then designs the new processing system using the computer in place of conventional machines. When his design is complete he documents it and passes the specification to the programmer. While the programs are being written, the analyst will concentrate on the noncomputer parts of the system such as training staff, producing manuals, organising stationery supplies. When the programs have been written and tested, and the noncomputer procedures are proven, the analyst will test the system as a whole until the user and the auditor are satisfied that it produces the required results correctly. He then hands the job over to the operating department and starts work on his next project.

Programmer

The programmer works in a team with the systems analyst on system projects. When the new computer system specification is passed to the programmer by the analyst, he will identify each computer run and proceed to write a program for it, if it cannot be covered by some existing standard software. The work of writing a program consists firstly, and most importantly, of solving the problem, that is to say, deciding what processing steps must be carried out and in which sequence, in order to produce the resultant output required by the specification. When he knows how to do this, the programmer expresses it in the form of a program logic flow chart, after which he codes each logic step into a suitable computer programming language.

Once written the program must be compiled (tested for errors of language and translated to machine code) and then data tested. When the tests prove that the program both produces correct results with good data and rejects bad data, then the programmer documents the programs and produces operating instructions. Each program thus completed is then ready for the full systems testing carried out by the analyst.

Data preparation operator

Data can be prepared for input into the computer in many ways. However, most of these involve the operation of a keyboard, the data being read from a source document in much the same manner as copy typing. The machine may, as a result of the key depression, punch holes in punched cards or in paper tape or it may make magnetic impressions on magnetic discs or tapes. It may, if the objective is verification, merely sense if a hole or magnetic spot is present or not. Whatever the medium, the job of data preparation consists of loading the machine, depressing keys according to the data on a source document and then unloading the resultant computer medium.

Ancillary machine operator

Some ancillary machines are used in data preparation after the computer input medium has been encoded. This could be to prepare the data further by sorting it or merging it or getting it ready in some other way for online input into the computer. Other ancillary machines process the results output by the computer before they are passed on to the user department. Still other ancillary machines are media conversion machines e.g. magnetic disc to printout.

Whatever the machine, the operator's job is that of machine loader, minder and unloader.

Computer operator

Computer operators normally work in pairs and often may have to do shift work if the computer is run, for economic reasons, twenty-four hours a day. They will work to a fairly rigid schedule, planned by the operations manager, saying what jobs must be run at any particular time. The work on any production run will consist of obtaining the operating instructions for that job and, from these, identifying which files, programs, input data and output media are required. The programs and files will be obtained from the database control, the input data and the output media from the processing control. The various peripherals are then loaded, the program read into the IAS and the start command given. From this point the operator must mind the computer, read any messages output at the operator's console and take the required action (e.g. load more input, change files, call the engineer) as indicated on his operating instructions.

When the job is finished, the files must be returned to the database and the input data and result information handed over to the processing control section.

Processing control

This is a clerical job concerned with two main aspects: ensuring the source data arrives on time and the output information gets back to the right people at the right time; and making sure that no errors occur or additions and/or deletions take place in data from the moment it arrives in the department until the results go back to the user department. The main controls are schedules, log books and control slips which are checked, written and maintained by the control clerks. The actual work involved may vary from company to company depending on the control procedures employed.

Database control

This work is similar to that of an ordinary librarian except that instead of books, the controller looks after files containing either programs or master and reference file data held usually on reels of magnetic tape and/or on exchangeable magnetic disks. These must be stored, retrieved, booked out and in according to a safe and accurate control system. In addition the librarian looks after blank file media for use in intermediate processing, and keeps records of wear and error rate on each physical file for replacement and maintenance purposes.

If the database is one large nonredundant file being shared by many functional application users, it is desirable to have some organisational function to take an overall viewpoint and act as arbiter between functional interests. This function is that of database administrator and will include a database manager and the necessary clerical support. Aspects of physical and organisational security will fall to this section, including the provision of good, standard documentation, and in particular the compilation of data directories to provide an indication of what data is available on the database and how the user can access it.

Introducing change

The systems analyst provides a service to the management of other departments in the business, who have the ultimate responsibility for the effectiveness and efficiency of the systems they operate. To improve these systems implies making changes and the analyst must know how to introduce change with the cooperation of the members of the user departments.

To introduce change successfully the analyst must not present any direct conflict or problem to the group but starting from current group attitudes generate a creative atmosphere by introducing new information which will stimulate the group members to think. As soon as the project is announced some information will be circulating in the group. It is the analyst's job to ensure that these facts are both accurate and reassuring.

The facts that must be covered with particular care are:

(a) Public image of computers–usually distrust and fear
(b) User's perception of analyst's role–possibly as an inhuman efficiency expert
(c) Company history of employee relations–fear of redundancy
(d) User's own suitability for job–both present and future work
(e) Previous computer systems–the effect on previous employees
(f) Purpose of present system–how this affects staff attitudes
(g) Effectiveness of present system–in terms of job satisfaction

Consider how change can be introduced:

Authority

If you want a subordinate (say a child or a member of staff) to do something you can simply tell him to do it using your authority to ensure it is done. What if he does not want to do it? You can force him by threat or use of punishment, but then you will need to supervise constantly to ensure he actually does it. He will also hardly behave with any great enthusiasm. If he is strongly against doing it he will also, if forced to submit, find some way of retaliation by direct or by indirect sabotage of your objectives. The systems analyst acts in an advisory capacity and does not have authority over the staff operating or managing the system. Even if this were so how could authority be of use in trying to influence the behaviour of superiors? The use of authority as a means of introducing change does not work.

Manipulation or sales techniques

Another approach has been developed as an adaptation of sales techniques and is frequently used by practising analysts. This is typified by the 'make them think it's their idea' attitude. There is no doubt that up to a point this approach works. People are susceptible to manipulation and can be persuaded to do things they would not normally want to do. There comes a time, however, when people realise they are being used and react accordingly. Professional ethics apart, this approach does not work and is therefore not effective.

Collaboration

The reason for the failure of both the authoritarian and manipulative approaches is the fact that no-one can change anybody else. People must change themselves. The only effective role that the analyst can play is that of one who shows the way and helps people to change themselves. Change involves learning and we only learn when we assimilate the new behaviour into our personality. This third approach is one of collaboration with the staff concerned. The analyst reveals and explains the problem and assists the user to understand and select the alternatives available to him. Providing there are benefits in terms of need satisfaction to the user in adopting a course of action, he will readily accept the change because he wants to. It is the job of the analyst to demonstrate how the objectives of any proposed system align with the user's own objectives. The collaboration approach works in practice on the basis of two heads being better than one and that, if treated as a responsible adult, the user can, with the analyst's help, be as useful as the analyst himself in solving problems. If people are put in situations of conflict with no way out they will become hostile whilst if the analyst shows the alternative solutions to them they can make adjustments and learn to change (Unit 4).

The standards environment

Just as for other departments, there is a need in the data processing department for some rules and guidelines as to the quality of the work performed there. In general, these rules are needed to:
(1) Protect all of the interests of the company and individuals concerned
(2) Effectively communicate ideas and enable speedy development and adoption
(3) Ensure the problem-free interchangeability of staff.
  To achieve these aims, each computer department should adopt and formalise a set of rules and procedures that conform as closely as possible with the relevant industry, national and international standards. These rules will be brought together to form a departmental manual covering standards for legal requirements, audit requirements–and management requirements.
  As with any system of rules, it is not enough to just state the targets required. The aims of the standards manual must be incorporated into a working system of control involving regular reporting and appraisal.
  The standards covered by the departmental manual should be devised
    to protect equally against errors both against and in favour of the company in all data processing systems
    to protect against: customers not paying accounts; suppliers making unjust claims; the criminal use of information gained by authorised staff; fraudulent staff; careless or lazy staff
    to protect: customers and suppliers against fraud or error in the company; user departments against fraud or error by the DP department; DP staff from unjust claims or dismissal
    to ensure compliance with current legislation
    to provide for the requirements of both internal and external auditors
    to provide for management control: to reduce the effects of labour turnover; to enable economic future planning; to enable economic review and amendment of systems and programs; to enable work to be fairly and economically distributed amongst DP staff; to provide performance standards for scheduling, costs and budgets, staff selection, review and development, machine utilisation, management control of all resource utilisation.

The standards manual

To produce a standards manual and system which will achieve the above, rules are needed for the following specific areas:

the source data
the files maintained
the programs used ⎫ work
processing the data
distributing the data
data processing staff ⎫ resources
data processing machines and environment

With regard to the work performed by the department the standards are concerned with accuracy, timeliness, relevance and security. Standards covering the resources of the department are aimed at ensuring high effectiveness and utilisation together with flexibility and good communication.

The contents of the standards manual will cover:

Organisation
 Company
 Department
 Aims and responsibilities
 Terms of reference–for job functions
Department administration
 Discipline
 Secretarial facilities
 Training and development
 Planning and reporting
 Records and files maintained
Department resources
 Hardware specifications
 Software specifications and manuals
 Sample forms and records
Working methods for:
 Systems analysts
 Programmers
 Data preparation and operators
 Control clerks
Performance standards for:
 Machines and equipment
 Systems analysts
 Programmers
 Data preparation and operators
 Control clerks

The working methods standards will be used by the staff in the daily performance of their respective jobs. They will contain not only instructions as to which charts, symbols, etc., are used but also what additional procedures must be built into the systems and programs they devise to ensure compliance with the legal and audit requirements of accuracy and security.

Resource	Target	Methods standards covering	Performance standards covering
EDP manager	To achieve an effective and efficient department	Planning Organising Coordinating Controlling Motivating Innovating	Budgets Throughput User satisfaction Labour turnover
Systems analyst	To successfully design and implement effective and efficient data processing systems	Problem definition Problem analysis Solution synthesis Solution implementation Amendments	Project duration User satisfaction System reliability and efficiency System security and accuracy System cost/effectiveness
Programmer	To successfully design and implement effective and efficient computer programs	Program design Program coding Program testing Documentation Amendments	Project duration Program accuracy Program efficiency Program duration Program storage utilisation
Data preparation clerk	To prepare error free data on a suitable computer input medium	Data preparation Data verification	Throughput Errors
Ancillary machine operator	To produce correctly organised computer input data, output results and storage information on a suitable medium	Data preparation Machine operation	Throughput Errors
Computer operator	To produce error free result information from input and stored data and computer software	Housekeeping and logging Machine operation	Job throughput Machine utilisation Errors
Processing control clerk	To ensure the timely availability of error free source data and distribute computer results accurately within time requirements	Data acquisition Data control Information distribution	Holdups Routing errors Timeliness Data errors
Database control clerk	To ensure the availability and security of stored master and reference data with maximum ease of access	Database security Database availability Database accuracy	Unauthorised access Retrieval speed Loss and corruption of data
Machines	100% utilisation	Machine operation	Machine utilisation Breakdowns Malfunctions

Figure 125   Methods and performance standards

Using standards

The use of standards which measure the actual utilisation of the machines and staff of the department enable the EDP manager

to gauge training effectiveness and speed

to evaluate potential DP staff

to amend, progress and plan current DP jobs

to project future applications

to project future DP machine and staff requirements

to establish realistic budgets

to estimate cost of new development

to estimate cost of proposed changes

to introduce full cost accounting control.

In order to obtain reliable figures to use as target standards the manager or appointed analyst will

develop initial standard by estimates; judgement; experience and measurement

plan, using initial standards

record actual values and compare

take action–correct failures for future performance or amend initial standards.

He will continue to adjust the standard used until it is found by experience to be correct.

The areas to be included for analysis of machine utilisation may simply be 'working' or 'not working', or alternatively a more complex breakdown such as the following might be used: productive time; assembly time; set up time; testing time; preventative maintenance; down time; maintenance or failure; rerun time; demonstrations; training; idle time.

When setting utilisation standards for staff it is necessary to break down the work into segments of like elements involved, e.g. fact finding, logic diagram preparation, and then by estimation or work measurement techniques evolve a standard elemental time. Each task allocated to the staff can then be allotted a standard based on an analysis of the estimated number of elements involved multiplied by the standard elemental time. It is important to make the standard realistic by allowing for outside factors such as interruption and unavailability.

System control

In addition to the methods and performance standards with which the analyst must comply, he will also be concerned with controls to be built into his system and its operating environment. The aspects to be covered by these controls are

physical resources–buildings and services; machines and equipment; unused media and supplies; staff; media holding information

know-how–staff expertise; software

data and information–held on physical media.

These require protection against a variety of hazards.

accidental loss–fire, flood, etc.
deliberate loss–theft
accidental damage–general accidents
deliberate damage–vandalism, sabotage
accidental error–corruption of data
deliberate error–fraud
unauthorised access–invasion of privacy, espionage, blackmail.
The controls and safeguards required to combat these hazards must be

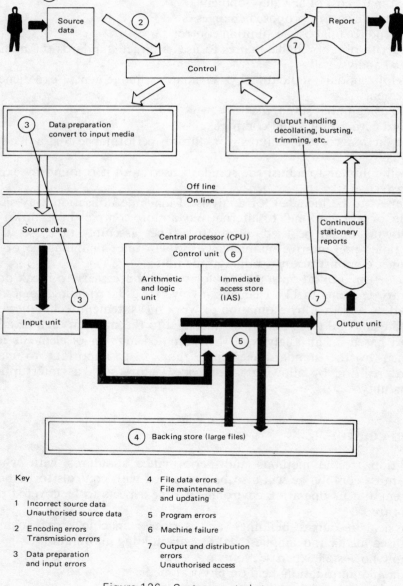

Figure 126   System control stages

adopted both during systems development and operational running. They include

> environmental controls–fire detection and prevention; safes and locks; alarm devices; air conditioning
>
> organisational controls–guards and supervision; documentation, log books and passwords; training and work scheduling; staff segregation and rotation; stand-by facilities; database control, indexing and labelling.
>
> system and software controls—see below.

The environmental and organisational controls need to be enforced in all the departments concerned–the source department, the processing department and the user department. The stages requiring special attention for the introduction of systems and software controls are illustrated in Figure 126.

The types of control employed in a system include

> source data validation–authorisation, credibility, completeness, legibility, precision
>
> transmission–parity, transposition, transcription
>
> encoding–check digits, format, picture
>
> data preparation–visual or mechanised verification
>
> input validation run–control totals, sequence checks, check digit, range limit, parity, parameter checks
>
> file security–physical and data labels, duplicates and generations, journals, file audit, block and record counts, parity, maintenance and update, suspense accounts, balance totals
>
> program security–system and program testing and documentation, program library security, link and interface testing
>
> hardware control–failure aborts, dumps and restarts, parity
>
> output control–common data cross checking, exception reporting, range limits, identification, distribution checklists.

The workload environment

The analyst will be working within organisational and control constraints to employ his productivity techniques on a variety of problems delegated to him by the EDP manager. The most common type of job he will be called upon to perform is the investigation of an existing man/machine processed system with a view to putting this on to the computer if benefits can be obtained by so doing.

Most systems can be computerised but the question of the advisability of this has still to be proved in each individual case. As a general rule, the use of a computer is practical:

(1) where there is a large volume of data involved in substantial calculations

(2) where the speed of result output is more important than the cost in man hours

(3) where the problem is too large or too complex for it to be solved by normal manual processing

(4) where there is a large enough workload and frequent enough processing to justify the expense

(5) where large data files that remain fairly static are used in normal updating procedures

(6) any case where the benefits can be quantified and on evaluation shown to outweigh the cost.

The main areas of work in which computers are employed are:

Calculation

Calculation involves solving equations and formulae for scientists, mathematicians, engineers and technicians. The main advantages of the computer here are: certain new methods of processing are possible; calculations of greater magnitude can be processed; far greater speed of calculation. Time shared, immediate access systems or local microprocessors are usually best in these situations.

Information processing

Serial processing–where large volumes of data involving limited calculation, heavy input and output, use of backing files, are processed on a regular basis, e.g. payroll, ledger accounting. Magnetic tape file, batch processing is normally used.

Data arrangement–regular or irregular processing of large volumes of input for combination and analysis with no files, e.g. sampling, questionnaires, statistics. Large IAS, fast input and output machines are required.

Information retrieval–large data files of information interrogated to provide content or index to content on a random basis, e.g. ticket reservation, libraries. Large direct access files are required with fast interactive terminal facilities. For frequently changing file contents, a real-time system is most suitable but expensive.

Process control–automation of machines and processes to provide automatic response to input stimuli, e.g. furnace control, drilling tools, automatic guidance systems. This is usually outside the scope of the systems analyst, using hybrid digital controlled analog devices of a specialised nature.

Evaluation and choice making–decisions and planning based on collection and analysis of past results. Usually requiring mathematically based programs to calculate probability of future events for various courses of action, e.g. sales forecasting, network analysis, production planning. A fast processor with large IAS and minimum peripherals is usually sufficient. VDUs and graph plotters may be useful.

Simulation–using mathematical data models to represent real situations and so observe the results of changing various parameters singly or in combination, e.g. structural design, management games, vehicle routing, profit optimisation, etc. The configuration here will vary according to the particular problem simulated ranging from desk analog computers for structural analysis, through normal digital batch processors to specialised peripherals such as light pen terminals, etc.

Computer bureaus services

In addition to the normal systems project, the analyst is quite often asked to provide help with the introduction of computing facilities into an area which has neither an in-house machine nor access to one in another part of the organisation. This may lead him to recommend that a computer and its attendant resources are installed in that area or he may suggest that a computer bureau should be employed.

Any body or organisation offering any service related to computing, either as a main line of business or as a sideline, can be considered a computer bureau in the broadest sense. These generally fall into four main categories: professional computer bureaus; computer manufacturers; private firms with spare capacity; universities, local government and public bodies.

Some bureaus specialise in a single service, others provide a complete range. Five main categories of service can be defined.

Hardware
(1) Hands on, do it yourself, workshop service. Machine available to be worked by own staff
(2) Closed shop processing service. Data is taken to the bureau, processed by bureau staff, and results returned
(3) Time sharing. The customer has terminals on his own premises linked by phone to the bureau's machine. Two methods of working are possible: interactive working, where the computer works under the command of the user at the terminal; remote batch job entry, where the terminal is used to transmit batches of data to the bureau for offline processing and return of results via the terminal or postal or courier service at some later time
(4) Media conversion. Bureau will convert data from one medium to another, e.g. data preparation, card to magnetic tape conversion.
(5) Specialised hardware services, e.g. output on to microfilm MICR, graphics.

Software
(1) The writing of operating systems and compilers to order
(2) The writing of specialised package programs
(3) Writing user programs to order
(4) Providing the use of software packages and library routines.

Consultancy
(1) Advice on buying and installing an in-house computer
(2) Investigations into productivity of computer usage
(3) Brokerage. Arranging for computer time, software and secondhand machinery.
(4) Providing systems analysis and/or programming assistance
(5) Computer information services
(6) Facilities management—running customer's computer installation
(7) Troubleshooting—emergency service.

Computer staffing
(1) Staff training—punching, operating, programming, systems, clerical
(2) Appreciation courses—staff and management
(3) Selection and placement services.

Security and courier service
Note: in addition some bureaus provide a full printing, duplicating and mailing service for clients.

Bureaus–advantages and disadvantages

A detailed list of problems in which bureaus can be of assistance would include
(1) computer staff shortages
(2) expansion of computer workload
(3) seasonal peak periods and other workload fluctuations
(4) where expensive specialised computing hardware is required
(5) where subject expertise is required
(6) at times of new file creation
(7) when a bureau is in a more suitable geographical location than the customers own facilities
(8) when the customer's equipment is out of date or under-powered
(9) preparing programs and files prior to the customer getting his own facilities
(10) where there is some computing requirement but not enough to justify the customer obtaining his own facilities (in-house)
(11) Where a time and/or cost saving can be made by using an already available software package
(12) to gain expertise prior to the customer obtaining his own facilities
(13) as a stand-by at times of breakdown of in-house facilities.

Against these advantages of using a bureau, the following problems should be considered.
(1) The service is not under the control of the customer and can therefore be inflexible and impersonal
(2) As bureaus need to make a profit, their services might be more expensive than in-house facilities
(3) A facility used by many customers (possibly competitors) can give rise to problems of secrecy, privacy and security
(4) Like an off the peg suit, bureaus can provide compromise solutions to individual problems
(5) Relying on someone else's facilities and know-how can prevent the building up of experience in the customer organisation
(6) Some bureaus in the past have proved unreliable and have even gone out of business.

Choosing a bureau

You do not buy the first car you are offered, but shop around for a good reliable bargain. Similarly, in selecting a computer bureau, it is as well to proceed in a logical manner.
(1) Decide what jobs you have for the bureau, if they will be regular or once-off, and, if possible, work out a time estimate for doing them.
(2) Prepare a benchmark job and approach several reputable bureaus or use a broker to obtain prices and detailed quotations. Word of mouth recommendations can be very useful. Among the details you need to ascertain are
adequate hardware available and compatible
adequate operating systems and software

experience and reliability of bureau and reputation and financial stability
real service provided and extras
confidentiality, security and insurance arrangements
delivery dates and turn-round time
availability of stand-by facilities.

(3) Select, train and appoint a bureau liaison man in the customer organisation. He will bargain prices and negotiate contracts with the chosen bureau. Prices may be on a fixed price job basis or on a time (hourly) rate. The contract should allow for changes in circumstance and indicate responsibility for errors, late delivery, breakdowns etc. Other factors considered are program copyright, documentation provided and an arbitration machinery for contractual disputes.

(4) Once the contract is signed, occasional checks on the standard of service and financial position should be made. In addition the liaison officer should keep an eye on the bureau market as a whole for new developments, both technical and organisational.

Other projects

Occasionally the systems analyst may be called upon to assist in **operational research** (OR) projects or he will become involved in using some of the more well-developed and defined OR techniques in his work. Operational research is the collective name for a field of activity which embraces several techniques, all with a similar approach to different problem types. Fundamentally OR solves problems by the abstract analysis and evaluation of mathematical models of real situations

The main steps in an OR project are:

(1) *Exploration* A study of the environment of a problem and the definition of the problem in terms of this environment.

(2) *Model building* This is a time-consuming job with the OR analyst building a mathematical, statistical (or sometimes even a physical) model of the problem.

(3) *Model testing* The model once built must be tested against the environment and data collected to evaluate against the model and introduce improvements by changing various factors.

(4) *Model solution* When the model has been validated against test data it can be used further to evaluate the results of theoretical changed conditions

(5) *Check solution* Before accepting the results obtained the OR analyst will attempt to check thoroughly that all steps have been correctly evaluated

(6) *Selling the solution* Management have now to be convinced that the improvement will work

(7) *Implement the model*

(8) *Monitor results* This step is to check if other factors have occurred since the model solution was evolved thereby invalidating or distorting the results.

The steps for an OR project, therefore, line up very closely with those of a systems project.

A brief synopsis of the various established OR techniques follows.

Queuing theory This technique originating in the study of telephone networks, is now applied to a wide range of problems which occur due to queues being formed waiting to use limited resources, e.g. traffic flow

Linear programming This technique is used for solving optimum resource utilisation problems and others involved in balance and mix factors, e.g. animal feeding, machine shop loading

Dynamic programming This is possibly more useful for problems in business which tend to be concerned with dynamic rather than static situations, in attempts to provide a flexible plan for the future, e.g. farm crop rotation, capitalisation

Game theory This originated during the second world war in an attempt to work out strategy and counter-movement. Its application is the development of a plan of reaction to a competitive movement. Its relation to business is obvious.

Inventory theory, stochastic (random) theory (probability), *replacement theory* and *flow theory* (simulation) are other OR techniques.

One final OR based technique which has gained great popularity in the world of business is *scheduling theory* better known to non-OR people as network analysis or critical path method. It is quite possible that the systems analyst could be involved in using this technique.

Network analysis

Network or critical path analysis is a technique to facilitate control of any isolated complex project.

Basic rules:
All **events** are depicted by a circle
All **activities** are depicted by an arrow connecting events
An activity cannot start until all activities leading to it are completed
An activity cannot lead to an event from which no activities depart unless it is the objective event
The network cannot contain loops
Events are numbered from one to the objective event, and all numbers must be accounted for
The problem must be clearly understood and the objective event known
No two activities can link the same two events.

Constructing the network
(a) Draw up a list of all major activities needed to achieve the objective event
(b) Break down each major activity into a sequence of minor activities indicating which must be completed prior to the next activity commencing
(c) Allocate realistic time values to each activity based on knowledge or estimates with no regard at this stage to the required date of the objective event. This involves a knowledge of what resources (e.g. man-power) will be allocated to the activities
(d) Construct the network commencing with the objective event ensuring all necessary activities are present with the correct relationship to each other

(e) The **critical path** will be one or more paths through the network that take the longest time. Starting from the date of commencement this will show the earliest date of the objective event with the current use of resources.

Using the network

(a) All activities not on the critical path will contain some slack or float, and these activities can be allocated earliest and latest start dates

(b) If the completion date of the objective event is unacceptable then the only way to improve it is to allocate more resources to the critical activities, probably from activities with slack

(c) Adjustments to the resources and, therefore, the time scale of the critical path may well result in the formation of a different set of activities becoming the new critical path

(d) It will be seen then that the process of adjustment and re-evaluation will continue until a satisfactory objective event date is reached

ACTIVITIES FOR BUILDING A PETROL STATION					
Activity Number	Activity description	Activity time	Critical	Float Total	Float Free
1–2	clear site	4	✓	0	0
2–3	excavate for tanks	5		7	0
2–4	dig trenches	6		8	0
2–5	deliver tanks	7		9	2
2–8	excavate for foundations	5	✓	0	0
3–5	construct tank walls	4		7	0
4–7	construct pump plinths	8		8	1
4–12	dummy	0		9	9
5–6	install tanks	3		7	0
6–7	asphalt forecourt	3		7	0
7–15	install pumps	3		7	7
8–9	dummy	0		4	0
8–10	erect walls	7	✓	0	0
9–10	erect window frames	3		4	4
10–11	erect roof	3	✓	0	0
11–12	dummy	0	✓	0	0
11–13	dummy	0		2	0
11–14	install electronics	3		3	3
12–14	install plumbing	6	✓	0	0
13–14	install cupboards	4		2	2
14–15	plaster walls	4	✓	0	0
15–16	paint	6	✓	0	0
16–17	clean out	4	✓	0	0

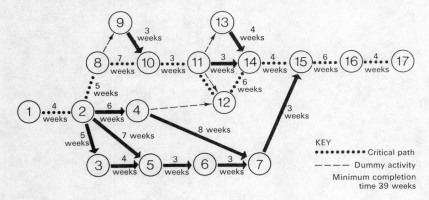

Figure 127   Network analysis chart and table

(e) No network is a static once off exercise because the main purpose of it is project control. On a regular (weekly, fortnightly, monthly) basis actual progress must be used to update the network and re-evaluation must be undertaken to ensure all activities are on schedule and, therefore, the objective date is being met

(f) Because of the re-evaluation required computers and software package PERT programs are normally used to produce the control information.

Assessment tasks

1 Prepare a recorded lecture on the history and development of systems analysis.

2 You have been asked to prepare a report to the personnel department on the implications of the proposal to purchase an in-house computer for your company. The Audit department have also expressed concern. Prepare the report with a copy for the auditors, allaying their fears.

3 Investigate a small data processing system (at work or college) and produce an annotated wallchart indicating the areas requiring the protection of controls and the kind of control you think suitable.

4 Produce an analysis of the computer bureaus in your area with details of the services they provide, charges, etc.

5 Draw a critical path analysis network for planning a wedding. What is the critical path?

Unit 12
Problem definition

Learning objective

To be able to plan the stages of a typical systems project and be able to conduct and report on a simple feasibility study. To be able to define a systems analysis problem and conduct fact finding investigations to gather the information required for the analysis of the problem leading to an improved systems design.

The stages of problem solving projects

Having been allocated a systems project, the analyst must proceed on a series of tasks which will lead him to the solution of the problem in the form of a more effective and efficient data processing system which has been accepted and implemented by the user department. The stages in this often time-consuming task are as follows.

Problem definition
The original idea
Preliminary vetting
Planning the feasibility study
Conducting the feasibility study
The feasibility study report and acceptance or rejection
Defining the problem and planning the systems survey
Fact finding and data collection

Problem analysis
Data organisation and analysis
Critical examination and evaluation of alternatives

Solution synthesis
Design: detailed determination of outputs, inputs, files and processing
Design: determination of work and decision elements
Design: block diagram sequencing of work and decisions
Design: allocation of work to men or machines
Design: systems charting; manual and mechanised runs
Design: alternative design evaluation and testing

Solution implementation
New system specification, report and acceptance

241

Planning the changeover
Forms design and materials acquisition
Staff appreciation and training
File making and conversion
Organising standby facilities
Manual run data testing, correction and documentation
Programming: machine run logic and logic testing
Programming: coding and coding check
Programming: source to object program conversion and correction
Programming: error and correct data testing and rectification
Programming: operating instructions and documentation
Complete system testing, evaluation and correction–parallel running
New system acceptance, changeover and security installation
System maintenance–planning and control systems
Evaluation audit for achievement of management system objectives
Maintenance updates and corrections as necessary

The feasibility study

When there is a computer in a company, someone somewhere will always be coming up with suggestions for possible workloads for it. Most of these jobs will be feasible, that is possible, for the computer to perform but this does not necessarily mean that it would be desirable or beneficial for it to do so. The computer and its associated staff have only limited time available and therefore work must be sifted and arranged into priorities.

The EDP manager will first vet any ideas put forward and only if they sound at all promising (based on his knowledge and experience) will he allocate a systems analyst's time to conducting a preliminary feasibility study.

The practical analyst will always try to establish first the reason why he is being asked to carry out the study. This can be most enlightening as the original idea can have been introduced from many sources and for many reasons, both valid and invalid as far as the company aims are concerned, for example:

(1) Ideas from company management may be due to
   good well-informed management
   keeping up with the Joneses, e.g. competitors use computers
   course attendance, reading or ideas from a consultant.
(2) Ideas from interested bodies, such as O & M, work study, punched card installation, may be due to
   a genuine belief that they can help the company
   empire building desires
   professional interest and career prospects.
(3) Ideas from user departments, such as accounts, sales and production, may be due to
   genuine attempts to solve problems, cut costs, etc.
   wishing to pass problems on to somebody else
   the feeling that all else has failed so let's try computers!

Having decided who are to be the recipients of his report and what their real motives and prejudices are (if any), the analyst is ready to make a start. Either directly or through his line management he must obtain the involvement of one or more members of the company's higher management. If the move came originally from this area then this is already done but if the idea originated in user departments or other departments with a professional interest then the analyst should realise that at some stage management approval will be required and it is best to involve them at an early stage to avoid much wasted time later on in the project.

The best way to ensure that the investigation has management approval is to adopt a formal approach to the request before any work is commenced. The analyst should make an appointment to meet the manager who is responsible for the work system in question and at this meeting work out the initial terms of reference which are crystallised on a regular request form and signed by the manager. An example of a form of this kind which has been combined with a summary feasibility study report for inclusion in the systems documentation is given in Figure 128.

Feasibility study request/report cc4		System code no.
Request		
Study requested by	Signature	Date
Name	Position	Dept.
Precise description of system to be studied :		
Reason for request (survey aims)		Date required by :—
Departments affected	Input documents	Outputs required
Report		
Study conducted by	Signature	Date
Report :		

Cost of changeover	Systems investigation	Man days
	Programming	Man days
	Other costs (Materials)	£
Running costs	Present system	£
	Proposed system	£
	Saving	£
Proposal accepted by applicant	Signature	System code number

Figure 128   Feasibility study request/report

Planning and conducting the study

Once the analyst has completed his initial interview he will have a good idea of the area of the survey and exactly what the manager hopes that the computer will achieve. He can now commence to plan his feasibility study within his existing workload and the time limits required by the requesting party.

At this stage a further item of control documentation, the project control summary (Figure 129) will be raised and thereafter used as the basis for progress reporting over the duration of the survey. If, after the feasibility report is submitted, it is decided to carry out a full scale survey this document will be updated with time estimates for the further systems and programming work required.

Using the techniques common to all systems analysis projects (interview–observation, etc.), the analyst must now proceed to obtain certain facts covering the area under investigation.

Assuming an existing non-computer system is in operation these facts would include:

PROJECT CONTROL SUMMARY 28/A12/9	System code no.
Project title	
Commissioned by	Date

Short description of system

Objective and system benefits

Related projects	
System code no.	Project title

Staff allocated	
Systems analysis	Programming

Figure 129　Project control summary.　(a) Front

(1) A block diagram outline of the system

(2) Organisation chart of the area involved

(3) Facts on present utilisation and costs: man hours and labour costs; materials used and costs; space involved and costs (annual); machines and equipment and annual depreciation

(4) Limits on present system: accuracy required; timing of inputs and outputs; frequency of processing; input–file–output data statistics volumes, content and capacity

(5) Problems on present system: staff availability; work volume fluctuations; complaints from customers or managers and other departments; any other problems (e.g. future requirements).

Having obtained his facts and details, the analyst must now use all his past experience to project how this system might be processed by the computer and he will proceed to build up block diagrams and cost tables for this proposed method. This must always start with the work and results required and encompass all aspects of the resources needed for the new system.

ESTIMATED WORK LOAD AND TARGET DATES									28/A12/9-2
Phase		Man weeks			Start week no.			Finish week no.		
		Est	Act	Var	Est	Act	Var	Est	Act	Var
1	System feasibility study and report									
2	System investigation and analysis									
3	System design, specification and approval									
4	Programming :—logic development									
5	Logic chart									
6	Coding									
7	Compilation									
8	Data testing									
9	Documentation									
10	Non computer planning									
11	File creation and conversion									
12	Pilot and parallel running									
13	Training and implementation									
14	Production running and handover									
15										
16										
17										
18										
19										
20										
21										
	Total work load				Target completion date					

Figure 129   Project control summary.   (b) Reverse

The following is an example of the possible steps to be followed: the outputs required; the files required; the inputs required; the processing required–manual and machine (block diagram); the staff required–organisation charts; the cost of staff required; the machine time and equipment required; the cost of machine time and equipment; the materials required; the cost of materials required; the space required for the staff, machines, materials; the cost of space required; operating costs table; the systems analysis time required (costs); the programming time required; the clerical changeover costs involved; the program testing time costs involved; changeover materials and contingency costs; parallel running period and additional cost; changeover cost table; time scale for systems investigation and changeover.

When the analyst has built up a detailed summary of the proposed system he will have a close comparison to make with the existing system to evaluate if in fact the computer will produce the benefits required by the originator of the feasibility study request.

It is unlikely that the choice will be a straightforward one however. It may well be that although the computer will not achieve what was originally required, it will provide benefits of a different kind. Or again, it may be found that although the proposed computerised system will achieve all that was required, it may also pose some even more drastic disadvantage problems.

The feasibility study report

In theory the analyst need only report back conclusions in an impartial manner for the requesting management to interpret and act on accordingly. In practice having become deeply involved with the situation, the analyst will, with the advice of the EDP manager, have strong views as to the advisability or not of proceeding with a full scale systems project. These views will of course influence the tone of his report and his verbal action in the role of adviser to the user department.

A formal summary of the report can be included in the systems documentation form but it is likely that there will be a separate report document and even a visual presentation. The last word will remain with the manager of the user department (who will sign acceptance of the report as a formal request to continue with the project if agreed) and with the EDP manager who must agree to the priorities for committing his staff to a lengthy detailed assignment.

Example feasibility study report   20.1.1984

TERMS OF REFERENCE

Requested by:	J. Smith, Chief Accountant
System outline:	The production of payslips for hourly, weekly and monthly paid staff, with stamp lists and coin analysis for hourly and weekly paid staff.
Study aims:	Reduction of processing costs. Smoothing of peak load working. Improvement in resource utilisation.
Departments affected:	Payroll department
Report by:	P. Brown, Systems Analyst. DP department.

CONCLUSIONS

The payroll system **is** a feasible computerised system and a major systems project is recommended for the following reasons:

(1) Computerisation will produce an annual estimated processing cost saving of £14 450 p.a.

(2) Payslips, stamp lists and coin analysis can be produced within 3 hours of receipt of clock cards, if required (against 2.5 days for present system)

(3) The proposed system will release 17 valuable trained personnel for other company duties

(4) The computer system will reduce the number of errors (and therefore queries) by 90%

(5) The streamlining of the payroll department will release 800 square feet of valuable office space

(6) The computer can absorb the fluctuations in workload with minimum time and cost penalties

(7) Whilst there is spare capacity on the computer, the proposed system will release 7 expensive book-keeping machines which can be used in other parts of the company and defer further captial expenditure on equipment requests.

NOTE: If the feasibility report was given a visual presentation, each of the above points would be backed up with a present/proposed diagram

CONTENTS

PRESENT	PROPOSED
Organisation Chart 'A'	Organisation Chart 'B'
Block Diagram 'A'	Block Diagram 'B'
Cost Summary 'A'	Cost Summary 'B'

COST OF CHANGEOVER

1)	Systems investigation	100 man days	£ 800
2)	Programming	60 man days	£ 360
3)	Computer program testing	10 hours	£ 250
4)	File conversion	50 hours data preparation	£ 100
	File conversion	30 man days clerical	£ 120
	File conversion	2 hours M/c time	£ 50
5)	Parallel running	up to 3 months	£3100
6)	Additional queries and contingencies		£1220
		TOTAL	£6000

IMPLEMENTATION

This system has already been installed with success at the Manchester Group Branch and it is not therefore expected that any major problems will be encountered. We can expect full co-operation from Manchester and possibly the services of a system advisor from the team which installed their system.

With this in mind, it is proposed that if this report is accepted, systems work can be commenced by 1.5.1984 and the new system can be fully operational (and therefore the benefits obtained) by 30.10.1984.

Signed P. Brown, Systems Analyst

On the supposition that the feasibility study report was positive and that the applicant accepted its findings and wished the full-scale project to be carried out, the following sequence of events will now occur:

(1) The EDP management will, upon receiving a formal documentary request from the authorised applicant, accept the new project as part of the workload of the department and allocate a systems analyst or team leader to be responsible for the project.

(2) The analyst appointed will obtain the feasibility study report and proceed to carry out the following broad steps: detailed definition of the problem; plan for conducting survey; fact finding and data collection; data organisation and analysis; critical examination of present system; detailed determination of new system outputs, files, inputs, processing and decisions; logical sequencing of work and decisions by a block diagram.

This sequence of work will culminate in the completion of the business oriented design aspect of the new system's workload and is about half-way to the final completion of the project.

Detailed definition of problem

The analyst will commence by reviewing the original problem definition as stated in the feasibility study. It is very likely however that as a result of facts discovered and forecasts made during this initial study, the requirements of any proposed system will have been totally or partially amended.

With the original requirements in mind the analyst will:

(1) *Establish criteria*

By interview and investigation he will determine the real reasons for the systems survey, i.e. the expected benefits of the new system

Initially these may be stated as improved service to management, improved service to customers, and improved service to company departments.

However these answers are vague and indicate that the problem has not been probed in sufficient detail. Improved service resulting from computerisation is the result of one or more of the following potential benefits of computers.

speed–quicker results
accuracy–improved quality results
cost–reduction in overall processing costs
space–reduction in space utilisation from centralisation
staff availability–overcoming specialised labour shortages
presentation–clarity and neatness but coding problems
work capacity–smoothing peak work loads, adjustment for growth
work complexity–new techniques impractical manually

It should be realised however that these are only **real** benefits if they are required, e.g. quicker results may cost more whilst not being used any earlier.

The following may also be a motivating force:

security–secret or valuable information or resources
computer utilisation–spare capacity on an expensive machine
modernisation–replacement of obsolete equipment or systems
human reasons–status, power, image, ignorance, etc.

The aim of the survey is to produce a system that satisfies the stated criteria, which must be specified as to both type (speed, cost, etc) and value (money, units, times, etc.). Multiple criteria must be ranked in priority sequence.

(2) *Establish system subject and objectives*

The general subject is obtained in answer to the question what is the system concerned with?

In any business system there is likely to be more than one answer to this, producing specific subject subsystems. These may be apparently independent of one another or dependent due to overlapping, nesting, timing or common data.

Where nesting occurs further breakdown is required until a complete list of subsystems is established. This list must be priority ranked based on the effect of each subsystem on the overall system.

The overall system objective is determined by the questions why is this system performed, what are its outputs.

The list of outputs produced should be validated by asking the question why is that done, repeatedly subjecting the answering statements ('to…') to this same question, until an answer which coincides with the objectives of the business as a whole is arrived at.

The outputs thus validated will now indicate the termination points of the specific subject subsystems which should now have their specific objectives specified by asking what does this system do.

Possible system types and objectives are:

Receptor system–to detect and capture data
Storage system–data retention and retrieval
Classification system–to quantify and measure unknowns
Process system–to convert data or resources
Communication system–to transmit information
Effector system–to convert data into action
Control system–to stabilise within given limits
Any combination of above

(3) *Establish constraints on system*

A constraint is a limitation on finding the perfect system solution imposed within the area in which the system will operate. The analyst must produce an optimised balance between these constraints and the perfect system. Amongst these will be:

effect on and by other manual and DP systems with which this system is directly integrated
any requirements additional to the existing system outputs
any known and potential difficulties with the existing system
any system of priorities imposed over and above the established criteria.

(4) *Establish system restrictions*
A restriction is a limitation of the area allowed for seeking a system solution. Facts to be established include:

time limits on survey
organisational limits on survey area
personnel limits on survey area
available and potential resources for system processing (including hardware and cost limits).

(5) *List assumptions to be made*
All problem solutions assume certain probabilities. List all assumptions made other than the obvious, e.g. that the firm continues to operate, that the validity of the system remains. The problem should now be defined in enough detail to enable survey planning to commence.

Survey planning

The first step will be to review and amend the terms of reference first defined for the feasibility study. As with the problem definition this is liable to have been considerably changed by the new facts and circumstances revealed by the preliminary study.

The analyst should be working within the framework of a set of methods standards for systems analysis as laid down in the department standards manual. If this is not the case then he must at this stage define methods standards for all working procedures during the survey.

Having defined the problem he will now be in a position to list all the various steps envisaged in conducting the survey. Whilst there is a general pattern for conducting all systems surveys the exact details will obviously vary with each individual project.

The analyst must now estimate the man hours involved in carrying out the above steps. This will involve consultation with programmers or the chief programmer with regard to the nonsystems work. On average the completion of the systems specification to the installation stage will take about one man day for every ten program statements involved.

The analyst in charge of the project will have defined his time limits for the completion of the various stages of the survey and must now work out the various systems and programming resources he has available to work on these procedures. If more man hours are required he must negotiate these with the EDP management.

A schedule for the conduct of the survey must now be prepared allocating the resources to the project steps against planned time limits. The method used for this will vary according to the size and complexity of the project and may be either by using specialised forms, bar-charts or even critical path analysis. As the time required for any workload depends on how thoroughly it is performed the analyst will now set standards of quality, duration and effectiveness against each individual stage.

A good control system must be set up with regular reporting of the progress made in conducting the planned steps of the survey. No good plan is ever rigid and obviously there will be circumstances which will cause work to fall behind target or below standard. By a regular reporting process where members of both the EDP and user departments are represented, these problems can be discussed and amendments made to the original plan to optimise the situation.

In preparation for the first stage of the project the analyst will prepare checklists, or use standardised forms, of the information types required and sources of information available.

All these plans should be formalised into documentary form and the analyst should obtain written agreement to his plans from both the line management concerned and his own DP management. This in fact is the first step in the project control system. Having obtained agreement the analyst will proceed to conduct the project according to the planned and timed stages.

Introduction to staff

In nearly all cases the project will involve obtaining facts about an existing system and this means visiting offices and interviewing managers, supervisors and possibly staff members. Rumours on the grapevine can be very harmful to the success of the project, and the first thing the analyst should do is organise a meeting of all staff concerned through the line management. This meeting will enable the analyst and his team to be introduced to the staff by their own superiors thus putting them in the position of friendly visitors rather than hostile intruders. At the meeting the analyst will outline the reason for and aims of the project, remembering to put these into the context of benefits to the staff rather than abstract or technical reasons. A frank and open discussion should follow with the analyst making it clear that he is always ready to meet staff or staff representatives and discuss any part of the project providing that this is channelled through the normal line of authority in the area concerned. This last is essential if line management authority is not to be usurped.

Sample introduction

To illustrate the human relations approach and for use as a class discussion exercise the following sample introductory talk to user department staff is given:

Example

'The purpose of this survey is to give yourselves and your supervisors an opportunity to improve the work that you have to do, removing the drudgery by mechanisation and rebuilding the manual work into interesting, worthwhile jobs with proper rewards.

During your day by day work I expect you have often had ideas for improvements which you may not have had the time or opportunity to develop. Our role as systems analysts is to assist your supervisors to develop improvements by offering our time and training in specialist techniques. We would therefore be grateful if you would bring forward any ideas you may have to your supervisors and ourselves.

Any changes resulting from our joint efforts will be fully discussed and approved by your representatives and management before being introduced.

We are not only investigating conditions and working methods in this system, but also the way that work comes into the system, and we would welcome hearing any problems that affect your work in this respect. We will also be assisting your supervisors to establish the best office layout, and will be investigating conditions, space and equipment problems.

Changes may be introduced on a trial-run basis and no change is irreversible, so your comments will be welcome at all times during the survey. Apart from actual changes in working methods, a real benefit comes from writing down and clearly defining what work is required and who is responsible, and on completion of the survey we will publish procedure and training manuals.

As far as the results of the survey are concerned I would like to make it quite clear that the company has guaranteed that no one will become redundant as a result of this project. All investigation will be carried out by job function and not by individual person. We are only concerned with what work is performed and not how well that work is done by Mrs Smith or Mr Brown.

During the survey you need not fear that we will be constantly standing over you watching you work. Apart from the fact that you would naturally dislike this, it is also only one of many ways of collecting facts.

To outline the survey to you briefly, we will first of all sit down with your manager and supervisors to produce detailed charts of all work being performed in the system. We will then discuss and agree with all concerned the best method for producing this work in the future.

During this time we will need to obtain various volume and frequency information and it may be necessary to ask you to keep simple counts on various items. This is to ensure that due allowance is given to the many queries and, 'exceptions to the rule' that always occur in clerical work. To sum up, we hope to produce a plan for the future to improve both the conditions and the effectiveness of this system. The amount of success we will achieve depends on how well we work together so if you have any questions, problems or comments please let us hear them'.

Fact finding and data collection

In order to be able to design a complete system, whether manual or computer, it is first necessary to know very detailed facts about the purpose and nature of the system.

Fortunately there is usually an existing system or systems from which much valuable experience can be obtained and, providing certain precautions are taken to ensure facts are accurate and that only strictly valid limits are accepted from the present system, this is the normal area for data collection.

This stage of the survey can be regarded from two distinct aspects: what facts are required? these must be complete, correct and valid; how and where these facts can be obtained?

Check list of facts required for systems survey is as follows:

Agreed, detailed definition of purpose of the system

Detailed sequential steps of system, procedures and methods for both routine and exception processing

Detailed existing standards and limits for both the data processed and the processing steps with regard to: legal requirements; audit requirements; management policy; quality standards; timing schedules

Details of maximum, minimum and average volumes, sizes, frequencies, units and related statistics of the data processed

Details of existing (and future) problems encountered in processing and the effectiveness of the present system

Detailed costs of each step of present system

Details of all machines and equipment used in the system processing

Plans and details of the physical environment of the system giving space, distances, locations and conditions of the areas involved in processing system data

The framework within which the system operates, consisting of: the systems interaction with other systems of the organisation and the relationship of the processing department(s) with other departments; The detailed organisation chart for the processing department(s) showing position, staff, grade, responsibility, names; the normal working hours and maximum, minimum and average hours for each position on the organisation chart

Details of all media used for holding data, giving origin, distribution, material and format, e.g. forms, reports, files, ledgers, registers etc.

Details of existing coding systems in use in the system and any other coding systems in the company that may relate to them.

Sources of data and methods of collection
Interview
The following should be observed when fact finding by interview:

Place of interview should be suitable bearing in mind the confidential nature of the items discussed and the availability of backing information together with freedom from constant interruption.

The correct person to interview must be the person who can give accurate, detailed facts of the present system whilst knowing where this deviates from written policy if applicable.

The method of interview should be based on good human relations principles and should be a questioning approach to ensure accuracy and provide indications of possible improvements.

The interviewer must be prepared, impersonal, objective and unbiased to any preconceived solutions.

The timing of the interviews should be convenient to both parties avoiding peak periods or times of stress when cooperation would be difficult to obtain.

Facts obtained by interview can be recorded by means of: note taking; tape recording; rough charting; document collection; questionnaires and check lists.
Observation
Observation can be either direct when the analyst observes actual working or indirect when some other person (manager, supervisor, staff) observes and records the data and passes it to the analyst.

When obtaining facts by observation the staff being observed must be fully aware of the purpose and methods used to obtain full cooperation.

Observation fact finding is accomplished by: charting and diagrams; photographic recording; special record keeping, e.g. tally sheets; activity sampling.

Document analysis

By reading and analysing various records, forms, instructions and charts, facts on the existing system may be obtained, particularly volume statistics and various standards and limits. Care must however be taken to ensure the accuracy of this information as the documents found are invariably out of date.

Data may be obtained by: taking sample copies, e.g. form and document collection; analysing and extracting statistics; note taking; photocopying.

Visualisation and synthesis

In certain cases either the existing system will be unavailable for study or it may be impractical to do so. Facts may be obtained by visualising the process and the analyst performing it, or alternatively facts can be built up by synthesis from a known factor or factors.

Data may be obtained by self observation, synthesis from tables, synthesis by calculation.

Summary of fact-finding techniques

(1) Written notes and sketches
(2) Tape recording
(3) Photographic recording: cine–memomotion (time lapse); cine–micromotion (frame analysis); still–cyclegraph; still–chronocyclegraph; still–document photocopying
(4) Document collection: budgets; manuals; O & M reports; plans and layouts; policy instructions, minutes, etc.; personnel files; equipment lists; past performance records; plans and schedules; charts, etc.; questionnaires and checklists; special records, e.g. tally sheets, data and time counts etc.; work distribution charts; copies of working documents, e.g. forms and registers
(5) Activity sampling
(6) Synthesis: tables (PMTS, etc.); calculation
(7) Charting

Questionnaire design

The questionnaire should be in three parts:
(1) Heading data, e.g. date, interviewer
(2) Classification data, e.g. sex, age, status, area, occupation
(3) Subject data–the required information to be classified by the above.

The interviewee should be quite certain as to the purpose of the questionnaire as this can influence the validity of the answers. The correct person should be chosen for interview. All questions must be answerable by facts unless it is an opinion survey. The answers should be required in unmistakable uniform units, e.g. tons, gallons, not just weight or capacity. Questions should not be ambiguous, e.g. age or date of birth. Answers should not require calculation. Questions should not contain words that may not be understood by the informant. Answers should cover a stable, representative period. All questions should be capable of being answered with precise data, e.g. yes/no, numbers, dates, places. The questionnaire should not be too long or too complex. Before use the questions should be validated by a trial run using the questionnaire on a few people who know nothing of its preparation.

When fact finding by questionnaire, the problem should never be approached by first deciding which questions will be asked. This always leads to confusion and overlapping of data when the accumulated answers are tabulated. The correct approach is to first decide on what result tables and facts are required, e.g. what is the subject material and what are the classification headings, and from this to proceed to what questions need to be asked to obtain the answers.

Tally sheets

A variation of the questionnaire approach where simple count or time data is required is to design special purpose forms to be used for cumulative collection of data as events occur. These are normally filled in by the staff concerned and should therefore be kept simple and convenient to complete. An example is given in Figure 130.

Activity sampling

In some cases the analyst may wish to determine the frequency of a certain activity or occurrence, e.g. the amount of time spent by clerks on a particular aspect of the system or the frequency with which a certain type of document occurs in a file. To do this can involve him in a great deal of time consuming fact finding work if he has to conduct a 100% survey of the subject and it will be preferable for him to obtain his results from a sample observation only.

His main problem is how many samples must be taken to be sure his data is representative of the whole to within a given accuracy. Fortunately there is a formula for finding this which has been evolved by statistical methods.

The steps in taking a sample are:

(1) Carefully choose a representative area and time in which to conduct the survey.

(2) Obtain an estimate of the expected frequency occurrence by interview, advice or pilot study.

(3) Calculate the number of samples required by using the formula:

$$n = \frac{4P(100 - P)}{L^2}$$

where
n = number of samples required
P = estimated percentage of activity occurrence
L = percentage limits of accuracy required

TALLY SHEET								
Phone calls			Dates : From *7·4·84* to *11·4·84*					
Description		Frequency						
PO outgoing date :		7ᵀᴴ	8ᵀᴴ	9ᵀᴴ	10ᵀᴴ	11ᵀᴴ		totals
(A)	phone outside source no look up	lll	✚✚	l	ll	l		12
(B)	phone outside source look up records (either end)	l	l		l			3
(C)	phone outside source and negotiate	ll	ll	✚✚	ll	ll		13
(D)	phone outside source no. engaged	l	lll	l	l	lll		9
Internal outgoing								
(E)	phone internal source no look up	lll	llll	lll	lll	l		14
(F)	phone internal source look up records (either end)	ll	✚✚ l	llll	ll	lll		17
(G)	phone internal source and negotiate	l	ll	l	lll	l		8
(H)	phone internal source number engaged	l			lll			4
PO & internal incoming								
(I)	answer phone and reply no look up	✚✚	ll	lll	llll	✚✚ ll		21
(J)	answer phone and reply look up records	ll	l	l	lll	ll		9
(K)	answer phone and negotiate	ll	l					3
(L)	answer phone and transfer call	ll	ll	ll	lll	l		10
Name : *S. Eagle*			Function : *Secretary*					

Figure 130   Typical tally sheet

e.g. expected percentage of rectification working $= 10\%$. Accuracy limits required $\pm 5\%$

$$n = \frac{(4 \times 10)(100 - 10)}{5^2} = \frac{40 \times 90}{25} = 144$$

$n = 144$ samples required to give accuracy $\pm 5\%$.

Note: The above formula is correct for 95% confidence limits. That is the answer will be correct $\pm 5\%$ in 95 cases out of 100. There are other formulae for greater or lesser confidence limits but this is most common.

(4) Prepare a schedule of samples to be taken on a completely random basis. If observations of work are to be made, these should be at random time intervals. If a file is to be searched the documents chosen must be selected at random intervals in the file sequence. The most common way to arrive at these intervals is to use the numbers printed in published random number tables.

(5) Armed with a preruled study sheet, the analyst will proceed to conduct his survey. All observations must be made instantaneously and without bias.

(6) On completing his sample the analyst must work out his results to give the observed percentage frequency over the number of samples taken.

(7) The next step is to validate the accuracy of the result by substituting the observed percentage frequency for the estimated frequency in the original formula calculation. If when using the new frequency the number of samples required works out the same or less than the actual number of samples taken then the result is reliable to the limits required. If not then the analyst must take the additional samples required and then revalidate.

Physical layout diagrams

Usually the analyst will want to know something about the physical environment in which the existing system is operating. He will collect organisation charts for the area and to supplement these he should obtain physical layout diagrams. These are usually available from the works engineers

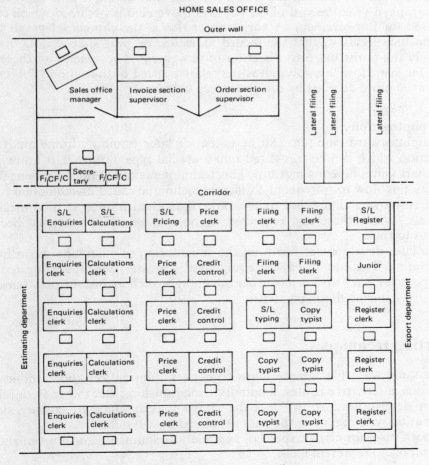

Figure 131   Physical layout diagram

and maintenance department but if no blueprints are held the analyst will find it useful to prepare his own diagram. These may be useful as a base for straightforward layout planning and space saving analysis. Figure 131 gives an illustration of a selfprepared layout diagram.

Film and tape recording

One rarely used method of fact finding is to make a visual record of the situation for later analysis at the analyst's leisure. In cases where intense physical activity is involved or where activity is so gradual as not to be readily apparent to the human eye the use of visual recording techniques can pay dividends. A brief outline of these follows.

Cyclegraphy

By attaching battery powered lights to the fingers, hands, or legs of a subject or to the appropriate moving parts of a machine and taking a time-exposed still photograph, a visual record of the paths of movement is obtained which can be analysed for improvement. A variation of this is the **chronocyclegraph** which uses flashing lights so that the record indicates, by pear shaped dots of light, not only the paths but also direction of movement. The spacing of these dots (wide for fast, close for slow) gives the relative speed of the action. This can be made even more detailed by use of a stereo camera.

Cine photography

A straightforward cine film can be taken for later frame by frame analysis of the action which can be translated into a special type of flowchart known as a simochart (simultaneous motion). This technique is called **micromotion**. Where the action is slow or infrequent a different technique called **memomotion** is used which employs a time-lapse unit to take individual frames at time measured intervals. When these are projected at normal speed the activity becomes obvious to the eye.

One later development has been the substitution of videotape recording for cine filming. The cost of capital equipment is greater but tape being reusable soon pays for itself and it has other advantages such as instant play back and monitoring during filming activities.

Charting techniques

In the same way that we use maps to convey information about traffic flow, directions, alternative routes, landmarks, relationships, etc. rather than rely on written descriptions, so we use the charting techniques to convey similar information with regard to the data processed by a system.

In both cases for clarity, speed of assimilation, simplicity and convenience we use symbols to represent facts.

The main uses of charting are:

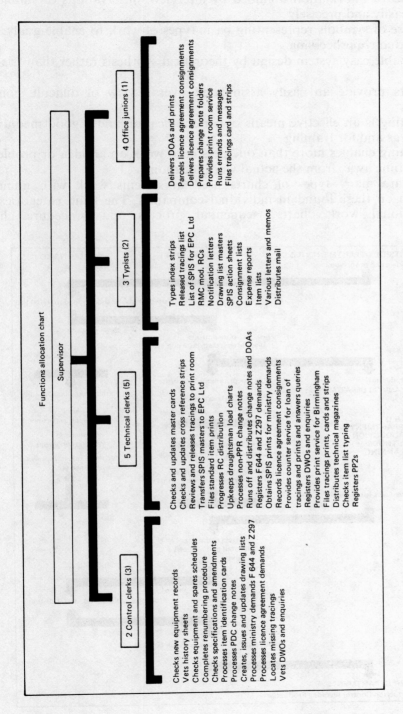

Functions allocation chart

Supervisor

2 Control clerks (3)

Checks new equipment records
Vets history sheets
Checks equipment and spares schedules
Completes renumbering procedure
Checks specifications and amendments
Processes item identification cards
Processes PDC change notes
Creates, issues and updates drawing lists
Processes ministry demands F 644 and Z 297
Processes licence agreement demands
Locates missing tracings
Vets DWOs and enquiries

5 Technical clerks (5)

Checks and updates master cards
Checks and updates cross reference strips
Reviews and releases tracings to print room
Transfers SPIS masters to EPC Ltd
Files standard item prints
Progresses RC distribution
Upkeeps draughtsman load charts
Processes non-PPR change notes
Runs off and distributes change notes and DOAs
Registers F 644 and Z 297 demands
Obtains SPIS prints for ministry demands
Records licence agreement consignments
Provides counter service for loan of
tracings and prints and answers queries
Registers DWOs and enquiries
Provides print service for Birmingham
Files tracings prints, cards and strips
Distributes technical magazines
Checks item list typing
Registers PP2s

3 Typists (2)

Types index strips
Released tracings list
List of SPIS for EPC Ltd
RMC mod. RCs
Notification letters
Drawing list masters
SPIS action sheets
Consignment lists
Expense reports
Item lists
Various letters and memos
Distributes mail

4 Office juniors (1)

Delivers DOAs and prints
Parcels licence agreement consignments
Delivers licence agreement consignments
Prepares change note folders
Provides print room service
Runs errands and messages
Files tracings card and strips

Figure 132 Functions allocation chart

to record information obtained by interview, observations or simulation, quickly, easily and precisely

by use of symbols representing basic types of work to enable analysis for more productive processing

to enable easy system design by theoretical synthesis rather than trial and error

charts provide an easily assimilated overall view of difficult, complex situations

charting is an effective means of communication and a good medium for selling ideas and for training

charting enables more than one person to work on an idea or problem at the same time away from the actual work location.

There are many types of charts used in systems work with numerous variations on these found in individual companies. The main categories are: organisational work charts; sequential process and procedure charts–

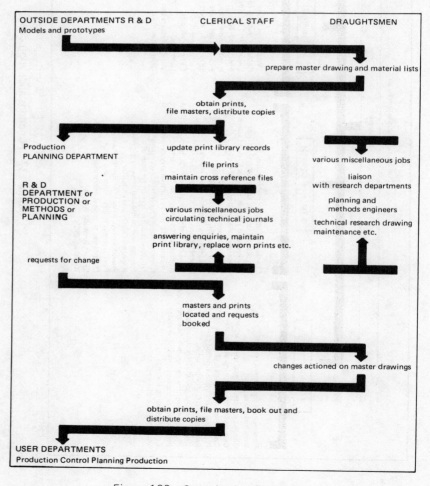

Figure 133   Organisation flowchart

flowcharts; analysis charts and diagrams; pictorial presentation charts and diagrams; creative design charts; control charts.

Organisational work charts

The main version of this is the normal organisation chart discussed previously. A variation on this is the **functions allocation chart** which consists of the normal organisation chart with, under each function box, a list of the procedural tasks performed by that function (Figure 132).

The **organisation flowchart** is a further variation, this time depicting the sequential flow of a system or procedure against an organisational function grid (Figure 133).

The final type of organisation work chart is the **work distribution chart**. This is more concerned with the distribution of staff hours amongst the various procedures performed in the office (Figure 134).

DRAWING OFFICE – 472 D

Procedure	Total Man hours	Draughtsmen Operation	Man hours	Section leader Operation	Man hours	Typists Operation	Man hours	Junior Operation	Man hours
drawing amendments	101	checks and redraws	80	approves and checks	5	raises amendment from request / prepares for distribution	6 / 4	retrieves files / distributes	4 / 2
enquiries	34	answer technical questions	28					obtains records and files	6
renumbering procedure	17			issues advice notes	5	types new record cards and file reports	10	issues number lists	2
new drawings	142	draws and prepares parts lists / checks spec lists	72 / 10	attends specification meetings / issues file lists	20 / 8	raises file record / types file list card	20	obtains print copies / files prints	10 / 2
house-keeping	28			attends routine standards meetings	2	opens mail and date stamps / types general letters	6 / 10	run errands / distributes mail	7 / 3
Totals	322		190		40		56		36

Figure 134   Work distribution chart

Sequential process and procedure (flow) charts

Process charts are derived from work study and all use five basic symbols joined by flow lines:

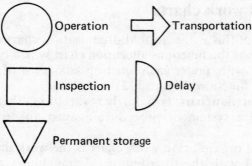

Operation — Transportation

Inspection — Delay

Permanent storage

There are three types of process chart and it is important to be clear which type is intended as the symbols must only refer to one resource, e.g. Man process chart; Material process chart; Equipment process chart.

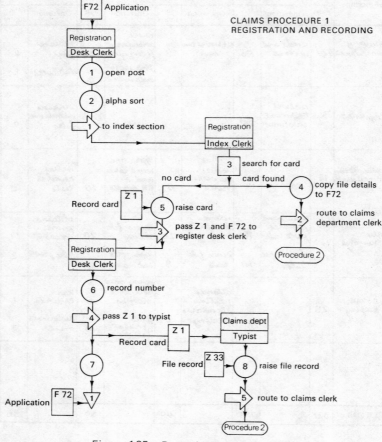

Figure 135   Procedure chart (O & M)

Developed from these are various types of **procedure chart** which are of more relevance to the systems analyst. The procedure chart is a cross between a man process chart and a material (information) process chart. However, in addition to the five symbols above there are added symbols to represent the media carrying the information and organisation function symbols. Figure 135 illustrates a typical procedure chart.

There is a simplified version of the process chart which uses only the operation and inspection symbols to indicate the main processing involved. These are called **outline process charts.** There is an equivalent of this for procedure charts using only a single circle or box symbol for manual processing instead of the five manual symbols.

This outline procedure chart is shown in Figure 136. There are probably more variations of procedure charts than there are pages in this book. Among the most common variations are the **multicolumn procedure chart** which is a two-dimensional matrix chart showing document flow against a time scale or

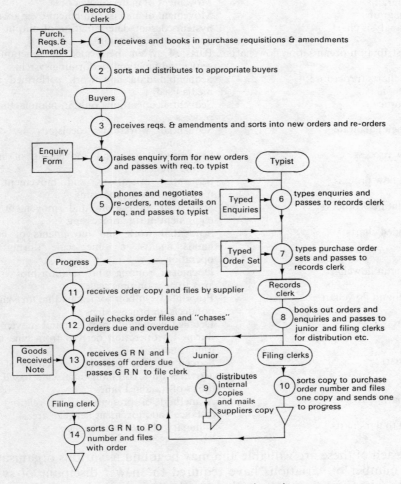

Figure 136   Outline procedure chart

against a department breakdown, and the **single column flow chart** which has preprinted sets of all five basic symbols down a page with spaces by the side for annotation. The analyst completes these charts by joining the appropriate symbols and making brief notes against each operation step.

The following is a summary of the main types of chart that the systems analyst has inherited from the fields of work study and organisation and methods.

Chart type	Main purpose
Organisation charts and function allocation charts	Functions, responsibility, relationships, staffing
Bar (Gantt) charts	Scheduling, comparisons
Multiple activity charts (man/ machine charts)	Relative activity against a common time scale
Layout diagrams	Scale plan view of area
Flow diagrams	Movement of material over area
String diagrams	Movement of men or equipment over area
Output analysis chart	Systems design–determination of output, file and input specification
Work distribution/organisation flowcharts	Parts of system performed by function or sequential functions performing system
Systems charts (procedure)	Sequential data flow–work performed and media used
Outline process	Sequential operations only in manufacturing process
Block (logic) diagram	Sequential work and decisions in data processing
Man flow process	Sequential work and movement of men during processing
Material flow process	Sequential operations and movement of materials during processing
Equipment flow process	Sequential utilisation and movement of equipment during processing
Two handed charts	Sequential work and movements of both hands against a time scale during an operation
Multicolumn flowchart	Document routing and relationships from area to area on time scale
Single column flowchart	Preprinted symbols joined by line for simple nondecision process steps
Simocharts	Detailed elemental chart of hand movement during an operation derived from cine film frame analysis
PMTS chart	Sequential time element bar chart of all activities on a common time scale based on tables of standard times
Travel chart	A method of presenting data relating to distance and movement between areas
Various tabular charts	Summary of facts for reference

Whilst each of these are valuable and may be found in various organisations, the large number of variations have required the newer discipline of systems analysis to simplify and reduce the standard charts adopted. Figure 137

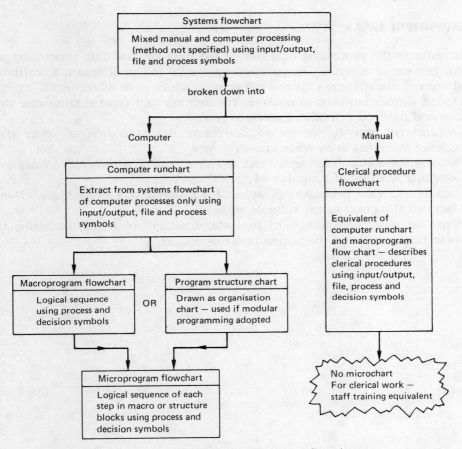

Figure 137　Systems and programming flowcharts

indicates a logical approach to systems and programming flowcharting. Examples of each of these charts are to be found in the documentation samples or by means of the index.

The only symbols needed in this simplified system of charting are

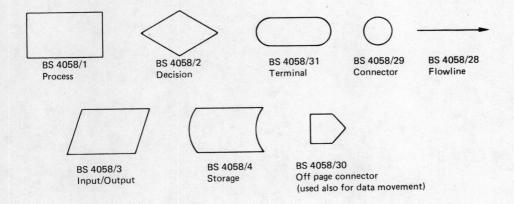

Assessment tasks

1 Investigate the processing of a simple but high volume data processing jo being performed manually in your workplace or college. Prepare a feasibilit study report in a manner that will sell your conclusions to its recipient.

2 Design a questionnaire to discover the number and type of telephone cal placed and received in a office known to you.

3 Conduct an activity sample to determine the utilisation of office dat processing machines in an office known to you.

4 Perform simulated interviews (with a video camera if possible) to discove the working routines of a number of clerical workers.

5 Prepare a clerical procedure flowchart for a simple office procedure. Obtai the facts for this chart in any suitable manner.

6 Write an essay on the subject of systems project planning, including th areas to be planned and the project controls desirable.

Unit 13
Problem analysis

Learning objective

To be able to organise the facts collected relating to an existing system or a proposed new one so that they are in a suitable form for analysis. To understand the process of analysis, including the grouping into like elements and identification of relationships in order to be able to analyse sets of facts in preparation for critical examination. To be able to perform the process of critical examination in order to produce alternative solutions and to have the ability to compare and evaluate the alternatives for the most satisfactory solution.

Analysis

To analyse something is to break it down to its constituent parts and to identify these and the relationships between them. This is necessary to understand how a thing works and, therefore, the necessity for each of the parts and their relative importance. If, for example, a chemist is asked to analyse a substance, he will perform certain tests to establish the chemical elements of the mixture. This may be in order to find out why the mixture has certain effects or it may be in order to improve the effectiveness.

Having made his tests, he will be able to establish the various sequential chemical reactions between the substances and from there proceed to calculate the effect of varying the relative volumes of each. He may also find impurities which either do not contribute to the desired effect or in some cases even act to inhibit it. Whatever the result, the analysis will enable him to predict the most effective mixture and quantities of ingredients for any desired result.

To take a further example, a military officer may capture a piece of enemy weaponry which is totally unfamiliar to him. By stripping it down into its component parts, he can then identify each part and by comparing these with the similar parts of weapons within his experience he can proceed towards an understanding of how the device functions and how to use it effectively.

In the problem definition stage, the systems analyst has identified his battleground and has then proceeded to collect his subjects for analysis. In this next stage he must organise all the facts he has collected so that he can then commence to break them down into component parts.

Data organisation

Before the analyst can make use of all the facts he has gathered about the existing system it is necessary to formulate them into some meaningful statement upon which to go to work. He will therefore prepare a summary of these facts in the following manner:

System description

(1) Outline sequential **block diagram** of system with total cost, departments and other systems affected, outputs and volumes produced, and major problems encountered, indicated for each block.

(2) For each block on diagram detailed **systems charts** using standard symbols, and against each symbol where appropriate the following information: person performing work-title, grade; volume of total file, statistical frequency of data; volume and statistics of documents processed; man hours for operation; distance travelled and time taken (and man hours if different); time delayed or file retention period; limits of check accuracy and quality; time and day of processing and limits; indication if a problem (or peak) operation; details of machine or equipment involved; indications of legal or audit 'musts'; total cost of operation.

System environment

Purpose of system

Organisation chart(s)–functions allocation

Index of charts (procedure list)

List of major problems

List of machines and equipment

List of forms, reports and files

Layout plan of working area

Cost summary of system

Organisation flowchart/work distribution chart

Details of existing coding systems

File of working documents

Rough charts, document, form and register copies, etc.

Analysis of present system

Whilst the analyst has been gathering the facts on the present system he will have been questioning each item of data obtained as to its necessity and validity. This will have resulted in some improvements so that the summary resulting from the data organisation will in fact be, not the actual present system but a slightly improved proposed system.

Prior to any further analysis it is necessary to consolidate the ground covered so far by getting the system description charts and system environment facts sheets thoroughly checked and agreed by the line management responsible for the system. This ensures that any further work performed by the analyst is not wasted and, to ensure that the checking is thorough, it is a good plan to get each sheet signed and dated by the checker.

Once the summary is agreed the analyst will proceed to examine it critically in order to reduce the work content of the new system to the minimum required for effectiveness.

There are several techniques which the analyst can use to assist him in his breakdown of the problem. The various charts already mentioned are, in themselves, both fact finding and analysis techniques. The use of separate symbols for different types of operation or medium, identifies the component parts.

Lists and tables are also devices for breaking data down into elements, some of which we have already discussed. Further charting and tabular techniques that can be useful follow.

Layout and movement charts

In problems involving physical layout relationships and movement of men, materials or information there are three complementary techniques which may be found useful. They are flow diagrams, string diagrams and travel charts.

Flow diagrams

These are a combination of the flowchart and the floor layout plan which detail the movement, operations and delays over a physical area. The analyst will prepare his diagram by obtaining a floor layout plan and by interview or observation (or by development from a normal flowchart) will locate the

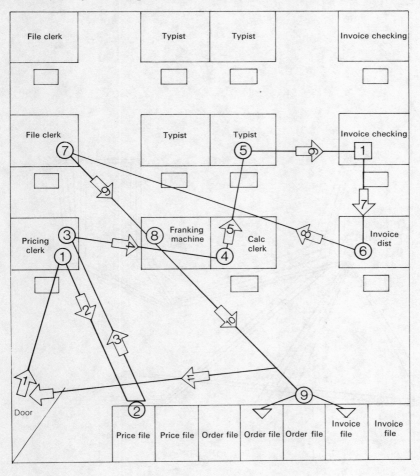

Figure 138   Flow diagram

movements and delays between the various work stations involved. He then draws these onto the floor plan using the inter-connected flowchart symbols. Figure 138 makes this technique obvious.

String diagrams

While flow diagrams indicate the work, movements and delays involved in one cycle of a system they do not convey the volume of movement over a period. The string diagram which is again based on the floor plan does just this, highlighting at a glance the areas of highest activity. While the flow diagram is useful for eliminating procedural delays, the string diagram is a tool for determining the problem areas in location relationships with respect to work flow. A string diagram is made by inserting pins into the layout plan at the work stations and other points along the route normally travelled and joining these with coloured cottons, the number of strands representing the work volume. For comparison with the flow diagram, a string diagram is illustrated in Figure 139.

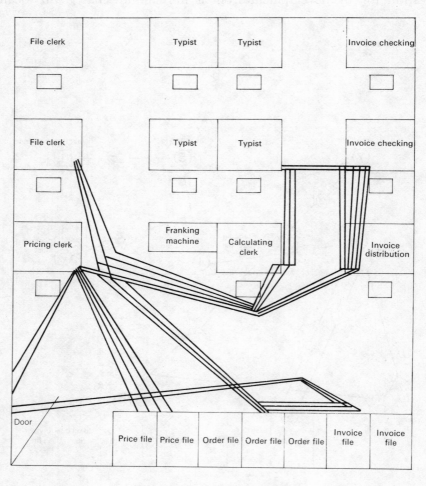

Figure 139   String diagram

Travel charts

The string diagram makes it obvious where there are long or high volume journeys taking place but does not offer any quantitative evaluation of these. One tabular technique that is useful as it is easily understood by nontechnical staff yet at the same time condenses data about work flow in a concise manner (rather like decision tables) is the travel chart.

The principle is the same as that used in the distance tables between towns found in the motoring organisation handbooks. In the example (Figure 140) the upper part of the entry squares contain the distances in any appropriate unit between the work station/department/location supplying the data and the receiver of the data supplied. The lower half of the entry box can be used as the analyst requires to indicate actual volume of data or percentages. The value of the chart is in concisely presenting all the facts so that the analyst can aim at improving location relationships to minimise movement.

The technique can be further enhanced by the inclusion of various summary tables.

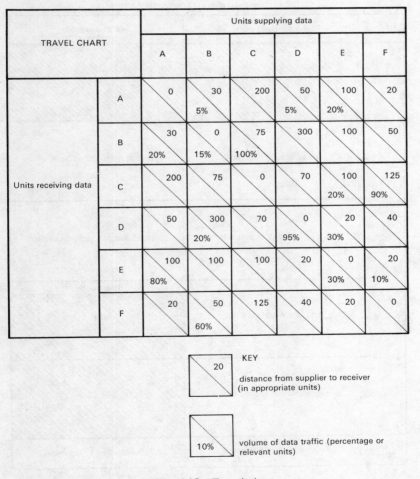

Figure 140   Travel chart

Multiple activity charts

If the analyst has a problem relating to the coordination of several activities performed by either men or machines or a combination of both, the use of a multiple activity chart (sometimes called a man/machine chart) will enable him to see clearly the relationships involved and allow him to devise and evaluate better relationships.

The essence of the technique is the combination of a time scale and a bar chart. The analyst will gather data relevant to one or more cycles of the activity for each man or machine involved. He will then draw up a chart with an appropriate time scale and plot out the times working on various activities or simply work and not working for each function analysed. Each type of activity will be indicated by a separate colour or hatching.

Figure 141 is a multiple activity chart representing the well known problem of toasting three pieces of bread under a grill which only holds two slices at a time. Students will understand the technique better if they can solve this

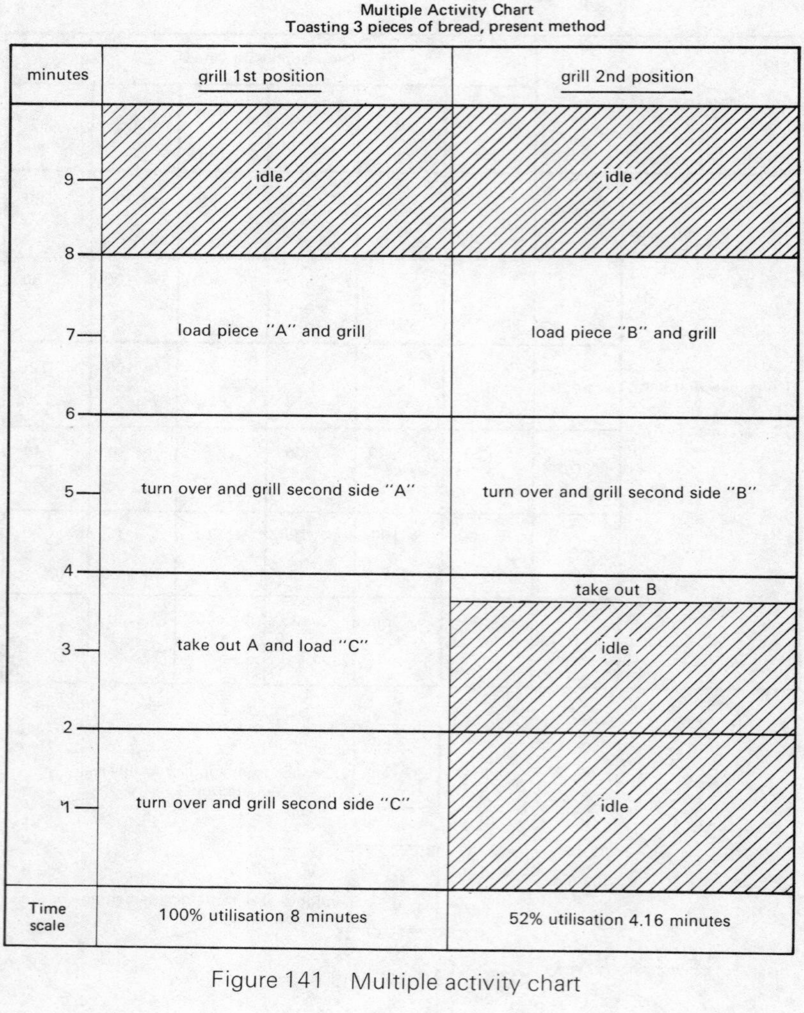

Multiple Activity Chart
Toasting 3 pieces of bread, present method

minutes	grill 1st position	grill 2nd position
9	idle	idle
8		
7	load piece "A" and grill	load piece "B" and grill
6		
5	turn over and grill second side "A"	turn over and grill second side "B"
4		take out B
3	take out A and load "C"	idle
2		
1	turn over and grill second side "C"	idle
Time scale	100% utilisation 8 minutes	52% utilisation 4.16 minutes

Figure 141   Multiple activity chart

problem using the chart and produce a chart indicating how to toast the bread in approximately 6 minutes instead of 8 minutes.

Output analysis charts

A major technique in the analysis and design of system files and their content, the output analysis chart is very simple to construct and understand. It is based on the fact that data produced for system outputs can be derived only from three sources–direct input, maintained files or computation. If, therefore, outputs are collected for the present system and listed on a chart with an analysis of their field content, the analyst can easily spot duplication and natural grouping and thus build up a list of preferred files, inputs and computation operations for use in his new system. Although the technique is so simple that an illustration (Figure 142) makes it selfexplanatory the student should not underestimate the usefulness and power of this charting technique in systems design.

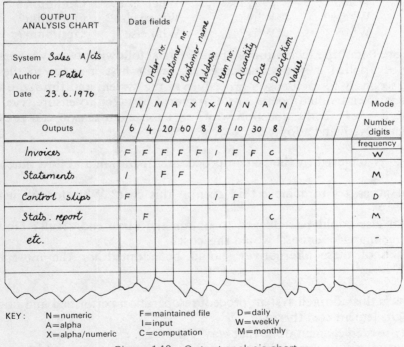

OUTPUT ANALYSIS CHART — Data fields	Order no.	Customer no.	Customer name	Address	Item no.	Quantity	Price	Description	Value			Mode
System *Sales A/cts* — Author *P. Patel* — Date *23.6.1976*	N	N	A	X	X	N	N	A	N			Mode
Outputs	6	4	20	60	8	8	10	30	8			Number digits
												frequency
Invoices	F	F	F	F	F	I	F	F	C			W
Statements	I		F	F								M
Control slips	F				I	F		C				D
Stats. report		F						C				M
etc.												-

KEY:
N=numeric F=maintained file D=daily
A=alpha I=input W=weekly
X=alpha/numeric C=computation M=monthly

Figure 142 Output analysis chart

Simplification

The next stage in the analysis of the facts is to examine each component part produced by the lists, tables and charts, to eliminate all unnecessary aspects (impurities) and to generate a series of alternatives for comparative evaluation.

Critical examination

One technique which is common to all productivity improvement functions is that of questioning all aspects of the present system in order to find out the real necessity for the work involved and to find the simplest and best procedures to adopt. In some cases this questioning approach is an unconscious one but for greatest impact it is better to adopt a more formal approach.

In practice the more experienced the analyst the less he tends to approach problems in the comprehensive manner that will be set out here. Although this is a fact it is regrettable for by working systematically through the following set of questions the analyst can be sure that no alternative has avoided his net.

Critical examination is a set of questions to which successively detailed stages of the system are subjected. It consists of primary questions to establish exactly the present method and reason for processing and secondary questions to develop alternatives and solution methods. The format is

Primary		*Secondary*	
What?	Why?	What else?	Optimum?
How?	Why?	How else?	Optimum?
When?	Why?	When else?	Optimum?
Where?	Why?	Where else?	Optimum?
Who?	Why?	Who else?	Optimum?

In more detail the technique is applied in the following twenty stages, which should be applied in the sequence given, in the first instance to the overall system, secondly to each costly procedure in the system and thirdly, if the cost justifies it, to individual operations. Care must be taken to ensure true, honest, accurate answers to the question why? as a mistaken reason can prevent the best alternative being adopted.

Purpose

(1) What is achieved by the system/procedure/operation and how much does it cost?

(2) Is it necessary to achieve this, even at this cost? Why does it justify this cost?

(3) What else could be achieved to obtain the same end result? How much (including changeover cost) would this cost?

(4) Which of these alternatives should be adopted for the most effective system?

Means

(5) How is this adopted system/procedure/operation performed and how much does each element cost this way?

(6) Why is each element done that way?

(7) What alternative methods of performing each element could be used and how much would these cost (including changeover cost)?

(8) Which of these alternative methods should be adopted on each element for the most effective method?

Sequence

(9) At what time during the month and in what sequence is this adopted system/procedure/operation performed and what costs due to this time/sequence are incurred, e.g. peaks, overtime, delays, storage, rehandling?

(10) Why is this done then or in that sequence and does the reason justify the cost?

(11) When else could it be done and what would this cost or save (including changeover cost) on the existing time/sequence?

(12) Which of these alternatives should be adopted for the most effective sequence?

Place

(13) In which department(s) and physical location within the department is this adopted system/procedure/operation performed and what costs does this incur, e.g. walking, mailing?

(14) Why is it done there and does the reason justify the cost?

(15) Where else could it be done and what would this cost or save on the existing location (including changeover cost)?

(16) Which of these alternative locations should be adopted for the most effective location?

Person

(17) Which department, function, machine and person performs this adopted system/procedure/operation and how much (including overheads if charged) is their hourly cost?

(18) Why does this department, function, machine and person perform it and does this justify the hourly charge?

(19) What other departments, functions, machines or persons could perform this work and what cost or saving on the existing cost (including the cost of changeover and training) would be incurred?

(20) Which department, function, machine or person should perform this work for the most effective staffing?

When all alternatives have been considered the most effective system (in theory) will evolve. It should be noted that most effective does not always line up with the immediately less costly method as an extra cost at one stage may produce an even greater overall benefit on a company wide basis.

Further investigation

The analyst will apply the critical examination technique in the following sequence; to the overall system; to each block on the block (logic) diagram; to each symbol on the detailed systems charts.

His aim is to examine each part as to necessity, effectiveness, performance and cost.

In doing so he will eliminate work, reduce work load, simplify tasks and add missing work as required.

In conjunction with this examination of the system description charts the analyst will investigate the system environment facts thus:

Organisation chart(s)–for the best span of control; to ensure all functions present; to remove duplication; to improve communication and control

List of problems–to solve or optimise

List of machines and equipment–to assess suitability

List of forms etc.–to reduce variety and to improve design

Physical layout–to improve work flow and to improve conditions

Cost summary–to highlight major areas

Coding systems–to rationalise and integrate.

Evaluation

When the analyst comes to the secondary questions, what should be done and how, etc., he will not make his decisions on guesswork or judgement but on facts. He will use quantitative units of cost, time, volume, etc., to compare one against the other. Having defined his criteria at the start of the project, he will then have a good basis for objective evaluation.

It is at this stage that the analyst might need to use the various statistical techniques detailed in Unit 7. One further graphical technique that can be useful is the decision tree (Figure 143).

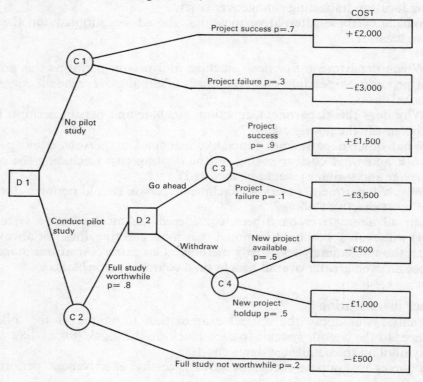

Figure 143　A decision tree

As each item is questioned and improvements devised the analyst must obtain the agreement of the line management concerned. As has been stated previously the best way to do this is by working at the improvements as a team with the changes developing naturally and therefore accepted from the start.

Quite often this may not be possible however and the analyst will be in the position of selling his proposals. The best approach here is one of honesty, clarity and tolerance. It cannot be stated too often that the analyst must view the change in terms of benefits to the recipient rather than from abstract or technical viewpoints.

When the period of analysis and change is complete (with the obvious amendment and recharting involved) the analyst will be left with a half-way, paper system which represents neither the actual existing system, nor the final proposed system but the best (in terms of minimum effective workload) system, regardless of processing method or sequence.

Data arrangement for design

The next step is to organise this **minimum effective workload** so that the best system with regard to logical processing sequence can be devised. To do this the analyst now prepares the following:

(1) A detailed (content:field, character, digit, symbol, size) specification of all outputs in the system required to satisfy the legal, audit and management requirements of the system as to content and timing.

(2) A detailed (as above) specification of all files of permanent data required in the system to produce the outputs directly or through processing.

(3) A detailed (as above) specification of all inputs of transaction data into the system required to update files and produce output directly or through processing.

(4) A detailed description of all work elements and constants required to produce output from input and file data.

(5) A detailed description of all decision elements required in the processing of input and file data.

The problem analysis stage

The problem analysis stage is probably the most important aspect of the systems analysis project. It is here that all the dead wood that has accumulated over the years in systems that have just grown with no real overall planning is cut out. It is at this stage that all the omissions that have made a potentially effective system prove, in practice, to be less than satisfactory are noted for inclusions. It is here that all the problems, hold-ups, inefficiencies and other defects are revealed.

The reason for the small amount of technology provided in this Unit is that the critical examination technique is both simple and plain common sense. In essence it just says 'what is going on' and 'what should be going on'. It is as simple as that. The fact finding techniques described in Unit 12 are also analysis techniques.

Assessment tasks

1 Take a simple item, e.g. a biro, pencil sharpener, or preferably something unfamiliar to you, such as an item from a woman's handbag for boys, an item from a man's toolkit for girls, and take it apart. Make a list of the component parts, grouping like items, e.g. screws, nuts, springs, and then write beside each item set a list of alternative uses. Describe a new device from your list of alternatives.

2 Perform the above task on a collection of any six filled-in business forms.
3 Produce (or take an existing) clerical procedure flowchart and subject it to the critical examination technique, working from macro to micro. Produce a report on your findings with any recommended changes you think fit.
4 Draw a layout chart of your office or classroom. Turn this into a flow or string diagram or travel chart and subject this to critical examination as above.
5 Draw a decision tree for your own career prospects.
6 Produce a multiple activity chart for the use of a time sharing terminal by manual entry only. Use a chart (not your intuition) to devise a more effective method.

Unit 14
Solution synthesis

Learning objective

To be able to identify the stages involved in systems design and to distinguish the various system types and their suitability for particular user requirements. To be able to design simple systems and depict this design by means of systems flowcharts, clerical procedure flowcharts and computer run charts. To understand the factors influencing file design and to be able to apply this understanding to the design of data elements, records and files within a database. To be able to define and apply design criteria in the field of environmental design. To be able to evaluate various system solutions for optimum effectiveness and efficiency.

The stages of solution synthesis

Having analysed and critically examined all the factors related to the problem, the analyst should be left with the minimum effective workload in terms of lists of output, file and input data elements and lists of the processing and decision tasks required to produce the system information from the data resources.

Solution synthesis entails using this data analysis to produce a well-designed system which will satisfy the aims of the user and the host organisation and at the same time make the most economical use of the business resources. The following are the main stages to be worked through: establish system type; overall system design; database and file design; input/output design; environmental design; system evaluation.

In order to arrive at a satisfactory solution, the analyst must be aware of the criteria of good system design and bear these in mind at each stage of the design process, particularly at the evaluation stage when each solution may meet some but not all of the requirements. It is at this stage that he must accept compromise with the priority that practicality is more important than design elegance. Perfection is an ideal to strive for but this must not be allowed to hinder achievement.

In general, the analyst should aim to satisfy the requirements of

effectiveness–the system must produce exactly (no more and no less) that information required by its recipient

response–the system must produce the information exactly (no sooner, no later) when it is required

throughput–the system must produce information as frequently as it is required

efficiency–the system must meet the above aims with the minimum use of the business resources possible

279

reliability–the system should function whenever required without break-down at any point. If breakdowns do occur, there must be adequate standby facility available

flexibility–the system must be designed to allow for ease of modification in changing circumstances with the minimum disruption

ease of implementation–the system should be as simple as possible and allow for easy implementation with existing resources or at least available resources.

System criteria

With regard to the computer processed parts of the system, the following, more detailed criteria should be adopted.

(1) The system should require the minimum clerical time, computer time and set-up time

(2) The system should make the best use of computer time by balancing input, set-up, processing and output

(3) Where possible the maximum data should be held on one master file and not duplicated on several files

(4) The system should be constructed in self-contained modules for ease of modification and run-time scheduling

(5) Each module or computer run should achieve a positive result (sorting and merging do not change data and should be minimised) and should have a distinctive function.

(6) Security and accuracy controls should be built in where necessary but only to achieve the required quality level cost effectively

(7) All processing should be designed with regard to the effect on and from other systems in the integrated systems network

(8) Manufacturers and library subroutines should be used whenever possible

(9) Master files should be processed as infrequently as possible in serial access processing

(10) Input data should not be entered into the system until required and output data should be dumped as soon as convenient

(11) Slow output devices (consoles, terminals) should only be used where no alternative exists or where the business oriented system makes this essential

(12) Restrict manual intervention between computer runs and aim for a simple manual–computer–manual system whenever possible

(13) Incorporate foolproof standby procedures for use in the event of breakdown

System types

The analyst will be designing his new system within an existing organisational framework. This framework will consist of certain hardware and software resources being applied to the existing mix of system applications. It may be that the ideal system he is aiming at will fit nicely within this framework or it could be that the requirements of the new system imply the necessity for change. As described in Unit 6, there is a range of system implementations from simple, local processing work units to organisation-wide processing networks. Usually it is not so difficult to fit a local requirement into a network system, or by-pass the system network and make local arrangements, but if the new system involves the setting up of a processing network for the first time, this can be a very involved, arduous process, particularly if a shared database system is envisaged.

An analysis of system types must cover

application types–processing, data capture, information retrieval, process control, simulation, etc.;

application mode–batch or real-time;

implementation method–individual local, centralised remote network, hierarchically distributed network, horizontally distributed network.

Any application type may be performed in any mode by any of the implementation methods. An individual application within any of the types will determine the best mode and implementation method but these will be restricted initially to the existing hardware, software and know-how resources of the organisation. If the analyst wishes to go outside these limitations, he will still need to work within the available (outside the organisation) technology and he will need to put forward a very good case for the additional resource requirements and organisational upheaval involved. This case must be based on the benefits to the user and the overall organisation which may be amongst those listed in Figure 49 or may be one or more of the following.

quicker processing–better management control

reduced processing cost–running cost/job cost

better management information–for profit planning and control

improved quality DP–reliability

present equipment replacements (obsolescence or inadequacy)

space saving

staff saving–clerical labour cost or scarcity

better service to customers

ability to absorb increased workload and reduce peaking

equipment compatibility in all parts of organisation

paperwork savings

machine utilisation–capital tied-up in office machinery

diverging systems and procedures standardised

introduction of more sophisticated techniques–OR, market research, etc.

In order to prepare a case for the acquisition of additional resources, it is necessary for the analyst to conduct a facilities study which, in itself can be a major project if the required changes are costly or involved.

The facilities study

On the assumption that the resource requirements are not just local but have organisation-wide implications, the analyst will not attempt to assume full responsibility for the study but will act under instructions from a steering committee. This committee will probably be chaired by the EDP or management services manager and its members will comprise representatives of all the organisational functions involved, including at least one member of the top company management.

The analyst returns to the steering committee with fully detailed (quantities, time constraints, etc.) flowcharts covering each proposed area of computerisation. The committee will discuss these with the analyst, noting any problem solutions that can be effected manually, and then the final list of systems to be computerised is prepared.

This committee should meet regularly to review the progress made by the analyst and to approve further investigational areas and terms of reference. The wide area covered by the steering committee members should enable cooperation to be gained more readily in all areas of the company for the analyst in his investigation.

Quotations from manufacturers or bureaus

Armed with full details the analyst and steering committee are now ready to approach the various computer manufacturers or bureaus to obtain hardware specifications and cost quotations.

The first problem is to decide which sources to ask for quotations. Undoubtedly bargains can be had by firms with enough computer experience to be able to shop around, but for the company with no previous computer experience it is wiser to restrict the choice to large well-established manufacturers or consultants.

In the first instance general enquiries should be sent to those companies selected asking for publicity material and advice. The replies to this initial request should be judged as indicative of the standard of customer support to be expected. Look for lack of enthusiasm, too quick sales representatives, and young inexperienced representatives; look at material quality supplied, and vet material for real content.

In addition to judging the results of the general enquiries, the analyst should organise visits for himself and the steering committee members, to similar companies to their own who have equipment from these manufacturers or who use those bureaus. The opportunity to ask for unbiased opinions on sales support, reliability, etc. should be taken as well as using the visit to borrow ideas and learn from the mistakes of others.

The analyst, although working under the control of the committee, will be expected to provide expert technical advice for decision and should keep himself up to date by reading the computer press and books covering hardware ranges and prices.

When enough information has been gathered to be able to judge between the companies concerned a final choice of a maximum of four manufacturers or bureaus should be made and these should be approached for quotations.

Asking for quotations

When the contact has been made each company chosen should be supplied with identical job folders containing:

List of all systems proposed

Index for each system listing all procedures or break points

Flowchart using conventional symbols of each procedure within each system

List of all inputs, files and outputs in each procedure with frequency; timing; volumes (average); average number of items; accuracy and other limits.

Used copies of all documents used in each procedure.

An accompanying questionnaire should be drafted laying out the following questions asking for answers in detail as appropriate:

(1) Proposed systems computer flowcharts for each system/procedure given with run timings (approximate)

(2) Computer utilisation bar chart over month showing each job quoted for input devices, CPU, output devices

(3) Estimated man hours to systems analyse, program and test, convert existing files and test full system

(4) Estimated bureau hours required to test programs

(5) Complete list and technical performance specifications of all hardware (including data preparation and output handling) required to run proposals; IAS size in bits; CPU speeds; Peripheral speeds

(6) Comparative costs for each item of hardware if purchased, or if rented; and maintenance (if additional–and if extra outside working hours)

(7) Costs if run on bureau basis as alternative

(8) What free support is offered, such as training (including/excluding accommodation); testing time; systems support (analyst experience, duration)

(9) What training is available, duration and cost and quality

(10) Is any systems analysis/programming aid available and costs

(11) Costs of program testing and what bureaus available (with configuration as quoted)

(12) What nearby configurations for standby arrangements

(13) What peripherals are available on this configuration and how does it expand with costs and technical specifications

(14) With what other configurations (or machines) is this configuration compatible (without reprogramming)

(15) What is the availability (delivery date) of this configuration

(16) What is the main programming language. How efficient is it. How long is the training course. Is it ready now. Date implemented. How much store does it require. What is the minimum configuration

(17) What high level languages are available on this configuration and other configurations. How much store is required and how efficient are the compilers. Dates of first implementation

(18) What software, e.g. DBMS, teleprocessing, packages, etc. is available

(19) How much store does operating system take up

(20) What special equipment is required, and approximate cost. What installation support services are offered

(21) Estimated cost of all materials required

(22) Proposed staffing.

Vetting manufacturers' or bureau replies

This stage will call for all of the analyst's experience and knowledge as he is the key man who will advise the steering committee as to the validity of the proposals received. He must make his judgement on the following factors:
How much of the above information is given
The quality and evasiveness of the replies
Personal experience or user advice on manufacturers
Any company policy or political decisions (e.g. nationality)
How well the proposals meet the original aims, in order of priority of the requesting party, including cost
The similarity and differences in differing company solutions
As a result of careful vetting, comparison and the clarification of any unclear or doubtful points the analyst must prepare a report for the steering committee in which he will recommend: either, no action, purchase, leasing, rental, the use of a bureau or the use of an outside consultancy (hardware/software).

When coming to his decision he will consider, with the help of accounting advice: tax disadvantages of leasing and renting; overall cost advantages of purchase; obsolescence advantages of rental; uncommitted experimental advantages of bureaus; cost and convenience advantages of bureaus; other pertinent company considerations (geography, reciprocal trading, etc.).

Having decided on what must be done the analyst will then choose the supplier best suited to satisfying the aims of the proposed systems. In addition to the factors previously mentioned the analyst will make use of several techniques to attempt to verify the manufacturers' proposals.

To test the relative computing speeds he may use instruction mix benchmark tests which will indicate the times expected for typical machine processing. In addition to calculating mix speeds the analyst may make use of standard tests (commercially available) or a set program devised by the analyst's company, representative of the typical company system.

This will entail a live run and timing on the recommended hardware but will give a better all round idea of the overall processing time including peripheral and set-up times. The disadvantage of benchmark tests is that no program can be really representative of the whole range of a company's systems.

The feasibility report

Having made all of his calculations and comparisons the analyst must come to a decision as to which manufacturer or bureau is favoured. He is now ready to put his proposals and reasons forward to the steering committee in the form of a report. The following points should be noted:
(1) Make report show the equipment as part of overall plan for cost reduction and problem solving and not as a panic measure
(2) Show that if 'in-house' equipment is obtained, it will have high utilisation
(3) Provide facts and plans to show when and how savings will recover capital expenditure
(4) Show the alternatives considered and the reasons for your choice.

(5) Plan report along the following lines: title and reason for report; index; narrative body; appendices.

The feasibility report body should have the following contents:

the proposal–brief outline up to one page only;

the expected benefits and justification–this should be as visual (charts, diagrams, colour etc.) as possible and can be backed up by a presentation with charts, models, film shows, etc.;

the basis of decision–listing all alternatives considered and the reasons for the final proposal;

costs of implementation including: siting and installation, hardware capital costs, staffing for operation, systems and programming costs prior to operation, training costs, materials, program testing and parallel running costs.

plans for the implementation of the proposal–with detailed time schedules (bar chart, critical path diagrams etc.);

five-year development plans after implementation–systems computerisation and integration, hardware enhancement, staff loading and requirements, space requirements, future predictions;

a request for action on the proposal by a given date with details of savings lost by delay for each month after.

System design

Having determined the type of system to be designed (and having ascertained the hardware, software and know-how resources available for its implementation), the analyst will have a choice or mix of design techniques to follow. If the system is centred around the implementation of a shared database then he will probably be primarily concerned with the database design, after which he will design his system to utilise this. If there is an existing shared database, then he will devote his energies to designing a system to utilise this facility fully. If the system is to have its own local files, then he will first tackle the overall system design followed by the design of the individual files it uses. We will consider here the overall system design considerations and talk about database design in conjunction with file design later on.

The first step in the synthesis of a new system is the identification and sequencing of the work and decision functions. In doing this, the analyst must make provision for three system areas: routine processing; exception processing and controls.

System block (logic) diagram

Having produced the various detailed specifications the analyst is ready to proceed to the most important phase in the design of his new system. This is the stage which determines exactly what the new system will be. This is also the stage where most junior analysts fail, in attempting to rush on to the method of processing and thus constricting the optimum solution with preconceived bias.

The purpose of the system block diagram is to establish the optimum sequence of fundamental processing elements and thereby determine the system workload and simplify the choice of optimum processing methods.

As with programming logic, there is no simple way of teaching students how to produce optimum logical sequences. This is an ability which some people have and others have not. It can be acquired over long periods given the aptitude for this type of work but the best we can do here is to look at the way skilled analysts instinctively approach the task.

Separation of functions

Working from the lists of work and decision elements required to produce the system outputs, the analyst will classify these in terms of basic processing functions, e.g.

Decisions	—	classification and checking
Work	—	recording (writing)
Work	—	reproducing (copying)
Work	—	sorting (sequencing and merging)
Work	—	calculating
Work	—	storing (filing and retrieval)
Work	—	communicating

Grouping of major processing blocks

The analyst now goes on to identify those elements on the list that most naturally occur together thus creating the major procedures in the system. He will now attempt his initial rough diagram of the system using the same symbols as for program logic charting.

After the Start symbol he will decide the first procedure in the system and draw this and subsequent logically sequenced work boxes on to his diagram until the first major decision diamond is reached. He will follow one path only from this decision until it is exhausted, returning then to trace the second path to its conclusion. This process is continued until all procedures on the list have been charted.

There now follows a stage of checking, amending and redrawing the rough chart until he is satisfied that all steps are covered, that the processing will produce the required output exactly and that all steps are in the best possible logical sequence.

Sequencing of processing elements

Once the analyst is satisfied that the major blocks in the system are logically sequenced he will go on to repeat the process for each basic function box and diamond within each procedure. This will involve producing further rough diagrams until the most satisfactory solution is reached. During this process it is likely that compromises will be made between the grouping of like elements for the most efficient processing and the separation of like elements for the most simple, direct processing. At all times the effectiveness and flexibility of the system should guide the analyst's decisions.

The final chart evolved from this process will include input/output symbols, file symbols and process and decision symbols for all processing, with no

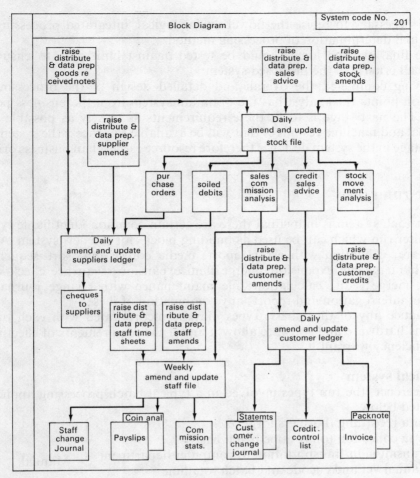

Figure 144   Block diagram

attempt to define the processing method. This is the system flowchart (see Figure 151).

Allocation of functions

The final stage of systems charting is to annotate the system logic with the optimum processing method for each step, based on the analyst's experience and knowledge of:

the resources available–men, machines, computer

the relative advantages and disadvantages of each available resource

the particular objectives and criteria of the system, e.g. reduce cost, improve speed

the interrelationship of each procedure in the system.

Each work and decision block is allocated to one of the following levels of processing: manual–by hand plus single element machine and equipment; mechanical–using large multi-element office machines; computer. It may be found necessary to revise the flowchart for logical, integrated processing after the initial determination of processing method.

The final evolved logic should be tested against limit data to ensure this meets all criteria of the proposed system.

Having completed the overall and detailed design of the processing and decision points the analyst has the optimum system from the business point of view. The next stage is to fit these requirements as closely as possible to the manual and machine resources that will be available to process the system. This final stage in the system design is therefore resource rather than business oriented.

Basic run types

Whilst each system is individual there are certain common identifiable types of computer run which can be used as building blocks for the new system. Among these are: validation with error report; media conversion; sort–sequence or special; merge–file expansion; merge–item expansion; sequence check–check, resort, merge; edit; calculation; file maintenance with change journal; file update; interrogation and report; any combination of these.

In practice any of these basic types may be incorporated with each other if systems hardware and software allow it and if the requirements of effectiveness and efficiency warrant it.

A typical system

For reference, the run types involved in a typical batch processing application are listed below:

(1) Data recording (business forms etc.) ⎫
(2) Data collection (on routine batch basis) ⎪
(3) Transmission/transportation to computer department ⎬ Manual
(4) Manual vet and encode and batch totalling ⎪
(5) Data preparation ⎪
(6) Verification ⎭
(7) Input/validate/media convert run ⎫
(8) Sort run (or sequence check) ⎪
(9) File expansion or item expansion or file update run ⎬ Computer
(10) Calculation and file edit ⎪
(11) Interrogate or validate/media convert/output run ⎭
(12) Manual output handling (bursting, decollating etc.) ⎫
(13) Distribution/transmission ⎬ Manual
(14) Action in user department ⎭

The analyst now proceeds to prepare his first rough clerical procedure flowcharts and computer run charts (Figure 151). These will probably be modified as the result of subsequent design stages, until they are finalised after systems evaluation and testing.

Database and file design

The various database, file, block, record, field and element structures are discussed in Unit 6. It is within these structures that the analyst plans his design. His system will be a model of events in the real world which link things (entities) to other things, thus causing relationships within the data structures. A further relationship is that of the characteristics (attributes) of these entities. Everything in the universe is related to everything else in some way. It is only when we want to link certain facts together for a particular purpose (system) that these relationships need to be defined. The stored data model of a group (set) of related entities and attributes is called the database of a system. The essential characteristics of an information retrieval system organised round a database are

> the selection of the facts to be stored (dataset)
> obtaining these facts–data capture
> vetting the facts for accuracy–integrity
> classifying and storing the facts–logical structure
> preserving the facts from corruption–security
> reconstructing a damaged database–recovery
> vetting requests for information–validation and authorisation
> retrieving data upon request–access.

The selection of the dataset will be a fallout from the lists of file elements for each application system to share the database derived during the analysis phase. These lists must be scrutinised for duplications and the key entities identified together with their related atrributes.

The next stage is to identify the relationships between the various entities. This is often achieved by means of a **Bachmann diagram**.

Figure 145   Data relationships

Bachmann diagrams present a picture of the database design which can then be implemented using conventional software or special database management systems (DBMS) software. The diagrams use a simple set of symbols, a rectangle for records which can be accessed directly, a hexagon for records that are accessed via other records, an unbroken arrow joining records which are always members of a set (mandatory), a dotted arrow joining records which are sometimes members of a set (optional) and a small numbered circle with footnote to indicate the sequence key adopted for record access. Relationships between entities can be defined as consisting of **owner records** and **member records**. There may be many owner records using one member record or one owner record using many member records or much more likely a mix of the two conditions. The arrow (dotted or unbroken) indicates the one to many relationship direction. The resulting structure built up by the diagram can be a **tree structure**, where each record is only a member of one set having only one owner, or a more complex **network structure**, with records having more than

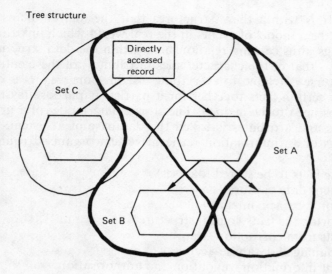

Tree structure

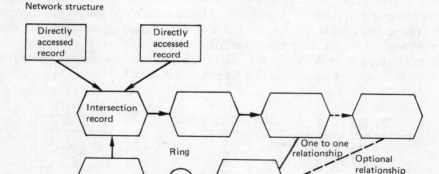

Network structure

S1 = Alphabetic sequence

Figure 146   Bachmann diagram conventions

one owner and therefore depicting more than one set. If any records have a one to one relationship, no arrow heads are used on the connecting line. If records have a many to many relationship, these may be depicted by arrow heads in both directions on the line but more often a dummy intersection record is used to join these records with no application data but record address pointers only. Pointers are frequently used to connect records from owner to members, members to previous and next in sequence members and members to owners. This device sets up flexible rings of related records for ease of access.

The database description provided by the Bachmann diagram and implemented by a data description language (DDL) is known as a **schema**. The subset of this schema which is the set of data related to one specific application is called a subschema.

Record structures

If the analyst is designing conventional files he will be less concerned with relationships (although field within record and record sequencing are still important) and more concerned with record structures and grouping. Two factors need to be considered: the data requirements of the system and the need for an efficient, balanced system. The analyst should aim at producing a system in which set-up time is reduced to a minimum, input/output and processing time is reduced to a minimum, and internal data transfer and processing time balances input/output time.

Starting with the data required by the business requirements of the system the analyst will find there are two distinct types of data; descriptive data and value data. Little can be done to reduce the amount of value data (arithmetic and logically processed facts) but descriptive data (names, headings, etc.) can be reduced by the coding techniques discussed elsewhere. When the analyst arrives finally at the irreducible minimum amount of data that must be entered into the computer system, he must then consider the best way to group this to achieve the desired efficiency.

To return for a moment to basic principles. Data processing involves producing output data either directly or in the form of updated master (maintained) files. This output can only come from four sources: direct input; direct maintained file data; direct program constant and literal data; processed interaction of any or all of the above.

Input and maintained file data is organised into a hierarchy of characters or digits; numeric or alphabetic words; multiple word fields; multiple field records; multiple record blocks.

The record is the basic unit in data processing. It is how these records are grouped and arranged that affects the balance and, therefore, efficiency of the system.

Record size

In establishing which of the essential data will be input, which on file and which built into the program the analyst should consider the following:

The size of the record determines the overall size of the unit of input and of the maintained file.

The larger the record the longer the input/output time, both via input/output units and backing store units.

Records may be of fixed or variable size.

Variable size records, or blocked groups of records, are more complex to process and therefore increase transfer/processing time. Fixed size records or blocks conversely decrease this time.

Fixed size records or blocks must be as large as the largest record/block size and are, therefore, wasteful of capacity and also increase input/output time. Variable size records hold only the minimal data and are, therefore, the opposite of this.

As a general practical guide, fixed size records and blocks tend to be used most frequently and are best suited to high activity files, low volume files, files with evenly sized records and infrequently run jobs.

Record grouping

We have seen that record size has most effect on input/output time. Record grouping and arrangement determines the transfer/processing times. As with size, the initial limitations derive from the business considerations of the system. To a large extent the purpose and type of the system (batch processing, real-time, etc.) influences the hardware configuration and this in turn, together with the available manufacturer's software, will limit the scope for the designer to arrive at an optimum solution.

In the first place the analyst may or may not be given a choice of processing records wholly in blocks as some machines are character addressable rather than word addressable. It is, however, possible for records to be grouped and processed in blocks which can contain: a fixed number of fixed size records; a fixed number of variable size records; a variable number of fixed size records; or a variable number of variable size records.

Given a choice the analyst will consider the following points when determining the optimum grouping of records:

With variable size records the block size will be variable and the IAS allocated must equal the largest block, which will result in poor storage utilisation and more complex programming

The smaller the block size the less data can be held on file due to interblock gap allowances

The maximum block size is limited by the amount of IAS available as well as the need for transfer/processing time balance

Transfer/processing time balance must be calculated making allowance for the normal activity rate of the file. The times for processing and for skipping individual records in a block are calculated by multiplying the average instruction time by the number of instructions in each case. These are then multiplied by the expected number of hits and non-hits respectively to give the total processing time for the block.

The time to transfer the block to and from the IAS is calculated by modifying the nominal quoted transfer rate by the block size and interblock gap, to arrive at an effective transfer rate for the block. Most manufacturers provide tables of effective transfer times.

As a general guide the use of the largest practical fixed record/fixed block gives: good IAS and backing store utilisation; fast transfer rates; simpler programming; reduced handling time.

Other considerations when designing files are flexibility for change, growth and security.

Input|output design

When the analyst has determined his new system inputs and outputs he will be faced with the task of designing the physical media on which his data fields will be represented. Another aspect of forms design is where an improvement can be effected without any other change in the system merely by simplifying and improving the document layout.

Regardless of whether the system is a manual or computer one the main means of communication in the data processing field is by means of the business form. Most students are unaware of the sheer volume of paperwork used in the typical business. A survey taken over a wide range of industries in the United States, which is far more computerised than the UK, revealed an average of 2926 varieties of forms per company. An accounting department covering just one geographical group of a UK company was found to be using 153 varieties of forms. This is the reason why good forms design is so important. In fact forms design is only part of another specialist activity known as forms control which is too complex to go into here.

In designing a form the analyst has two initial considerations in mind: design for ease of print production; design for effective, economic use. Of the two the second is far more important as it is normally accepted that the cost of using a form is about twenty times its production cost.

Printing considerations

The analyst should bear in mind the following points which the printer will need to know:
(1) Material type and weight–use standard materials
(2) Colour paper and colour ink required
(3) Size of form–business stationery is now standardised to eliminate wastage (see Figure 147)
(4) Style of production–any special type style, spacing, lines, emphasis, shading, etc. should be pointed out when ordering the forms.
(5) Special instruction–the analyst must also make sure the printer realises the need for such things as folding marks, serial numbers, filing holes, perforation and in a double sided form whether it is to be printed head to head or head to tail
(6) Packing and handling–the analyst should specify if the forms are to be in sets, padded, and if so joined on which edge, and also give packing instructions
(7) Volumes and delivery dates–the printer must know if volumes required are regular or once off and what delivery dates are required together with the maximum requirement at any time.

All of these factors not only ensure that the forms will be correct and delivered on time but also, if observed, will enable the printer to set up the most economic printing runs and therefore lower the cost of the forms.

User considerations

The following points should be observed with regard to the user's requirements.

Identification–all forms should have a title and form number. In addition company identification and serial numbering may be required

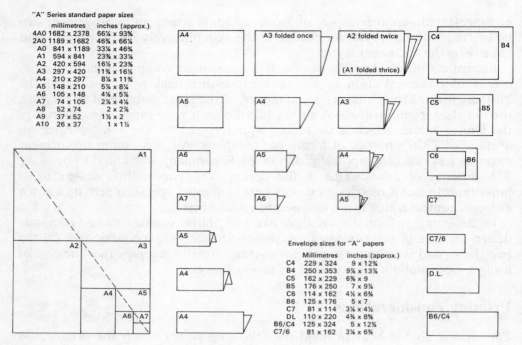

Figure 147   Standard paper sizes

Instructions–these may be required with regard to filling-in, routing and retention period. If so they must be placed so that the user will read them before acting

Introductory data–information regarding date, time span covered, destination or an explanation of purpose may be necessary

Logical grouping of content–the data should be arranged on the form for a purpose and not just to fill in the spaces conveniently

Filling-in form–the material should be chosen with regard to the method of entry (pen, punch, type, printer) and the environment it will be used in. Also considered will be the number of copies required and the method of producing them (one-time carbon, NCR paper, carbon back, etc.) Forms paper can be tissue, manifold, bank, bond or ledger and the weights (measured in grammes per square metre) from 27–114 g/m². The material is also important if any special photocopying or other requirements are to be met.

Another aspect is the spacing of any lines, boxes etc. which will vary according to the method of entry. Hand spacing should be 1/4″ vertical × 8 characters per inch, machine entry 1/6″ vertical × 10, 12, or 16 characters per inch and a compromise allowing for both 1/3″ vertical × 10 characters per inch.

As much information as possible should be preprinted and tick boxes and similar devices used. One most important aspect is the sequence of data entry which should line up with the layout of the source document. This is even more important when a mechanised process such as keypunching is to be performed from the form. A specimen key punching source document entry is illustrated in Figure 148

Code	Qty.	Item no.		Price		Qty.	Item no.		Price		Qty.	Item no.		Price	
A	tons	type	no.	£	p	tons	type	no.	£	p	tons	type	no.	£	p
1	4	8	11	15	18	20	24	27	31	34	36	40	43	47	50

Figure 148   Key punching source document

Using data–once filled in the form will be read, information extracted and possibly photocopied. The use of lines and spaces for grouping data to give easy visibility and prominence to important aspects and also the use of coloured paper and inks will be considered. In general the analyst will aim to achieve a simple, pleasing appearance that aids data retrieval and prevents clerical and reading errors

Concluding data–the form may require signatures, positions, department and date information

Filing and mailing aspects–as mentioned with regard to printer's instructions the analyst must consider the method of filing and mailing and, therefore, the necessity for and position of filing holes, perforations, serial numbers, etc.

General considerations

In tackling form design the analyst should aim to reduce the variety of forms required; reduce the number of copies per set; reduce the volume used; reduce the content of the form; reduce the form size.

In practice to design a form one would roughly follow the following steps:
(1) Decide what information is required
(2) Decide size in digits of the required data
(3) Decide the optimum sequence of data entry
(4) Decide on the printed questions and box labels that will be used. Ensure these are capable of direct coding and are not open-ended
(5) Decide on headings, instructions and concluding data
(6) Roughly draft the data on a large sheet of squared paper with scale suitable to the method of data entry
(7) Revise and redraw for appearance and smallest paper size
(8) Decide ink and paper colours, paper type and quality
(9) Prepare printer's instructions and final draft

Stationery types and quality
Computer output stationery can be subdivided into three main types: plain stationery (listing); preprinted stationery; special purpose stationery.
Plain stationery (listing)
This type of stationery is produced by suppliers as standard and therefore prices are correspondingly inexpensive due to bulk production. Although this is plain stationery in fact it comes in three styles, no printing at all, feints (3

lines to the inch) and flowline or screen listing (3 sets of seven fine lines to the inch). There is no price distinction between these styles but screen listing is normal and supply and distribution problems will be reduced if this is standardised on. Where possible this should be used in preference to preprinted stationery and headings, if required, printed out by the computer.

Preprinted stationery

For forms that have to go outside the company or where the amount of heading and static information is too heavy to lineprint, it may be necessary to use preprinted continuous stationery.

This type of stationery is much more expensive than plain stationery and all the normal economic aspects that apply to single forms apply here also. Prices increase as follows: as quantities decrease; as the amount of printing required increases; as the method of producing multicopies becomes more sophisticated; as certain non-standard special sizes are required; as the number of colours used increases; as special possible but expensive requirements, such as gumming and punching, increase; as the specifications of different forms become more divergent.

To obtain the most economical prices it is therefore necessary to comply, where possible, to the recommended standards in the foregoing sections.

Special purpose stationery

Most suppliers claim that any type of special stationery requirement can be provided. This is true but specials are usually very expensive and for short run work the setting up charge spread over few copies can be prohibitive. The aim should be to use standard stationery wherever possible and only to resort to special purpose if this can be proved to be a more economical overall method. Included in this type of stationery are gummed faces, continuous envelopes, continuous punched cards, special purpose folds and perforations.

The quality of output stationery is important and this should be suited to the line printer to be used. With online work it is false economy to use stationery of low quality or weight for the sake of cheapness, as breakdowns due to paper fouls can be very costly in computer time.

Environmental design

Gradually, from all his deliberations, the analyst will have evolved his final optimum system design. This culminates in the production of:

(1) A final systems chart showing each input, file, output record and the selected media. Also shown will be every computer run for which a program must be written together with full details of the manual processing required.

(2) For each input, file and output record there will be a written specification as to the data content, sequence and grouping of content on the selected media. If the new system design has required the installation of new computing facilities, or if this new system has resulted in large-scale organisational changes, the analyst may well find himself involved in physical layout design.

The actual technique of designing physical layouts is more the province of the architect than the systems analyst. However, the architect approaches the subject from a technical point of view rather than in relation to work flow and productivity. Often the analyst may be required to advise on the best layout from this angle even to the point of submitting draft layout plans.

There is no set method of approaching this subject. All that can be given are some points and hints on certain aspects. Usually the analyst will be concerned with one or more of the following: location of a building; characteristics of a building; location of individual offices within building; characteristics of offices; location of work stations; characteristics of work stations.

He will therefore obtain maps, floor plans, etc. of the physical area concerned and on these it is usual to superimpose scale models or paper cut-out representations of the items to be located and by trial and error combined with data analysis (distances, volumes, etc.) try to determine the best workable positioning of the area contents.

In addition to relative positioning the analyst must be concerned with environment characteristics, such as lighting, noise, etc., not only to satisfy the various legal requirements but also for the most productive conditions of working for men and machines.

A list of aims for optimum layout would include: maximum utilisation of space; minimum movement of work; maximum facilities for supervision control; minimum environmental interference; maximum safety and health conditions; allowance for possible expansion.

Among the items the analyst would investigate would be: lighting and colour schemes; temperature and humidity; noise and dirt; seating and furniture; machines and equipment; security and privacy; prestige (show place); access, stairs and lifts; communications, phone and transport; floor loading; toilets, cloakrooms, catering; power supplies and cleaning services; inter-office relationships; centralisation versus decentralisation.

On the final point, there are always debates as to the desirability or otherwise of centralised, usually open-plan, offices. The relative advantages of each type of layout are:

Centralised

Economic–high space utilisation; high machine utilisation; high staff utilisation

Specialisation of supervision and staff (lower labour grades)

Closer control over quality and quantity but with less supervision

Better training and promotional possibilities

Standardised systems, methods and targets

Fair, balanced work loading

Easier peak work load handling

Price advantage of bulk purchase (materials and stationery)

Better internal communications

Reduced duplication of information and processing

Specialised machines and environment conditions possible

Decentralised

High identity and status value

Tailor made systems and methods

Functional departments have more control over their own priorities

High privacy and quiet conditions

Higher natural morale in smaller units

Less external communication and work movement problems
Fewer distractions
More sensitive, flexible approach to change, and exceptions
Better overall job knowledge
No tendency for high grade staff to perform low grade work on do it yourself basis

Computing facilities environment

If the analyst is concerned with the installation of new computing facilities, there will be a special set of requirements to be considered. Each installation is of course a special case and must be considered on its own merits. There are, however, many areas of common ground in planning for the computer site and it is worth the analyst's while to work from the following check-lists at this stage to ensure no point is overlooked:

(1) **Allow space for:** computer room; engineer's room; air lock; air-conditioning plant room; space for motor alternator; data preparation room; ancillary machine room; space for control clerks; magnetic file library; output despatch area; data transmission room; space for programmers; space for systems analysts; management offices; viewing/conference room; bulk input/output storage; toilet facilities and rest area; area for future expansion.

(2) **Ensure correct environmental conditions:** access for machines and equipment; fire exits and security precautions; natural lighting for offices; quiet area for programmers; interview facilities for systems analysts; desk space for charting; visitor viewing and staff induction facilities; good work-flow, data preparation–computer–output despatch; effective supervision and control facilities; economy or showplace decor; expansion and building restrictions; area, height, floor rating, power supply, air pollution noise, vibration, flood damage, water supply, solar gains, electromagnetic radiation; standby facilities for air-conditioning, power, background heating and workload handling in case of failure.

(3) **Order machines, equipment and furniture:** air-conditioning plant; motor alternator; temperature and humidity recorder; fire detection system; data preparation machines; output handling–guillotines, bursters, decollators; data transmission equipment; office furniture and files; magnetic files media; shelving for bulk storage; engineer's work bench, equipment, files; work trolleys; media storage; fireproof master safe file; tacky mats; fire blankets and CO_2 extinguishers; telephones; special vacuum cleaner; paper tape winders, splice, handpunch; papertape collection bins; magnetic tape splice and adhesive; wall clock and time punch clock for run timing; reception/conference room fittings, projectors, etc.; bookcases, labeller, buro-box transports, etc.; vending machines (for shift work); cloakroom, handbag lockers, etc.

Evaluation

As the analyst proceeds through the various aspects of his new system design, he will be faced with problems of conflicting optimisation factors. Having designed his outline system and converted this to clerical procedures and computer runs, he will find when it comes to designing the physical environment, consisting not only of the special layout but also of the hardware, software and liveware processing components and data carrying media, that he will need to evaluate several compromise solutions. The main criteria to use will always be the initial systems requirements that he defined with the user management during his initial planning phase. These themselves will have been validated, in so far as they contribute to the overall attainment of the aims of the organisation.

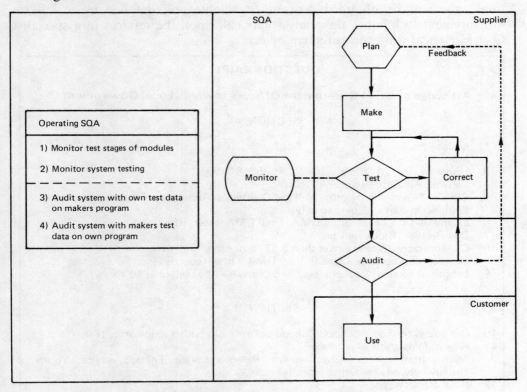

Figure 149   Software quality assurance

Having found the designs that satisfy these system objectives, the analyst may still find several suitable alternatives which may be employed and for this reason he will want to evaluate these to find the best design and, so, concurrent with his design development, will time each processing stage, both computer and clerical. A further reason for this timing evaluation is so that he will have data for the scheduling of the implementation and subsequent running of the new system and any balancing and coordinating that may be required.

The timing of system computer runs will depend on the particular machine configuration used. The analyst must be fully conversant with the specification and limitations of the machines he is dealing with. Particularly important will be the degree of simultaneity of CPU and peripheral operation which can range from none to fully simultaneous working.

There are many ways of producing timings for clerical work varying from stopwatch observed time study to tabulated sets of standard time data. Which of these methods is employed will depend on the skill and experience of the analyst and the use to which the derived data is put.

Where the timings are required only for planning purposes the analyst will find the simplest and most practical method is to attempt the job himself and note the average time attained over a number of cycles. By multiplying this average by the normal volumes of work a rough but sufficient estimate of the total time will be obtained. For more reliable and detailed clerical work measurement techniques the analyst may call upon the services of a specialist O & M clerical work measurement officer.

QUESTIONNAIRE

Attitudes of Local Government Officers towards Local Government

SECTION A

1. Male: Female
2. Married: Single
3. Under 21: 21–25: 26–35: 36–45: 46–55: 56–65.
4. Clerical: AP: Other (specify) ....
5. Clerk's: Treasurer's: Health: Welfare: Children's: Architect's: Education: Housing: Engineer's: Parks: Other (specify)...
6. *Examination*: Clerical: Inter DMA: Final DMA: Inter IHM.
7. Day Release: Block Release.
8. *Qualifications*: None: Fewer than 5 'O': 5 or more 'O': Fewer than 3 'A': 3 or more 'A': Degree: Diploma: Clerical: Inter DMA: Other (specify) ....
9. Length of service: 1 year or less: 2–5 years: 6–10 years: over 10 years.

SECTION B

10. *Did you enter from:* School: College or University: other employment?
11. *Why did you think of entering?*
Advice from school: Advertisement: Parent's advice: Friend's advice: Youth Employment advice: Other (specify) ....
12. *What attracted you?*
Pay: Career prospects: Security: Facilities for further education: Chance to serve community: Other (specify) ....
13. *If you entered from other employment what in your previous job did you dislike?*
Lack of opportunity: Poor working conditions: Inadequate pay: Poor career prospects: Poor relations with colleagues: Other (specify).......................
14. *What do you like about your job?*
Working conditions: Conditions of service: Staff amenities: Responsible work: Scope for initiative: Training facilities: Relations with members of public: Happy atmosphere: Useful work: Other (specify) ....
15. *What do you dislike?*
Pay not good enough: Too much/too little responsibility: Poor facilities for doing job: Not used to full ability: Don't get on with colleagues: Too much discipline: Promotion too slow: Other (specify)...
16. In your own words—What would lead you to consider leaving local government?

Figure 150   Questionnaire for assessment task

If the analyst is in the position of having software prepared by an outside agency rather than by a member of the in-house programming team, he should design a system of software quality assurance (Figure 149) to make certain that the full system requirements are met. There are two main reasons for this. Firstly, software purchased from an outside supplier is manufactured in exactly the same way as hardware, that is to time and budget considerations. Secondly, the hardware and the software are often made and tested separately by different suppliers and there is no guarantee that they will not contain certain incompatibilities. The role of software quality assurance is to audit the software during and after manufacture but before implementation to ensure all the necessary controls and test procedures are built into the system and that they function correctly.

Assessment tasks

1 Describe six different applications, each implemented by a different system type. Identify the reasons for the suitability of the chosen type for each application.
2 Provide an analogy for systems design by illustrating the same design stages found in systems design but using a product design task instead.
3 Draw a systems flowchart for any system of your choice. If possible chose some real but simple system that you can research within your own environment. Define the clerical processing and the computer processing and produce clerical procedure flowcharts and computer run charts. If it is not possible to use a real system, research a system description from a number of textbook sources and synthesise your answer.
4 Obtain detailed specifications, costs, etc. of a current processing configuration and present a report with reasons and details of a proposed application.
5 Draw a Bachmann diagram to describe the relationships of the contents of your telephone/address book.
6 Redesign the questionnaire in Figure 150.
7 Redesign your office/classroom and state your reasons for any changes.

Unit 15
Solution implementation

Learning objective

To be able to understand the stages necessary to implement a newly designed system. To be able to reproduce the necessary documentation required in a systems specification and to understand the reasons for each document. To be able to define the various tasks involved in implementation, in particular the area of thorough system testing. To be able to effect a systems audit after implementation to evaluate how well the new systems design is meeting its stated objectives.

Systems specification

Having completed a new system design based upon the best compromise solutions from the several alternatives he has synthesised, the analyst will draw together all the documentation he has been accumulating during his project and finalise the specification of the system. Initially, this specification will be used as the basis for both the programming effort and the clerical procedure definitions and training. Later it will be used as the reporting medium for obtaining systems acceptance from the user, computer operating and audit departments and, later still, for implementation and systems objectives audit. Finally, the systems specification is incorporated as the definitive statement of the system which will be used as the starting point for all modifications and changes.

In addition to the various flowcharts that the analyst has prepared, there are a series of preprinted forms for him to fill in together with a check list to ensure that the documentation is complete. At a later stage, the programmer will add his documentation for each computer run (program) to build up a comprehensive coverage. The operating department's systems work file will be composed of various documents selected from this specification. If clerical work manuals and handbooks are prepared, they too may be added to the file.

Systems report

Upon receipt of the systems specification the programming team will proceed to devise and test their programs (or incorporate library programs) for each computer run, as outlined in Unit 9. Meanwhile, the analyst will be occupied getting approval for his proposals and then preparing the detailed changeover of all the manual processing entailed.

SYSTEM SPECIFICATION AND JOB RECORD
CC2

System name   *Hourly Workers Payroll*

System No.   A φ 7

Systems team leader   F. Smithson   Int. tel :   297
Home tel :   698 - 4443

Systems analysts   J. Brown   Int. tel :   299
Home tel :   424 · 6741

Int. tel :
Home tel :

SYSTEM SPECIFICATION CONTENTS CHECK LIST CC3		System code No. A φ 7
Check list	Systems analyst	No. of sheets
✓	Title page	1
✓	System specification contents check list	1
✓	Feasibility study request/report	1
✓	System specification amendment record	1
✓	System acceptance record	1
✓	System scope	1
✓	Hardware specification	1
✓	Systems flowchart	2
✓	Computer run charts	2
✓	Clerical procedure flow charts	3
✓	Input, file and output index	1
✓	Media formats	19
✓	Data volumes and statistic	1
✓	Run timing	1
✓	Special procedures and control requirements	1
✓	Test data specification	1
✓	Glossary of special terms	1
	Programmer (for each run)	
	Program testing record	
	Pro____ess ___	

Figure 151   Sample systems specification

SYSTEM ACCEPTANCE RECORD CC6 System code no. A ∅7

1. Accepted by Systems department

   Date 31.1.84 Signature H. Andrews Title Systems Manager

   Date 31.1.84 Signature Perkins Title Analyst

2. Accepted by User-department

   Date 18.8.1984 Signature J. Smith Title Chief Accountant

   Date Signature Title

3. Accepted by Programming department

   Date 19.8.84 Signature B. Mann Title Chief Programmer

   Date 25.8.84 Signature H. Wright Title Programmer

4. Test data run result accepted by:— User department

   Date 30.9.84 Signature J. Smith Title Chief Accountant

   Date Signature Title

   Audit department

   Date 2.10.84 Signature C. Pearson Title Auditor Systems

   Date Signature Title

5. Accepted by D.P. Operating department

   Date 1.11.84 Signature B. Wheeler Title Operations Control

   Date Signature Title

FEASIBILITY STUDY REQUEST/REPORT CC4 System code no. A ∅7

Request

Study requested by Signature J. Smith Date 3.10.1983

Name J. Smith Position Chief Accountant Dept. 7461

Precise description of system to be studied:—

The production of payslip, stamp list, and coin analysis for hourly-paid staff. The maintenance of staff payroll records.

Reason for request (survey aims) To reduce processing costs + to smooth peaking problems in work load. Date required by:— 31.1.1984

Departments affected	Input documents	Outputs required
Production dept.	Clock cards F1238	Payslips F1240
Personnel dept.	Record amendments F1234	Coin analysis+stamplist F1240

Report

Study conducted by F. Smithson Date 20.1.1984

Report:— Feasible project. Will yield cost savings based on staff, machine and space savings. Also smoothing of peak work loads + reduction of turn round time.

Suggest project commences by end of April 1984 for implementation Oct/Nov 1984

Cost of changeover	Systems investigation	Man days 100 - £2400
	Programming	Man days 60 - £1000
	Other costs (materials)	£5260

Running costs	Present system	£30,500 p.a.
	Proposed system	£15,050 p.a.
	Saving	£15,450 p.a.

| Proposal accepted by applicant | Signature J. Smith | System code number A ∅7 |

Figure 151 Sample systems specification

HARDWARE SPECIFICATION — CC8

System code No. A ∅ 7

Quantity	Unit	Model	Speed	Specification
1	Central processor	XYZ 29	2 µs	16 K × 24 bit words
1	Console typewriter	XYZ 3/1	10 CPS	see manual
1	Card reader	XYZ 74	900 CPM	"
	Paper tape reader			
4	Magnetic tape unit	XYZ 18B	20 KC	"
	Magnetic disc unit			
1	Card punch	XYZ 6	100 CPM	"
	Paper tape punch			
1	Line printer	XYZ 99	1350 IPM	12"-120 char
	Graph plotter			
	Display unit			

Other machines (detail):—

Card punches and verifiers only.

SYSTEMS SCOPE — CC7

Sheet 1 of 1 System code no. A ∅ 7

Inputs

From department	Form no.	Description	Person supplying (title)	Last time in
621 (shop)	F1238	Clock card	Wages clerk	Wed. 3.30 P.M.
673 Personal	F1234	Record amendment	Records clerk	Daily 10.00 A.M.

Files and processing

1) Employee record file.

Daily: Staff amendments batched and data prep.

Weekly: a) Check amendment validity, sort to staff key amend file and delete transfers. Resort transfers and merge under new number.

b) Batch and data prep. Clockcards, validity check, sort to staff key and calculate payslips and coin/stamp analysis.

Outputs

To department	Form number	Description	Person receiving (title)	Last time out
Payroll 683	F1240	Payslips	Wages clerk	Thurs 3.30 P.M.
673	F1241 F1235 F1236	Coin, stamp analysis 'No. file amends Invalid amend list	Records clerk	"
673	F1237	Employee transfers	Stats clerk	"
621	F1239 P.C.007	Excessive hours Invalid clock cards	shop clerical	"

Figure 151 Sample systems specification

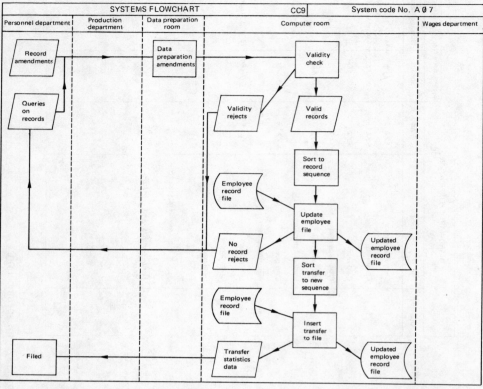

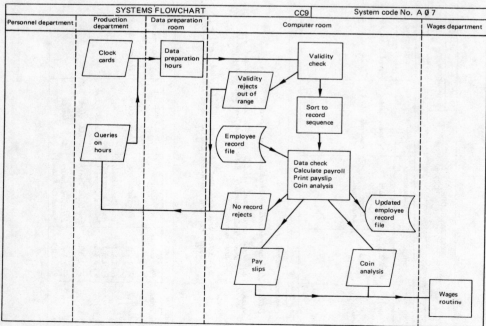

Figure 151   Sample systems specification

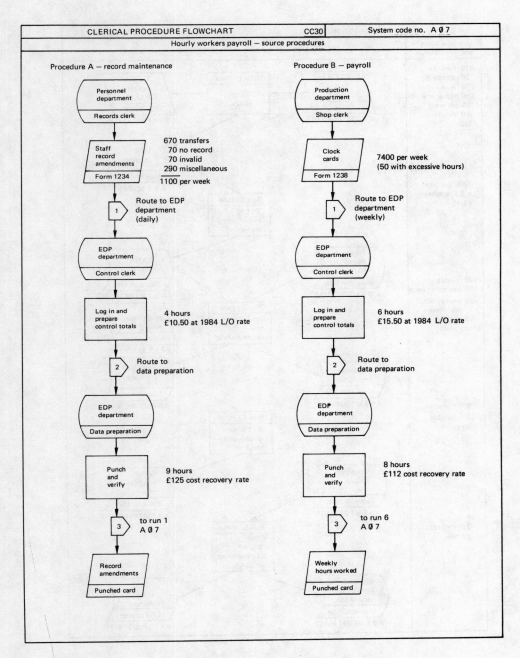

Figure 151 Sample systems specification

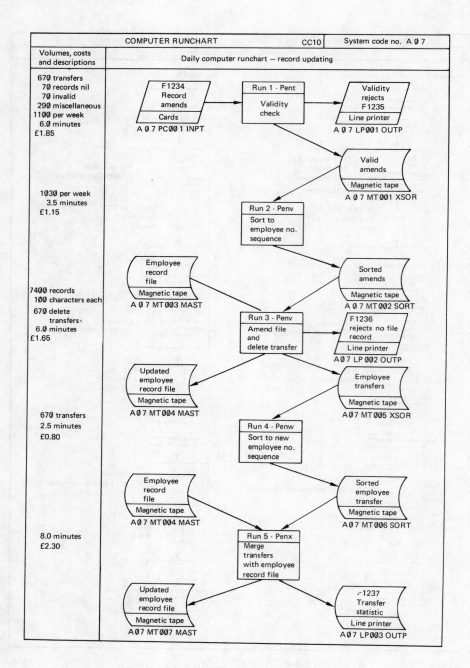

| COMPUTER RUNCHART | CC10 | System code no. A Ø 7 |

Volumes, costs and descriptions

Daily computer runchart — record updating

670 transfers
70 records nil
70 invalid
290 miscellaneous
1100 per week
6.0 minutes
£1.85

F1234
Record
amends
Cards
A Ø 7 PC00 1 INPT

Run 1 - Pent
Validity
check

Validity
rejects
F 1235
Line printer
A Ø 7 LPØØ1 OUTP

Valid
amends
Magnetic tape
A Ø 7 MT ØØ1 XSOR

1030 per week
3.5 minutes
£1.15

Run 2 - Penv
Sort to
employee no.
sequence

Employee
record
file
Magnetic tape
A Ø 7 MT ØØ3 MAST

Sorted
amends
Magnetic tape
A Ø 7 MT ØØ2 SORT

7400 records
100 characters each
670 delete
transfers
6.0 minutes
£1.65

Run 3 - Penv
Amend file
and
delete transfer

F1236
rejects no file
record
Line printer
A Ø7 LP ØØ2 OUTP

Updated
employee
record file
Magnetic tape
A Ø7 MT ØØ4 MAST

Employee
transfers
Magnetic tape
A Ø7 MT ØØ5 XSOR

670 transfers
2.5 minutes
£0.80

Run 4 - Penw
Sort to new
employee no.
sequence

Employee
record
file
Magnetic tape
A Ø7 MT ØØ4 MAST

Sorted
employee
transfer
Magnetic tape
A Ø7 MT ØØ6 SORT

8.0 minutes
£2.30

Run 5 - Penx
Merge
transfers
with employee
record file

Updated
employee
record file
Magnetic tape
A Ø7 MT ØØ7 MAST

⌐1237
Transfer
statistic
Line printer
A Ø7 LP ØØ3 OUTP

Figure 151   Sample systems specification

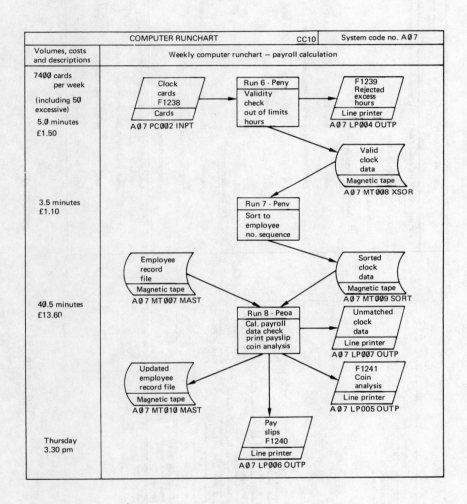

Figure 151 Sample systems specification

MEDIA FORMATS CC12	Sheet 1 of 19
	System code no. A Ø 7

For each item on the index sheet (CC11) there must be a format sheet specifying the record, block and file structure.

Details will include —

Record Specification

identity   description   medium used

fixed length size or variable length min/max size

key field(s)   field sequence   field level

field picture   field value range

File Specification

identity   description   medium and units used

type: input/master/output/working

organisation structure employed

fixed length size or variable length min/max size

block fixed/variable min/average/max size

key(s)   overflow organisation   copies

record sequence by identity   retention period

INPUT FILE AND OUTPUT INDEX CC11		Sheet 1 of 1
		System code no. A Ø 7

	Code	Description	Program name
Inputs	PC 001	Record amendment card	Pont
	PC 002	Clock data card	Pory
Files	MT 001	Valid amendments - Random	Pont - Ponu
	MT 002	Sorted valid amendments	Ponu - Ponu
	MT 003	Employee record file	C - Ponu
	MT 004	Updated employee record file - intermediate 1.	Ponu - Ponx
	.MT 0-05	Employee transfer	Ponv - Ponw
	MT 006	Sorted employee transfers	Ponw - Ponx
	MT 007	Updated employee record file - intermediate 2.	Ponx - Pora
	MT 008	Valid clock card data - Random	Pony - Ponz
	MT 009	Sorted valid clock card data	Ponz - Pora
	MT 010	Updated final employee record file	Pora - C
Out puts	LP 001	Amendment validity rejects	Pont
	LP 002	No file record amendments	Ponw
	LP 003	Employee transfer	Ponx
	LP 004	Rejected excessive hours	Pony
	LP 005	Error Analysis	Poa
	LP 006	Payslips	Pora
	LP 007	Unmatched clock data	Pora

Figure 151   Sample systems specification

SYSTEM SPECIFICATION AMENDMENT RECORD   CC5

Sheet 1 of 1   System code no. A ∅ 7

No.	Date	Sheets affected	Amendment description	Amended by
1	3.2.85	CC8	Hardware enhancement	J.B.

SPECIAL PROCEDURES AND CONTROL REQUIREMENTS   CC15

Sheet 1 of 1   System code no. A ∅ 7

INSTRUCTIONS In this section all dump routines, restart points internal checks, control total, auditing requirements and data validation checks that are required in the program must be clearly laid down in narrative form and each requirement given a number and checklist box for completion by the programmer.

TEST DATA SPECIFICATION   CC16

Sheet 1 of 1   System code no. A ∅ 7

INSTRUCTIONS This section must contain sample data designed to test each path of the system with MAXIMUM MINIMUM variables under ALL possible combinations of conditions. From the information given in this section it should be possible to produce test data input media.

GLOSSARY OF SPECIAL TERMS   CC 17

Sheet 1 of 1   System code no. A ∅ 7

Special term	Explanation

DATA VOLUMES AND STATISTICS   CC13

Sheet 1 of 1   System code no. A ∅ 7

Run No.	Form No.	Volume	Per	Related statistics
1-Port	F1234	1100	week	670 Transfers, 70 no record amends,
	F1235	70	list	70 Invalid amends, 240 misc.
				1 Validity rejects list/week
2 - Penu	-	1030	week	Valid amendments
3 - Pow	-	7,400	file	100 character employee records
		10,30	week	Valid amendments
	F1236	70	list	1 No file record list/week
		670	file	Employee transfers
4 - Penu	-	670	file	Employee transfers
5 - Penu	-	670	list	1 Employee transfers list/week
6 - Peny	F1238	7,400	week	Clock cards
	F1234	1,000	week	Clock data cards
		50	list	1 List excessive hours/week
		50		Vali..t data

RUN TIMING   CC14

Sheet 1 of 1   System code no. A ∅ 7

Run No.	Description	Set-up time	Peripheral time	Process time	Overall run time
1-Port	Read 1100 cards	1 min	1.5 min		2.5 min
	Print validity rejects	2 min	.5 min		3.5 min
	Media convert	1 min		.5 min	.5 min
	Processing				6.0 min
	Total				
2 - Penu	Sort	2 min	1.5 min		3.5 min
3 - Pow	Read amendments	1 min	.5 min		.5 min
	Read employee records	1 min	1.5 min		2.5 min
	Write updated file		1.5 min		2.5 min
	Print rejects				
	Write transfers		.5 min		.5 min
	Processing			.5 min	
	Total				6.0 min
4 - Penu	Sort	2 min	.5 min		2.5 min
5 - Peno	Read transfers	1 min	1.5 min		2.5 min
	Read employee file	1 min	1.5 min		2.5 min
	Write updated file	2 min	1.0 min		3.0 min
	Print transfers			.5 min	
	Processing				

Figure 151   Sample systems specification

To do this he has now to report back to the user department management in such a way as to enable them to understand what he is proposing and request that the proposal be implemented by the programming and installation stages. This formal acceptance is important as the analyst, no matter how good his system design, is still only an adviser with no authority for the actual working system. A second reason for this report is that it is still relatively simple and inexpensive to alter the proposal at this stage but once time and money have been invested into the program writing and testing, any change of mind by the user department can be very costly indeed.

Report writing has been covered elsewhere in this book but a few notes regarding this report should be made as it is usually of a special selling nature. Obviously the analyst wants his system accepted and should go about presenting his report in a manner most likely to achieve this aim. The best approach is to take a leaf out of the professional salesman's approach and write the report with regard to the following sequence:

(1) Plan the report carefully

(2) Start the report with a list of benefits to the user

(3) By appealing to as many senses as possible (colour diagrams, models, etc.) get the user to want the proposal implemented. After all you do not see lists of the latest car specifications in a showroom you see the brightest, biggest model in the range displayed for you to dream about

(4) Once the desire for the proposal is instilled, give the facts about it e.g. costs, plans, schedules, etc.

(5) Anticipate all possible negative questions and answer them in terms that the user will understand

(6) Finally clinch the sale while the customer is still hot. In other words request action on the recommendations in the form of a signature of acceptance of the proposed system.

Implementation

When the approval for the proposed system (with suitable modifications if required) is obtained the analyst, far from being finished, now enters into probably the most busy and complex period of the whole project.

Much of his time will be taken up in consultation with the programming team who will be developing and testing the program suite. In addition to this however the analyst must now take over the role of planner and coordinator of a many-dimensioned set of related implementation tasks.

The first thing he must do is to plan all of the various tasks in detail. These will include: clerical staff training and procedure manual production; file creation or conversion; form design and acquisition; equipment acquisition; organisation building; physical environment planning and conversion; standby facilities; the system changeover.

The planning may take the form of a Gantt bar chart or a critical path network and will entail a list of objectives to be achieved against a realistic time scale which is coordinated with the production of the computer programs so that overall systems testing can be carried out.

Announcement of plans for computerisation to company staff–this must be correctly timed as too early an announcement can cause speculative upsets whilst delay can result in exaggerated rumours and suspicions. Discussions and appreciation courses for staff and union representatives are preferred to plain notices in house magazines or on notice boards. As practice has proved this to be true, it is best where possible to promise no redundancy and to give as much detail as is required.

Staff involvement

The primary tool for effecting behaviour change is communication. However, what is communicated is not necessarily what is perceived by the receiver. The analyst must be sure that he is communicating the correct information in the best possible manner, but this is not enough. Perception is the selection and interpretation of sensory images by the receiver. People tend to see those things that will satisfy their needs and ignore those that do not. If a fire alarm goes one person may think there is a fire whilst the other one, not wishing to be disturbed, will write it off as a practice. People ignore mildly disturbing things only perceiving them if they become increasing and persistent. In the same way that groups adopt a role, individuals perceive their own role within the group as that which will enable them to manipulate their relations with others to achieve their own aims.

How the group perceives any proposed change is determined by how well the work of that group satisfies the individual needs. This itself depends on five aspects of the job:
(1) The job specification based on the technology concerned
(2) The group's leadership
(3) The authority and communication structure of the group
(4) The aims of the group and targets set
(5) The rewards and incentives provided.

If the group is satisfied by the work there will be a high degree of suspicion and resistance to any change of behaviour and a strong desire to preserve the identity of the group. If the group is not stable and not satisfied by its work, change itself will be more readily accepted but proposals will be very critically examined to ensure that it is not, in the user's perception, change for the worse.

To introduce change successfully the analyst must not present any direct conflict or problem to the group but starting from the current group attitudes generate a creative atmosphere by introducing new information which will stimulate the group members to think. As soon as the project is announced some information will be circulating in the group. It is the analyst's job to ensure that these facts are both accurate and reassuring. The facts that must be covered with particular care have already been discussed in Unit 11.

The analyst must demonstrate how the old attitudes of the group will no longer satisfy its members' needs in the new situation. This sets up dissonance in the group and the greater the impact the more willing the group members will be to change (or to dig in if the facts are not favourably presented).

The analyst should now conduct group discussion with the aim of encouraging participation in the evolution of the new system. During this discussion every individual should be prompted to participate and the analyst should use some form of visual listing (e.g. blackboard) as a form of collective group memory for proposals and ideas put forward. All ideas should be accepted and the analyst must protect individuals from group criticism which would stifle creativity.

The analyst must be careful not to force his own ideas or directly show preference for certain ideas put forward. He should instead develop the better ideas by means of probing questions whilst tactfully ignoring the others. In this way the group members evolve for themselves the reasons why certain proposals are desirable.

The analyst should not attempt to arrive at a solution too quickly but let this evolve at a natural pace. All ideas should be validated by the group and as each is accepted the analyst should ensure that each individual publicly commits himself to the change. At no time must any individual be faced with a dilemma that has no way out.

Staff training

The systems analyst is responsible for ensuring successful implementation of his systems including the training of staff to operate the manual procedures. Staff involved will be of all levels from delivery men to accountants. Before going into details on training methods let us be quite sure we understand a few basic terms.
Learning involves the assimilation of change into an individual's personality so that his behaviour in a given situation is altered.
Education is concerned with the communication of knowledge or facts to an individual.
Training is the communication of skills as opposed to facts.
Facts are just information, e.g. procedure instruction manuals and charts which tell the operator the step by step operations to be performed. There are two ways to learn facts, by rote (memory) or by understanding.
Knowledge is acquired by an individual who learns by understanding.
A skill on the other hand is a physical act which is not truly learnt until it becomes an instinctive habit performed by the body without any conscious thought, e.g. if the manual part of the system required data to be punched into cards then we require staff who have the skill of card punching as well as the facts or knowledge of what to punch, when and where.
A technique is the application of facts, knowledge and maybe skills to a certain pattern of behaviour. In our context it is simply a job or work station.

In common practice the term training is used to cover the teaching of a job requiring both facts and skills. We must consider here three aspects: who should train staff; what methods should be used; what are the stages in learning.

The analyst is the only person who will know exactly what must be done in the new system and why. However, the analyst has neither the time, authority, nor training to teach each operator. The organisation may have a training school or allow staff to attend local college or manufacturer's training courses.

These, however, provide education or skill training, not job training. What the staff must learn, to fulfil their role in the system, will depend upon the particular job they must do. The analyst must assess these needs individually and make arrangements accordingly.

Those who require facts or knowledge can attend college or manufacturer's courses whilst those who require a skill should be sent to an appropriate training school. When both the knowledge and skill have been obtained the job training can commence. The analyst will train the immediate line supervisors so that these in turn can train their staff. In this way the line of authority is not broken and the analyst's time is conserved.

Training methods

To ensure continuity and consistency the analyst produces a system specification stating each step clearly and exactly. One function of this specification is that of instruction manual, that is, of providing facts. However, how many of you have been given a manual and told to go away and read it? This is not education or training. It is time wasting. If it was a programmed text and you were trained how to use it and you wanted to use it that would be more useful.

Learning involves **communication**, i.e. transmitting and receiving information through the senses of touch, sight and hearing. Learning involves **doing**. For skills this means practical experience requiring about 65 per cent touch (practice), 25 per cent sight (demonstration) and only 10 per cent hearing (explanation).

The learning of facts is normally accomplished by sight and hearing in that order and again for the best results practice is most important. This takes the form of repetitious writing for learning by rote or working out problems for oneself for learning by understanding. One guide to the choice of actual method from the many available (e.g. lecture, film, book, manual, demonstration, teaching machine, discussion) is the factor of greatest sensory impact in the time scale and budget available.

Learning covers the following pattern:
  motivation–the benefits of learning
  induction–understanding of one's role
  explanation–facts and knowledge
  demonstration–sight and hearing
  goal setting–quality and quantity
  practice–sensory involvement
  checking–results against targets
  feedback–knowledge of results
  encouragement–reinforcing good results
  reward–reinforcing motivation

One term not yet defined is **teaching**. If learning is the assimilation of change and education and training are the communication of change, teaching is the enactment of the preceding steps to ensure that what has been communicated is assimilated.

No one learns anything unless he wants to. The individual must be motivated to learn and part of this motivation will derive from an appreciation of how his contribution fits into the system. This is the area where education and the normal methods of lecture, film, etc. fit in, as there are likely to be large groups of people involved. Explanation of the work to be done supplemented by the most visual training manuals is the next step, followed by the demonstration of what must be done with actual copies of documents, forms, etc. to be used.

The next stage is the setting of targets for the staff to aim at in their practical training. In the same way that run timing is calculated for the computer runs so the analyst must arrive at a standard time for manual processing based upon the standard quality required. Quality is stressed because it is a fact that speed tends to detract from precision and the effectiveness of any system depends as much on accuracy and clarity as on economy.

The trainee should not be set the final target immediately as goals in line with abilities lead to quicker learning, whereas a persistent history of failure promotes only frustration. The trainer should attempt to set individually realistic goals and as each is attained raise these until proficiency is reached. Also, some jobs are better as a whole whilst others are more suited to a part by part approach. The analyst must come to recognise which work can successfully be split into modules.

Where speed of learning is essential, concentrated learning by rote is the quickest. However, the most effective learning is by understanding where the training is distributed over a period of time (much in the same way as industrial sandwich courses are conducted). Practice must be accompanied by checking of the trainee's results against the methods and targets set. This checking is only of use, however, if the results are communicated back to the trainee. The more immediate this feedback the quicker the learning. This is one of the principles of programmed texts and teaching machines.

It is necessary to encourage good behaviour whilst not causing frustration through failure. To achieve this, encouragement should be given in the form of praise for good results with positive instruction to correct errors. When learning curves are plotted (results against number of practices) there are periods in the curve (plateaus) when no appreciable progress is made. These plateaus vary from job to job and person to person and it may be necessary to give further encouragement in the way of rest, competition or sometimes just straightforward change to effect an improvement.

Frequent revision of stages learnt should be incorporated with new areas of learning. To reinforce progress positively, rewards for achievement of the ultimate standards will greatly enhance the original motivation.

We should not neglect one very important influence–the analyst himself. He is also a person with needs and attitudes who will accept or reject information from his environment in the light of its effects on his own need satisfaction. How does he perceive his role in the group? How does he himself react to change?

It is the analyst's perception of himself that is the greatest influence on how he uses which techniques and, therefore, how effective his systems will be. It affects his relations with management, programmers, user's staff, in fact all the people he needs to do his job. His attitude to his job, how he views the role of the computer, whether as purely a technological god to be satisfied or as a tool to improve human lives, all of this will influence the way people react to him. As an individual in a group he will be subject to the pressures of group norms–company and department attitudes. But as an individual he also has the ability to influence these norms by being the creative deviant.

The aim of the systems analyst following the human relations approach should be to design systems that meet both the technological and human needs of the company, to act as an agent of change which results in a stable, satisfied working group.

File creation and conversion

This is a very large job in most applications which must not be underestimated. The tasks involved in this are: planning the file creation task; allocating the staff responsibilities; scheduling the time scale within cut-off date; developing conversion procedures in detail; developing control and error correction procedures; training staff for conversion; implementing and coordinating conversion.

In practice there are usually current files of data held on non-computer media which have to be converted (normally with modifications, additions and deletions) to computer media. This involves transferring the data clerically first to an intermediate form and then via data preparation onto the disk or tape file. If large volumes of data are involved this can take a long while particularly as the existing system must continue to run while conversion is going on. This results in the new files being out of date as soon as they are created (especially if the file is frequently updated) and so the analyst must also make provision for the capture of updating transactions while the conversion is taking place. These transactions will be collected until just before the actual system changeover is due to take place when they will be used to update the files prior to operational running.

System changeover

There are three basic types of system changeover that can be adopted depending on the application involved: once-off changeover; staged change-over; parallel running.

The once-off approach can only be adopted with confidence if the system is small and simple enough to allow complete testing prior to the changeover date. The staged approach is a phased series of once-off changes which can be used effectively if the system allows a convenient breakdown into simple modules. Parallel running is the most usual approach but the double cost of running two systems at the same time is the price that must be paid for caution.

Whichever method is adopted a full coordinated data and audit test must be conducted with all aspects–manual, computer, organisational and environmental, of the new system operating under normal running conditions. Only when

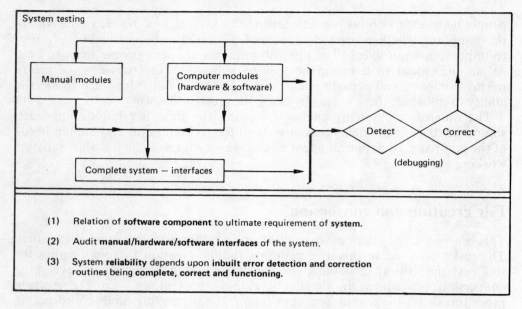

Figure 152   Systems testing

the audit department, the operating department, the systems department and, most important of all, the user department are fully satisfied to the point of signing acceptance for the system, can the analyst consider his project complete.

Systems maintenance

One final aspect of the systems project must be mentioned. This is the systems audit and evaluation which is conducted some time after the system has been installed and has had time to settle down. The analyst concerned with the original project will probably by this time be engaged deep in some other project and it is not unusual for specialist analysts or junior trainees to be engaged on the systems maintenance follow-up.

Basically this is a review to see that the new system is running smoothly and more important that it is achieving the aims and benefits that it was designed to achieve. During this study lists will be made of all items requiring amendment as well as any further or associated areas for systems study in the future. The maintenance analyst will be responsible for correcting any errors or deficiencies in the system and the amount of work required will be a reflection of the skill and care taken by the original analyst.

Assessment tasks

1 Prepare a half-hour tape-recorded talk on the subject of systems implementation.

2 Devise a plan for training a colleague to perform some job that you have experience of. This can be part of your work or a hobby. Follow your training plan and evaluate how successful you were.

3 Describe by means of a systems specification

(a) An invoicing system

(b) A real-time hotel reservation system

(c) An interactive stock control system

(d) A computer dating system

(e) Any other system that you are familiar with.

Index